ERRATA

GROWING UP TO BE VIOLENT

Lefkowitz/Eron/Walder/Huesmann

page 41 -- The paragraph under the heading
"Parent-rated Aggression" should read:

During the interviews with the parents
in the 3rd grade, each was asked several
questions about the child's recent
aggressiveness at home. For example,
"How often does NAME do things that bother
others in the family?" The parents'
responses to these questions, each on a
pre-coded five-point scale, were summed
to obtain an estimate for each parent of
the child's aggressiveness at home.

page 118 -- Line 8 should end "...early
aggression." Line 9 should begin "The
pattern of means..."

PERGAMON INTERNATIONAL LIBRARY
of Science, Technology, Engineering and Social Studies

The 1000-volume original paperback library in aid of education,
industrial training and the enjoyment of leisure

Publisher: Robert Maxwell, M.C.

Growing Up to be Violent:
A Longitudinal Study of the Development of Aggression

PGPS-66

———— Publisher's Notice to Educators ————

THE PERGAMON TEXTBOOK
INSPECTION COPY SERVICE

An inspection copy of any book published in the Pergamon
International Library will gladly be sent without obligation for
consideration for course adoption or recommendation. Copies may
be retained for a period of 60 days from receipt and returned if not
suitable. When a particular title is adopted or recommended for
adoption for class use and the recommendation results in a sale of
12 or more copies, the inspection copy may be retained with our
compliments. If after examination the lecturer decides that the
book is not suitable for adoption but would like to retain it for his
personal library, then our Educators' Discount of 10% is allowed on
the invoiced price. The Publishers will be pleased to receive
suggestions for revised editions and new titles to be published in this
important International Library.

PERGAMON GENERAL PSYCHOLOGY SERIES

Editor: Arnold P. Goldstein, *Syracuse University*
Leonard Krasner, *SUNY, Stony Brook*

TITLES IN THE PERGAMON GENERAL PSYCHOLOGY SERIES
(Added Titles in Back of Volume)

Also available: **Learning of Aggression in Children–L. Eron, L. Walder, M. Lefkowitz,** microfilm, microfiche, flexi copyflo, hard cover copyflo

The terms of our inspection copy service apply to all the above books. A complete catalogue of all books in the Pergamon International Library is available on request.

The Publisher will be pleased to receive suggestions for revised editions and new titles.

Growing Up to be Violent: A Longitudinal Study of the Development of Aggression

Monroe M. Lefkowitz, Ph.D.
New York State Department of Mental Hygiene
Albany, New York

Leonard D. Eron, Ph.D.
University of Illinois at Chicago Circle
Chicago, Illinois

Leopold O. Walder, Ph.D.
Behavior Service Consultants
Greenbelt, Maryland

L. Rowell Huesmann, Ph.D.
University of Illinois at Chicago Circle
Chicago, Illinois

PERGAMON PRESS INC.

New York / Oxford / Toronto / Sydney / Frankfurt / Paris

155.418
G884

Pergamon Press Offices:.

U.S.A.	Pergamon Press Inc., Maxwell House, Fairview Park, Elmsford, New York 10523, U.S.A.
U.K.	Pergamon Press Ltd., Headington Hill Hall, Oxford OX3, OBW, England
CANADA	Pergamon of Canada, Ltd., 207 Queen's Quay West, Toronto 1, Canada
AUSTRALIA	Pergamon Press (Aust) Pty. Ltd., 19a Boundary Street, Rushcutters Bay, N.S.W. 2011, Australia
FRANCE	Pergamon Press SARL, 24 rue des Ecoles, 75240 Paris, Cedex 05, France
WEST GERMANY	Pergamon Press GmbH, 6242 Kronberg/Taunus, Frankfurt-am-Main, West Germany

Library of Congress Cataloging in Publication Data
Main entry under title:

Growing up to be violent.

(Pergamon general psychology series ; 66)
1.   Aggressiveness (Child psychology)   2.   Aggressiveness (Psychology) 3.   Longitudinal methods.   I.   Lefkowitz, Monroe M., 1922-   [DNLM: 1.   Aggression.
2.   Violence.   BF575.A3   G884]
BF723.A35G76   1976   155.4'18   75-44349
ISBN 0-08-019515-6
ISBN 0-08-019514-8 pbk.

Printed in the United States of America

Contents

Preface

The present work is the culmination of a research endeavor initiated 20 years ago at the Rip Van Winkle Foundation in Hudson, New York. Proceeding on the assumption that aggression was one aspect of mental illness that could be studied systematically, the research team gathered data pertaining to the psychosocial development of aggressive behavior from a countywide population of third-grade schoolchildren and their parents. The design of the research was longitudinal: the intent of the researchers was to obtain a second wave of data when the children reached the 12th grade. The findings of the field study conducted when the children were in the third grade have already appeared in various journal articles and in a book. Hypotheses developed from this first wave of field survey data were tested ten years later by reinterviewing the subjects of the study when they were approximately 19 years of age. Inasmuch as we obtained measurements of aggressive behavior during two time periods — childhood and young adulthood — we were uniquely able to isolate certain child-rearing practices and environmental conditions that appear to be predictors of aggressive behavior in young adulthood. Consequently, we believe that our work provides important information where none previously existed.

During the decade that elapsed between the two periods of data collection, 1960 and 1970, violence appears to have reached epidemic proportions in the United States. This period witnessed the Vietnam War and the phenomenon of nightly violence broadcast live from the battlefield directly into our living rooms. Engendered by this war were the protests and counterprotests and the violence attending those events. Also related to the War and concomitant with it were the campus protests and the organized violence used to suppress them, eventuating in the student deaths at Kent State and Jackson State Colleges in 1970. This decade saw the assassination of major national figures: President John Kennedy, Senator Robert Kennedy, and Dr. Martin Luther King, Jr. Urban riots ranged across the country from Washington to Watts. Airline hijackings made sensational news, and a new form of violence emerged, which, like a contagion, spread to other parts of the world. In a less salient manner, but with monotonous frequency, the Mafia would perform its real-life version of the Hollywood "gangland murder." Cities were inundated with daily and often multiple occurrences of murder, rape, robbery, arson, and abduction. Meanwhile, violence was fast becoming a quintessential component of television entertainment. The situation continues to worsen so that presently the threat posed by violent crime is so menacing and so ubiquitous that it has drastically altered the lifestyle of individuals and is beginning to paralyze services and institutions.

Whether this seventh decade contained more or less violence than any of the preceding six is a question for historians and sociologists to ponder. But germane to our research was the fact that the eight-year-old boys and girls, the subjects of the study, grew to young adulthood during this period. Although we cannot demonstrate that this violent milieu systematically affected the behavior of our subjects, we do have evidence indicating that exposure to violence or violent models increased their aggressive behavior.

In democratic societies, where free enterprise as a system is apotheosized, the notion of controls is viewed as inimical to that system. But, if the level and spread of violence in the United States are to be reduced, certain controls are necessary. The situation seems directly analogous to the imposition of controls by public health systems when infectious disease threatens to imperil a population. It is on this note concerning the prevention and control of violence that we conclude our work of some 20 years.

In any work involving these many subjects over this amount of time, many people will have incurred our indebtedness. Financially, the ability to complete our study was made possible by contract No. HSM 42-70-60 from the National Institute of Mental Health. We are grateful to Drs. Eli Rubinstein and John Robinson of the U.S. Surgeon General's Scientific Advisory Committee on Television and

Social Behavior for their aid in obtaining this contract. We are also indebted to the full and continuing support received from the New York State Department of Mental Hygiene, which served as the sponsoring organization for the second wave of the study. Thanks are due to the Office of Child Development for their Grant, OCD CB 364, which permitted additional data analyses. Many individuals have earned our gratitude but above all we wish to thank the young men and women who cooperated with our research efforts ten years after their initial interview. In addition, we owe thanks to the school officials who cooperated with the second phase of our study. These were Mr. Hughes P. Dearlove, District Superintendent, Roeliff-Jansen High School, Hillsdale, New York; Mr. Walter E. Howard, District Principal, New Lebanon High School, Lebanon Springs, New York; Sister Margaret, St. Mary's Academy, Hudson, New York; Mr. John B. Vale, District Superintendent, Germantown High School, Germantown, New York; and Mr. Herbert J. Walsh, District Principal, Ichabod Crane High School, Niverville, New York. We are grateful to Mr. Victor Pompa for his diligent efforts as a research assistant and to Ms. Anne Karabin for her expert research and editorial assistance and for typing the preliminary draft of this manuscript. Thanks are also due to Dr. Paul Castellani for his skillful administration of our research funds and to Ms. Judy Holstein for her contribution as a research clerk. Finally, we wish to thank Ms. Ruth Nowell for her tireless efforts as research clerk, for her editorial assistance, and for typing the final draft of the manuscript.

Monroe M. Lefkowitz

Albany, New York

1
Theories of Aggression

What are the roots of aggression and violence in young adulthood? How do children develop so that they are viewed as popular and as leaders by their peers? How does early maladaptive behavior (like aggression) develop into psychopathology in young adulthood? What are the roles of family, culture, peers, and the media in shaping these behaviors? An attempt to formulate answers to these questions was begun through the design of a longitudinal study of aggressive behavior in 1955.

Although the psychosocial development of aggression was a major focus of the research plan, the import for society of studying human aggression was hardly as clear in 1955 as it is today. Omnipresent in American society — from the implacable hostility between whites and Indians in the Colonial period to the present-day barbarism of the My Lai massacre — violence, as Stokely Carmichael so aphoristically noted, is as American as cherry pie. The history of violence in this country has been adequately portrayed elsewhere (Brown, 1969). Suffice it to say that hardly a day elapses without significant acts of violence occurring throughout the land. To recite this litany of violence would in itself require more than one volume. Assassination of national figures or multiple deaths and injuries produced by one individual (such as Charles Whitman who, in 1966, indiscriminately shot and killed 13 people and wounded 31 from the top of the University of Texas tower; or Richard F. Speck who, in 1968, senselessly murdered eight nurses in Chicago; or Lieutenant Calley

1

who, in 1968, directed the massacre of civilians in My Lai) are the kinds of aggressive acts that occupy the limelight. Although internationally prominent, these few acts of aggression pale when juxtaposed with the daily but unheralded statistics of violence produced by wars, arson, rape, assault, murder, riot, police violence, child battering, and automobile deaths and maiming. The domestic scene is far from tranquil as evinced, particularly in urban areas, by the demand for new and sophisticated door locks, the advent of private neighborhood guards and vigilante groups, and the reluctance of individuals to venture out of their homes not only after dark but even during daylight.

This chapter is designed, among other reasons, to provide a broad and carefully examined theoretical context into which our study can be placed. It takes the reader on a wide excursion through a number of ideas about aggression in human and infrahuman organisms. While our longitudinal study will explore the relevance of situational factors in aggression, it was not designed to provide conclusive data on the contribution of biological variables to aggression.

SEMANTICS OF AGGRESSION

In the conversational sense, the connotative aspects of the term "aggression" are usually implicit in the context or are assumed. However, a problem arises when rigorous definition and operationalization of the concept of aggression are required. It becomes clear in any discussion of the topic that the term also contains a positive and negative valence, so that aggression can connote "good" as well as "bad" in the characterization of behavior. It is instructive in this respect to learn that the noun and adjectival forms of the term contribute to these connotative differences. *Webster's Third New International Dictionary* (1966) defined the noun form first as "an offensive action or procedure: a culpable unprovoked overt hostile attack." The fifth definition, however, is "healthy self-assertiveness or a drive to accomplishment or to mastery esp. of skills." One of the adjectival forms, the second, indicates that to be aggressive is to be "marked by driving forceful energy, ambition, or initiative: enterprising."

Whenever the topic of aggression is discussed, one of the first questions to arise is how it differs from self-assertiveness. "Aggressive" sales programs, "aggressive" investment policies, and "aggressiveness" in a male's pursuit of the female and other goals connote positive behaviors. In an open, competitive economy, aggression (in this sense) is not only viewed as laudatory but necessary. Presumably, bad aggression is easily recognized by its negative qualities as suggested by the foregoing dictionary definition. Yet, this is hardly the case since an offensive action or a culpable unprovoked hostile attack may also be interpreted as meritorious and heroic behavior and may be rewarded with the choicest premiums of society. For example, identical aggressive acts may in one context be defined as felonious assault and in another as counterinsurgency or effective police action. In yet another context similar behavior may be regarded as athletic skill and prowess.

Resolution of the casuistic question — the rightness or wrongness of aggression — is indeed a difficult task not only because of semantic considerations but because aggressive behavior can be justified as right from the frame of reference of the perpetrator, or as wrong from that of his victim. Moreover, right and wrong, with respect to the very same behavior, are reversed as a direct function of the reversal in roles of perpetrator and victim. Countless illustrations of this polarity in definition and its reversal may be drawn from the political, military, and sports arenas.

The ambiguity inherent in the concept of aggression may in part be traced to theories of its provenance. It is important to understand not only the scientific aspects of these theories but also their philosophical roots. The reason, as Eisenberg (1972) reminds us, is that belief systems about human behavior may not only influence responses to that behavior but also may become self-fulfilling prophecies. That belief systems shape human behavior is seen dramatically in the efficacy of the placebo or in our expectations of the performance of others. For example, it has been shown (Rosenthal, 1966) that a child's academic achievement varies in part as a function of the teacher's prior belief of the child's IQ. Similarly, a society's management and control of violence may vary with its belief that aggressive behavior is instinctual, is the product of aggressive drive which could be reduced by behaving injuriously, or is learned. Not only would the management of aggressive behavior vary with societies' belief concerning its origin, but the expression of the behavior itself might vary according to the actor's belief.

The ambiguous nature of the concept of aggression and the major theoretical formulations that attempt to describe and explain this phenomenon need to be understood because our beliefs about aggression may indeed influence the behavior itself. An analysis of the literature and current thinking of investigators in the field of aggression and violence indicates that theories concerning the origin of aggressive behavior fall into three basic categories: man is aggressive by nature; man possesses an aggressive drive engendered largely by frustration; man is born with the cognitive and morphological potential to act aggressively but whether or not he learns to do so depends on contingencies in his environment. A subclassification might be made of this last category to account for the possible occurrence of aggressive behavior due to pre- or postnatal insult to the central nervous sytem or to chromosomal anomalies.

AGGRESSION AND THE NATURE OF MAN

If individual violence (such as assault, murder, and property damage) or collective violence (such as wars) are attributable to biological determinism and the innate nature of aggression in human beings, then a garrison or quasi-garrison social structure in which such aggression could be successfully controlled would be the consequence. All of our written records about man tell us that concern with his essential nature has been paramount. These records and his lifestyle suggest that his nature was presumed to be bestial. Indeed a commandment to man stating "Thou shalt not kill" begs the question of the necessity of the commandment to forestall his killing. Furthermore, the notion of innate depravity is reinforced by the doctrine of original sin.

The manner in which people lived at least from the time of the barbarian invasions of the West during the third century A.D. to the present suggests the fear of unprovoked attack and the visitation of violence. Castles were ringed by moats, cities were walled, and city gates were locked at dusk. Homes were guarded by enormous gates of iron topped by menacing spikes. Variations on this lifestyle still prevail in urban areas throughout the world, and garrison states of greater or lesser degree are numerous. The violence wrought by the invasions of Europe and England by northern tribes of barbarians — Huns, Ostrogoths, Visigoths, Vandals, and Franks — can only be fully comprehended when studied in its proper historical context. We mention it simply as an attempt to relate the constant concern with attack to the belief system that holds man to be innately aggressive. If man is innately aggressive, then precautions are both necessary and realistic. If not, then a modification or restructuring of social controls may be indicated. Moreover, if aggressive behavior is only expected conditionally, then it may not occur unconditionally.

THE NATURE OF MAN AND THE SOCIAL COMPACT

The social philosophers of the 17th and 18th centuries, who were concerned with the legitimization of government and political authority, were very much enamored of the notion of a social contract (McNeill, 1963). However, the terms of such a contract were subject to varied formulations according to the particular philosopher's concept of man's essential nature. Thomas Hobbes is the best representative of the 17th-century thinking which held that man was essentially aggressive because of his impulse to self-preservation. In the *Leviathan* (1651 [1969 edition]) Hobbes attributes this impulse to two conflicting desires: preservation of individual liberty and dominion over others. Arising from this conflict is a war of all against all which makes life in the state of nature (free of government) "nasty, brutish, and short." Thus, the creation of a social contract in which man submits to a sovereign body and relinquishes his personal freedom results in self-preservation. Because the covenant restrains the desires for personal freedom and dominion over others, universal war is avoided. Under such a contract, tyranny and totalitarian rule are justified by their necessity.

Also concerned with a social contract and yet almost diametrically opposed to Hobbes in their views of man are John Locke and Jean Jacques Rousseau. Locke (1690 [1781 edition]) believed that man in his natural state was essentially virtuous. For him, therefore, a social contract would have different consequences. Repudiating the notion of innate ideas, Locke proposed that the mind is born blank — *tabula rasa*. He argued for the legitimization of government through a social contract not for the abrogation of universal war, as did Hobbes, but to remedy the inconveniences that arise in a state of nature. In that state every man is the judge of his own cause, whereas under government the judiciary, independent of the monarchy, renders these judgments. Under such a contract, the power of the government never extends beyond the common good; if necessary, the contract can be dissolved. We see that Hobbes' belief in man's aggressive nature would likely result in tyrannical rule and a garrison state, whereas Locke's belief in man's essential virtue would eventuate in a democratic social contract. Although these theories of man's nature would produce different consequences, both positions contain an essential similarity: man possesses an innate nature — aggressiveness or virtuousness — which is largely impervious to the effects of nurture.

Jean Jacques Rousseau began with the premise that man would be good; the institutions governing his life made him bad. In *Emile*, which appeared in 1762 (reprinted in 1911), Rousseau states: "God makes all things good; man meddles with them and they become evil." Left in his natural state without education, the child would, by his environment, be turned into a monster. Thus, throughout *Emile* the stress is on education with the goal of shaping behavior. What a child becomes, to use current terminology, is consequent upon his learning history. We see that the positions of Rousseau and Hobbes concerning the origin of aggression are antipodal. For Rousseau, aggressiveness is environmentally determined; for Hobbes, aggression is instinctual. Because of the pure condition in which the child is born, his education and the kind of society in which it occurs are vitally important in determining the child's future behavior according to Rousseau's theory.

The society advocated by Rousseau in 1762 in his *Social Contract* (1952) was democratic in form. Denied by Rousseau was the divine right of kings; sovereignty is rather the exercise of the general will. Because aggression potentially exists in the environment, men had to come together in some kind of association governed by a social compact. Rousseau's (1952) formulation is as follows: *"The problem is to find a form of association which will defend and protect with the whole common force the person and goods of each associate, and in which each, while uniting himself with all, may still obey himself alone, and remain as free as before,"* (p. 391).

The notion that man is born neither good nor bad places Rousseau in opposition to both Hobbes and Locke. Whereas Hobbes argued for man's inherent aggressiveness and Locke for man's essential virtue, Rousseau's philosophy rejects the idea that man has a fundamental nature. Rather, man is a malleable organism which, in the main, is molded by the environment.

We present this precis of social philosophy because of the parallel it holds for current theories of aggressive behavior. Perhaps equally important is the relevance of these social covenants, between those governed and their form of government, to social views of aggressiveness and consequently to the kinds of contingencies society effects to regulate aggression. In addition, the philosophy of the nature of man held by a society or government is related to the *Weltanschauung* of that society and thus to its expectations and interpretation of the expression of aggressive behavior.

Returning to the earlier statement of the three major theories of aggression, the idea that man is naturally aggressive accords with the philosophy of Hobbes about man's basic nature. Expectations that without rigorous controls he would behave aggressively implies a social contract in which government is absolute, such as absolute monarchies (which are all but extinct) or the more modern authoritarian forms of government, such as dictatorships. Under these forms of government, aggressive responses customarily solicit draconion measures such as capital punishment or corporal mutilation, as is the case in present-day Libya. In the parlance of learning theory, the contingency of a strong counteraggressive response from authority is employed in the attempt to control aggressive behavior. Moreover, a model of the aversive consequences of aggressive behavior is provided through exemplary punishment.

Any proposition arguing that man possesses some essential or fundamental nature or behaves instinctually in one manner or another must eventually, be able, to be explained biologically. If, as Locke proposes, man is innately virtuous, then ultimately the genetic mechanism whereby the characteristic of virtuousness (however defined) is transmitted within the species must be discovered. The same demand must be made for Rousseau's theory of fundamental goodness and Hobbes' theory of innate aggressiveness. Of the three, perhaps Rousseau is most attuned to the consideration of parsimony in the explanation of human behavior. Although he argues that man is fundamentally good, he attributes to environment — through education — the molding of a child's behavior. In this fashion Rousseau at least acknowledges the nature-nurture controversy and the likelihood that behavior can also be determined by environmental conditions.

Although it is difficult to establish any direct causal connection between the thinking of social philosophers of the 17th and 18th centuries and contemporary theories of aggression, ideas do not occur in a vacuum and historians and philosophers are convincing in their ability to trace the influence of ideas from one time period on another. For example, the influence of Attic Greece on present-day thought and behavior is readily demonstrable. In this regard it is interesting to note that Rousseau's ideas on education as expounded in *Emile* were very much influenced by the thinking of Plato as expressed in his *Republic*. Thus, it is plausible to assume that the ideas and theories concerning aggressiveness, fashioned by 20th-century thinkers in the biological, behavioral, and social sciences, were influenced by the views of man propounded by the social and political philosophers of the several preceding centuries.

INNATE AGGRESSIVENESS

Instinct theory is perhaps the most Hobbesian of the theories of human behavior which attempt to explain aggression. This theory, which holds that man is by nature aggressive, has many illustrious proponents. William James (1890) states that the human race was reared in a "gory cradle" and its members are the lineal representatives of successful enactors of slaughter and carnage. Thus, the instincts of pugnacity, anger, and resentment smolder within humans ready at any moment to erupt. McDougall (1908) also argues that man possessed, among many other instincts, an instinct for pugnacity. Freud (1922 [1955 edition]) states that cruelty and a desire to hurt others deliberately is a prominent feature of the human psyche. He attributes this desire to the death instinct, or *Thanatos* — one of the two fundamental human drives. From the moment of its inception, the organism is slowly but inexorably driven back to its lifeless form — a state of death. This drive toward death is not limited to its own host but is prevalent and affects relationships among human organisms and, ultimately, among societies. Powered by the libido, this drive, according to Freud, is the cause of war and a cause for pessimism insofar as man's future is concerned. In a letter to Albert Einstein in 1932 concerning war, Freud (1959) argued against the feasibility of ridding man of his aggressive instincts. The diversion of aggressive impulses so that they are expressed in other forms than war would be enough of an accomplishment. Although Freud was concerned about time running out, cultural evolution, he believed, is the means by which instinctual impulses will be restricted and displaced. In the main, the belief in man's innate aggressiveness is a common feature shared by those in the psychoanalytic school (see, e.g., Munro, 1955).

Those ethologists who extrapolate the results of their studies of lower animals to humans also tend to view man as an innately aggressive animal. In this sense, ethological theories of human aggression parallel in biological science the philosophy of Thomas Hobbes. For example, Lorenz (1966) argues that homo sapiens is even more aggressive than other animals because of his propensity for intraspecific aggression. In lower animals innate inhibitory mechanisms, such as ritualistic displays of appeasement, serve to constrain intraspecific aggression by fending off aggressors with little or no physical contact. In man, however, these mechanisms presumably have been rendered ineffective by the comparatively rapid advance of cultural evolution. Technological development has caused cultural evolution to outstrip genetic evolution. Aphoristically, Lorenz (1966) states that man has ". . . in his hand the atom bomb, the product of his intelligence, in his heart the aggression drive inherited from his anthropoid ancestors, which this same intelligence cannot control . . ." (p. 49). According to Lorenz, man, basically a harmless omnivore, lacks the physical structure with which to kill big prey. Concomitantly, he is missing the innate safety mechanisms that prevent carnivores from abusing their lethal powers to kill conspecifics. Genetically based, these powers or instincts rigidly program the organism. They serve natural selection by providing for a balanced distribution of a species over the available territory and in this manner they enhance food gathering. Also aggression, through rival fights, serves to provide the best mate and thus the best progeny. Aggressive instinct aids in the protection of these offspring. Thus, aggression as the "impulse to self-preservation" is the same for Lorenz as for Hobbes.

Lorenz' work and the extrapolation of the findings of ethology to human behavior have been sharply criticized by behavioral and social scientists. Before stating the major aspects of this criticism, however, we shall present a more moderate ethological approach to aggression, that of Tinbergen (1968). He raises the somewhat rhetorical question about the temerity of a student of animal behavior addressing himself to the problems of human behavior. To bridge these disciplines, he uses the history of medicine and points out that it has always been acceptable to study the bodily functions of infrahuman animals and the relation of these functions to human physiology. However, a great deal of resistance is encountered when zoologists generalize their findings on animal behavior to humans. Tinbergen cites the enormous interest in such books by Lorenz (1966) and Morris (1967) as an indication of the rapidly growing interest in the science of ethology. Yet he feels that these books are often misread and may stiffen the resistance against an ethological approach to human behavior.

Unlike other sciences of behavior, such as anthropology or psychology, ethology applies the method of biology to the phenomenon of behavior. This method allows certain questions to be asked of behavior: In what ways does it influence the success of the animal with respect to survival? What are the mechanics of behavior? How is it caused? What is the ontogenetic course of the behavior? What is the evolutionary history of these behaviors in each species? So, just as biology studies the functioning of organs responsible for digestion, respiration, circulation, etc., ethology studies the functioning of those organs responsible for movement or behavior. In this context Tinbergen (1968) defines aggression as the approach to ". . . an opponent and when within reach pushing him away, or inflicting damage of some kind or at least forcing stimuli upon him that subdue him" (p. 1412). The effect of such behavior tends to remove the opponent or at least to make him change his behavior so that he no longer interferes with the attacker.

In terms of survival, intraspecific fighting among animals serves to settle disputes about territory and mates and aids in food gathering and protection of the young. Most species other than man usually manage to settle these disputes without killing one another. Even bloodshed is rare. Man is the only mass murderer; in this sense he is a social misfit. The paradox is evident: in other animals intraspecific fighting has a distinct survival advantage, where as in man the contrary seems to be true. Tinbergen offers as an explanation the observation that cultural evolution has increased exponentially and has outstripped genetic evolution. Whereas genetically we have not evolved very much beyond Cro-Magnon man, culturally we are changing at an ever-increasing rate; the hiatus between both kinds of evolution is becoming increasingly great.

In other species aggression rarely occurs in pure form. For example, when the question of territoriality is involved, hostile clashes are controlled by an attack-avoidance system. When owners of a neighboring territory meet at a common boundary, both attack behavior and withdrawal behavior are elicited. In the course of evolution, this conflict of incompatible behaviors has acquired signal function. In effect they say "keep out!" Thus, animals are able to have all the advantages of their hostile behavior without the disadvantages.

According to Tinbergen, cultural evolution is responsible for man's uninhibited inraspecific aggression and mass killing. He cites the following factors as directly attributable to cultural evolution: (1) population density or overcrowding, which is the result of prolongation of life through medical science and the increase in food through agricultural science; (2) long-distance communication, which provides a continuous possiblity for external provocation of aggression; and (3) the upsetting of the balance between aggression and fear, which is a major precipitating cause of war. Soldiers are brainwashed, bullied, and dehumanized. Man's ability to make and use killing tools, especially long-range weapons, is a particularly lethal product of cultural evolution. A fist can only produce limited damage, while long-range weapons not only produce widespread destruction but also prevent the victim from confronting his attacker with appeasement, reassurance, or distress signals. To paraphrase Etzioni (1973), if Charles Whitman had possessed a coke bottle rather than a rifle atop the University of Texas Tower, he could have done little if any damage.

Cultural evolution is largely a function of the development of the human cortex. If reason is embodied in the cortex and instincts in the older brain or limbic system, then these two components of the human brain seem to have created a new social environment which, rather than insuring survival, seem to be enhancing destruction. Paradoxically, this social environment now seriously threatens the organism that created it.

Tinbergen attempts to reinterpret Lorenz' notion of an internal urge to attack as the causation of aggressive behavior in animals and men. He considers Lorenz' use of the term "spontaneity of aggression" as unfortunate. Both instinct and external variables produce fighting. Fighting derives as much from the situation as it does from aggressive drive. Moreover, there is a great deal of variability in aggressive drive and in the situational variables that combine to produce aggressive behavior. Aggressive behavior is by no means reflexive; rather, it is the result of a complex interaction between aggressive drive and environmental stimuli. In this respect Tinbergen agrees with Morris (1967), who proposes that aggressive acts are genetically governed responses to stimuli originating in others. Morris questions the existence of an innate spontaneous drive.

Agreeing with Lorenz that education cannot eliminate the internal urge to fight, Tinbergen argues for a crash program of eliminating or mitigating the situational or environmental variables that are partners to the aggressive act. Among the more salient situational variables are population density and depletion and pollution of our habitat. The balance of terror, the fear of lethal radiation, world organizations, international police forces, and redirection (sublimination) of aggressive drive (all products of cultural evolution) may prevent or mitigate man's intraspecific aggression and his ultimate annihilation. According to this theory, man has already begun to sublimate or redirect group aggression. As an example, Tinbergen cites the Dutch, who have united in their fight against the sea. A more current example is the "conquest" of space, a program that began independently in the United States and the Soviet Union as a national endeavor and has now become international.

A CRITIQUE OF THE THEORY OF INNATE AGGRESSIVENESS

Ethological theory has not gone unchallenged. The works, in particular, of Lorenz (1966), Ardrey (1966), and Morris (1967) have been widely criticized. The concept of instinct applied to man whether used by the Freudians or the ethologists is unproductive scientifically because it explains nothing. To label aggressiveness as "human nature" connotes immutability, and behavior so classified is placed beyond the limits of scientific investigation. Moreover, the exercise is tautologous: an emitted behavior is labeled aggressive and, as if this adds something, the aggressive behavior is said to be the result of an aggressive instinct which causes aggression. We have two concepts where only one is needed. Furthermore, the concept of instinct, which is employed to explain human aggression, takes on a metaphysical quality comparable to notions of vital forces such as entelechy, a notion of the ancient Greeks, or Bergson's (1911) *elan vital*. Indeed, Montagu (1968) likens these descriptions of man's innate aggression to the concept of original sin and innate depravity. (It is interesting to note in this respect that the title of Lorenz' book in its original German is *Das Sogenannte Böse* — the so-called evil.)

An example of how this Hobbesian notion of innate bestiality has influenced the thinking of even an enlightened journalist is illustrated in an article by the editorialist Tom Wicker (1969) on the apparent massacre at My Lai. In a section entitled "Letting Loose the Beast," Wicker says, "Songmy (My Lai) in fact proves nothing specific about Vietnam; it only shows once again what man is capable of once he lets loose the beast within himself" (p. 54). The implication of this theory for the structuring of society and garrisoning the beast has been alluded to above.

However, there are as yet no convincing genetic data — whether chromosomal, familial, or morbidity risk — to explain the hereditary transmission of the same amount of aggressive instinct in human beings. Ethologists tend to confound the evolution of man's morphology with his behavior. Few would argue that natural selection has determined man's morphology. To maintain, however, that the behaviors effected by such structure are also determined by natural selection is to argue *reductio ad absurdum*. Beyond the obvious relation between morphology and behavior is the relation between behavior and environmental contingencies. This latter relation has been used to shape the behavior of various species as well as man. Thus, Hinde (1967) has strongly criticized Lorenz for the notion of the spontaneity of aggression. He proposes that the principal determinant of fighting arises from the situation. To postulate causes that are internal to the aggressor is superfluous.

Obviously not all criticisms are pertinent to all ethologists because they differ among themselves. For example, Lorenz is criticized for ignoring the role of learning in shaping of aggressive behavior (Bandura, 1973a; Berkowitz, 1969b; Feshbach, 1970; Kaufmann, 1970; Scott, 1967). Few behavioral scientists would argue today that man's behavior is not influenced by his experience. Furthermore, even if there are constitutionally governed impulsive responses, these too can be modified by manipulating the environmental contingencies. Cultural anthropologists such as Alland (1972) note that although regulated by genetic limitations, human development is sociopsychological rather than solely genetic. Alland states:

> Genes are responsible for man's capacity to acquire culture. They are also responsible for the basis of other capacities, the potential for a wide range of behaviors. The expression of these traits depends upon the environment in which maturation takes place. Different human populations may have somewhat different potentials, particularly small isolated populations living in extreme environmental conditions, but it must be borne in mind that while genes may provide different probabilities for behavior they do not produce the actual behavior itself. Thus different environmental conditions (including education) can produce the same behavioral results on different genetic backgrounds. Individuals with very similar genetic backgrounds can be very different. We must not forget that anthropology has already demonostrated that major (even minor) behavioral differences between human groups depend upon culture. (p. 151)

In addition to the criticism that ethological theory ignores the effects of learning and the complex interplay between nature and nurture, the theory is further criticized for extrapolating from animal to human behavior and arguing by analogy. Moreover, the mechanisms accounting for aggression in man and animals and the stimulus antecedents to aggression across species are far from the same. Extrapolation and arguing by analogy are, according to Montagu (1968), the results of assuming that all of human behavior is phylogenetically based. This assumption fails to take into consideration man's unique ontogenetic development and the approximately one million years of his cultural evolution. Berkowitz (1969b) notes that ethologists such as Lorenz attach labels to patterns of behavior exhibited by humans that are similar to labels attached to animal behavior. For example, Lorenz notes that patterns of behavior in the greylag goose of jealousy, grieving, and strife are very similar to patterns in man. Consequently, he concludes that these actions must be governed by the same underlying mechanisms — instincts.

Scott (1967) argues that the ideas of instinct expounded by Lorenz are pre-Mendelian and prephysiological. For a concept such as spontaneity of aggression to be valid physiologically, chemical and physical changes must be demonstrated that would precede such spontaneous aggressive behavior. For example, the physiological concomitants of hunger are lowered blood sugar in the cells, stimulation of the brain cells, stimulation of the brain centers associated with this factor, and the consequent hunger contractions in the stomach which lead to food seeking and eating behavior. Such a mechanism has not been demonstrated with regard to spontaneous aggression as far as we know.

Thus, instinct theory generally and a theory of aggressive instincts in particular are lacking in credibility as applied to man. Such a theory lacks parsimony and is not empirically verifiable. Moreover, the hydraulic nature of the theory and the dire effects that putatively occur when pressure is forced out of the systems (a natural occurrence if aggression is generated spontaneously, as Lorenz claims) provide an ominous and Hobbesian augury for social control. Eventuating not only in a garrison state but a garrison world, this theory would also detract man's focus from what more likely would yield promising results in the control of aggressive behavior: manipulation of situational determinants.

The material presented thus far on the theoretical origin of aggressive behavior turns, in the main, around the idea of innate impellers to aggression. Aggression has survival value for the individual organism and for the species collectively. The phenomenon is programmed in the genes and arises spontaneously. For the Freudians, this innate programming carries the seeds of death and destruction but it may be temporarily sublimated. Depending on the particular ethological view, the behavior may or may not come under the control of situational determinants. However, all such theories would agree that the behavior is inborn and, in a manner of speaking, is phylogenetically ordained.

PHYSIOLOGICAL COMPONENTS OF AGGRESSIVE DRIVE

Departing from a strict phylogenetic approach to the provenance of aggression are those theories of aggressive drive that focus on aberrant and anomalous conditions of the organism. Concerned with such impellers to aggression as chromosomal anomalies, organs of the central nervous system, sex hormones and endocrinology, and psychopharmacology, these theories differ from the instinct theories of aggression in that they focus on specific physiological systems of the organism and the response of these systems to environmental stimuli.

The XYY Syndrome

Although the data are far from unequivocal, some investigators have attempted to adduce data to support the relationship between an extra Y chromosome — the putative super-male syndrome — and aggressive behavior (Cowie and Kahn, 1968; Jarvik et al., 1973; Telfer et al., 1968). Certain morphological characteristics (such as excessive tallness) and certain behavioral characteristics (such as low IQ were thought to be concomitants of the XXY syndrome, but this is now questionable.

Proponents of the argument that the XYY karyotype* is related to violence and criminality attempt to buttress their argument through epidemiological data. For example, Jarvik et al. (1973) have assembled data from the world literature on the XYY karyotype as well as from chromosome surveys of normal adult males. In the latter population the frequency of the XYY chromosomal anomaly is eight XXYs in 6,148, or approximately .13 percent. Approximately the same frequency occurs in chromosome surveys of newborn males. Out of some 10,000 cases surveyed, 13 newborn boys showed the XYY condition. By contrast, the chromosome surveys of approximately 5000 criminals illustrate that 98, or 1.90 percent of this group, manifested an XYY karyotype. This frequency is 15 times greater than that found in either newborn or adult normal males!

In data presented by Hook (1973) it is also evident that the XYY genotype is much more likely to be found in mental-penal institutions than in the normal population. However, even if there were a direct association between the so-called super-male phenotype resulting from the XYY condition and violence, this relation would account for only an infinitesimal amount of the variance in violent crimes. But the relationship between the extra Y chromosome and

*An individual's chromosomal complement as shown by a photomicrograph of a somatic cell in which the number, size, and shape of the chromosomes are displayed.

violence is far from direct and the possible existence of third variables require consideration.

The fact that the XYY karyotype occurs with significantly greater frequency in mental and prison institutions is explored by Hook (1973) for third variabls under three hypotheses. In the first, the associative hypothesis, he raises the question as to whether XYY males as compared to XY males are born more often in environmental situations that are conducive to a greater degree of social deviance. No such associative etiology can be demonstrated, he feels. The second hypothesis examines social etiology as a third variable in terms of the relationship between the XYY syndrome and physique. Usually these males are over six feet, and tall individuals who are also impulsive or who manifest a behavior disorder are more likely to be incarcerated than short individuals evincing similar behaviors. Simply, tall individuals who behave in a peculiar or erratic manner may appear more threatening to society than short individuals who behave in such fashion; thus, tall individuals are more often placed in one or another form of custody. Of course, this argument should also hold for tall XY individuals and on this point the evidence is conflicting. Some institutions do have a concentration of tall XY males, whereas other settings do not. The problem is further complicated by sampling bias. Since it was discovered that an association obtained between a tall physique and the XYY karyotype, some investigators sampled their institutional populations only for males above six feet in attempting to determine the incidence of the XYY phenomenon. Consequently, when only tall prisoners are screened for this condition, the prevalence of XYY is 2.7 percent. This compares to 1.8 percent when prisoners under six feet in height are screened for this karyotype (Hook, 1973).

Lowered intelligence may also be implicated as a possible third variable in that it is also part of the XXY syndrome. Specifically, lowered intelligence may have circumscribed the learning of non-aggressive or prosocial behaviors, limiting the XYY individual to a narrower repertoire of chiefly impulsive ways of behaving. In addition, lower intelligence may simply increase the probability of an individual being apprehended after the commission of a crime.

A third causal hypothesis advanced by Hook is that the XYY genotype is associated with a neurological deficit. Some trend to a greater frequency of electroencephalographic abnormalities obtains for XYY individuals; however, this finding merely represents a trend and is far from consistent. In the main, there is no evidence to support a neurological hypothesis involving brain or endocrine dysfunction in the association between the XYY genotype and deviant behavior.

Nongenetic factors, primarily familial and social, have not been adequately controlled. The association of these factors with the extra Y chromosome and the possible determination of the characteristics atrributed to this chromosome have yet to be delineated. Kessler and Moos (1969) make a strong statement in this regard when they say "that XYY males are uncontrollably aggressive psychopaths appears to be nothing more than a myth promoted by the mass media. When compared to matched chromosomally normal fellow inmates, institutionalized XYY males seem to be less violent or aggressive and their preadmission histories generally involve crimes against property rather than persons" (p. 442).

Thus we are faced with the epidemiological findings that the extra Y chromosome in the male is 15 times more frequent in prison populations than in normal adult males or in newborn males. However, before we can conclude that this extra Y chromosome is a genetic precursor to aggressive behavior, more than epidemiological data are required. Bandura (1973a) suggests that a satisfactory answer to the question can only be achieved through a double-blind prospective study of boys with the XYY genotype and a group of matched controls not possessing this condition. Periodic assessment in a longitudinal design should be able to clarify the relationship between the extra Y chromosome and aggressive behavior. Since the frequency of the XYY karyotype in newborn males is only one to two per thousand, the sampling problems involved in carrying out such a double-blind study tend to become staggering.

Cerebral Mechanisms and Aggression

Studies of brain functioning and aggressive behavior (Boelkins and Heiser, 1970; Kaada, 1967; Mark and Ervin, 1970; Morgan, 1965; Moyer, 1971) suggest that areas of the brain principally in control of aggression are thought to lie deep in the temporal lobes and in subcortical structures know as the old brain or limbic system. These structures include the cingulum, amygdala, hippocampus, thalamus, hypothalamus, and the septum. Studies on both animals and man suggest that these areas of the brain are integrally involved in both the elicitation and suppression of aggressive behavior. As shown by the implantation of electrodes in these areas, the focus for elicitation or suppression is extremely narrow, often within fractions of a millimeter. Stimulation of certain regions of the hypothalamus or the amygdala will provoke rage attacks in cats and other organisms, whereas the removal of these organs will reduce aggressive behavior. Dominant animals become submissive and the dominance hierarchy within a group can be changed through these techniques (Brown and Hunsperger, 1963; Rosvold, *et al.*, 1954).

Delgado (1967) has conducted experiments on aggression in rhesus monkeys using the technique of radio telemetry. Various parts of the brain of these monkeys are stimulated by FM radio signal sent by transmitter to stereotaxically implanted electrodes. Delgado has shown that agonistic behaviors of these animals can be modulated dramatically by this technique. He concludes that aggression can be definitely manipulated by direct stimulation of the brain. Since results obtained in experimental situations often do not apply to more normal social situations where animals are not isolated or restrained, caution should be exercised in generalizing such findings of infrahuman animals to man. Environmental variables, such as the hierarchical structure of the group, serve to modify aggressive responses. For example, in low-ranking monkeys painful stimuli fail to evoke hostility against dominant members of the group, so that even when the animal's behavior is being artificially controlled by radio stimulation, the animals still appear sensitive to the behaviors of other members of their social group. But conflicting data are presented by Robinson (1968), who was able to effect a fairly permanent reversal of the dominance relationship between two animals by telemetric stimulation of a nucleus in the hypothalamus of rhesus monkeys. In another experiment (Bandler and Flynn, 1974) electrolytic lesions were made in the thalamus of cats at the sites which produced attack on a rat when this dorsal midbrain region was stimulated. Destruction of this region, however, suppressed the attack elicited by stimulation of the thalamus.

These animal studies suggest that a portion of the variance in aggressive behavior may be accounted for by the particular functions of certain brain mechanisms. When we look at the data with human beings, there is further indication that brain mechanisms are implicated in the initiation of aggressive behavior and in its modulation and inhibition. Disturbances of functioning of the cerebral cortex in man disinhibit the subcortical centers such as the limbic system from higher control. Impairment of the neurological control of aggressive behavior has been attributed to various clinical conditions. Ontogenetically, the earliest damage to the cortex may occur during the perinatal period. Pasamanick and Knobloch (1966) and Knobloch and Pasamanick (1966) describe a pervasive condition which they termed the continuum of reproductive casualty. Insult to the central nervous system is sustained by the fetus as a result of various complications of pregnancy and delivery. Chiefly, diffuse damage to the cortex occurs from anoxia. The continuum has a lethal component manifested in spontaneous abortions and perinatal deaths and, they propose, a sublethal component reflected in disorders of the central nervous system, such as cerebral palsy, mental deficiency, and learning and behavior disorders. Thus, according to their concept, manifestations in such children of hyperkinetic behavior, aggressive temper tantrums, and rage behavior would be considered a sublethal part of this continuum. Behavioral development is disorganized and stress thresholds are lowered as a result of such damage to the central nervous system.

Another group of clinical conditions which releases the subcortical centers from cerebral control and results in aggressive outbursts occurs from acute drug intoxication, which includes chronic alcoholism. Along with head injuries, which may produce cortical pathology, these conditions eventuate in a wide range of aggressive behaviors, such as temper tantrums, irritability, and fighting and violence. Alcohol, which is believed to depress the cortical control functions, has been shown to have a strong association with violence. Tinklenberg and Stillman (1970) report on a series of studies showing that alcohol is present as a factor in between 50 to 55 percent of the offenders in a large number of criminal homicides. Alcohol has also been implicated in various forms of assault, nonfatal shootings, and suicides; it is also a major variable in motor vehicle accidents and the resulting injuries and deaths.

Still another clinical condition that culminates in violent attacks on others, sexual offenses, self-multilation, and destruction of property results from lesions in certain subcortical structures of the limbic system. Encephalitis lethargica, temporal lobe pathology, and tumors in the frontal lobe, the hypothalamus, the septal region, the anterior hypothalamus, the amygdala, the uncus, and the hippocampal areas are prominently associated with increased irritability and rage attacks (Boelkins and Heiser, 1970; Moyer, 1971). A sensational example is the previously mentioned case of Charles Whitman who on post mortem examination was found to have a malignant tumor in the amygdaloid structure of his brain.

Mark and Ervin (1970) define a clinical entity which they term "the dyscontrol syndrome." Violent acts, more often than not, they claim, are produced by brain disease involving damage to the limbic system or temporal lobe. They feel that the hypothalamus is most frequently involved. Characteristic of the patients they studied were four symptoms, which comprised the dyscontrol syndrome: (1) a history of physical assault; (2) senseless brutality precipitated by drinking even a small quantity of alcohol (pathological intoxication); (3) impulsive sexual behavior often including sexual assault; and (4) multiple automobile accidents and traffic violations (among those subjects who drove cars).

Although it seems clear that the cortical and subcortical centers are involved in the expression of agonistic behavior in animals and aggression in man, the relationship between these mechanisms and aggression is incompletely understood. The neurological control of aggression is an extremely complex phenomenon and is far from being systematized.

Hormones and Aggression

Hormones secreted by the endocrine system have been demonstrated to produce an effect on aggressive behavior. One of the consistent findings emerging from studies of animal and human behavior is that males are generally more aggressive than females. Social expectations, of course, play a role. Males are expected to be more aggressive than females and the difference may be a self-fulfilling prophecy.

An extreme point of view in this regard is afforded by Rader (1973), who argues that all violence committed by males is both sexually and politically motivated.

> There is a long history of female reinforcement of male impulses toward violence. From the time we are little boys, we are taught to look to women for the affirmation of our manhood. It is from them that judgment is rendered on our success or failure as sexual beings, as men. Women for centuries have marched their sons off into hopeless wars; it is the female auxiliaries of street gangs who incite boys to violence or often are the stated cause of deadly gang fights. It is women who teach young boys false conceptions of manhood, mothers and teachers and wives who goad their men into bloody role playing, who provoke and approve their violence. But it is the men who die.
>
> I am convinced that violence, all violence, is both sexual and political in character, and that its explanation lies in the psychosexual disfigurement of the young male. Violence is

rooted in emasculation, emasculation too often accomplished, intentionally or not, through the offices of women. Violence in the United States is indisputably synonymous with young male aggression: murder, rape, assault, gratuitous brutality.

Acts of violence by young men are political acts in the specific sense that they are long-delayed reactions against authority, against powerlessness before authority, authority usually presented to males in boyhood in the person of the dominant woman, the matriarch and teacher. Women comprise 85 percent of all elementary school teachers, and, with the abandonment of parental responsibility by middle- and upper-class white males, female dominance commands the home.

However, in addition to sex-role training and expectations, there are data supporting the hypothesis that male aggressiveness has a biological component associated with male sex hormones. Even Maccoby and Jacklin (1971), who take strong issue with existing stereotypes about sex differences, agree with the generalization that males are the more aggressive sex. Inferring a biochemical basis for these differences, they cite four factors to support such an inference: the cross-cultural universality of these sex differences, the fact that they are found as early in life as the behavior can be observed, the similarity of such differences in both man and the subhuman primates, the fact that females can be made more aggressive by administration of male hormones during the perinatal period.

The presence or absence of sex hormones during the embryological development of the fetus is of critical importance in the development of the genital tract (Boelkins and Heiser, 1970). Of the male hormones, the most important in its relationship to aggressive behavior is testosterone. During the embryological period of the fetus, the undifferentiated reproductive system will develop as a male's even under the influence of minute amounts of androgens, whereas, the absence of androgens will cause the genital tract to develop as a female's (Harris and Levine, 1965). These hormones are secreted appropriately either by the adrenals of the fetus or those of the mother. Not only the genital tract but also those neuromechanisms that mediate sexual behavior are also differentiated at this time through the action of testosterone.

Behavioral changes influenced by testosterone are not limited to sexual behavior as demonstrated by Young, Goy, and Phoenix (1964). By treating pregnant rhesus monkeys with testosterone during the second quarter of fetal development, these authors were able to effect changes in the behavior of female offspring. In many of its aspects, social behavior of these females became markedly masculinized.

In another study (Ehrhardt and Money, 1967) the behavior patterns of ten girls, four to 14 years of age, whose mothers received treatments with androgen-like hormones during pregnancy, were studied on the basis of sex-role preference tests. Based on the preference of these girls for boys' toys, on their athletic energy, their outdoor interests, and their minimal interests in typically feminine pursuits, nine of the ten girls were classified as tomboys.

Ehrhardt, Epstein, and Money (1968) studied 15 girls born with masculinized external genitalia. Because of a defect in enzyme metabolism during the fetal period, these girls experienced the effects of excessive amounts of androgens. Although these conditions were corrected by treatment with cortisone and surgery, the girls remained masculine in their play activities and interests and eschewed or ignored typical feminine pastimes. Because of early social learning, however, the long-term effects of fetal masculinization were tempered. Typical conceptions of romance, marriage, and motherhood were expressed by these girls at the appropriate developmental periods.

Castration has been shown to reduce fighting behavior in animals (Sigg, 1968) and, albeit drastic, this procedure has been used to control certain violent male sex crimes (LeMaire, 1956). Anti-androgenic substances have been developed which have the same effect as castration in the control of violent sexual offenses (Lerner, 1964). Although most of the studies suggest that the level of testosterone in the bloodstream is correlated with aggressive behavior, data are extant (Moyer, 1971) suggesting that the introduction of estrogens will mask the effect of androgens and thus reduce aggressive behavior.

Heightened irritability and feelings of hostility are thought to be part of the premenstrual syndrome (Hamburg, 1966). In one study of a women's prison 62 percent of the crimes of violence were committed during the premenstrual week compared to two percent committed at the end of that period. In another study (Dalton, 1964) 49 percent of all crimes were committed by women during the menstrual period or in the premenstrum. Although the physiological relationship between premenstrual tension and irritability is unknown, the syndrome is associated with a drop in the progesterone level in the blood during this period. In this connection it has been demonstrated that women who take oral contraceptives containing progestagenic agents are significantly less irritable than women using other forms of contraceptives or no contraceptives (Hamburg, *et al.*, 1968). Although the underlying physiological reasons are not clear, the data tend to support a relation between irritability (and perhaps aggression) to a decrease in estrogens in the bloodstream. However, Parlee (1973) raises serious questions about the scientific status of the hypothesis of a premenstrual syndrome. Critical of the methodology used in these studies, she concludes that on the basis of the present research "... it is difficult to predict anything about an individual's behavior from the fact that she is in the premenstrual or menstrual phase of the cycle" (p. 456).

Along with the effects of hormones on the increase or decrease of aggressive behavior, there is evidence that hypoglycemia may also be related to aggression. Few systematic studies exist, however, and the kinds of data are of the order which show that low blood sugar is related to irritability and unsocial or antisocial behavior in a greater percentage of subjects than those with normal blood sugar levels (Moyer, 1971). In studies of the relationship between sugar metabolism and crime, low blood sugar was implicated as a factor in hostility, aggressive tendencies, and crime (Moyer, 1971).

Under which of the theories of social philosophy advanced earlier can the preceding material on the physiological considerations of aggression best be encompassed? Inasmuch as these physiological conditions are chiefly clinical, the phenomena would not fit under the "essential nature of man" category propounded by Hobbes or Locke since it is implied that clinical conditions are not normal. Theoretically, clinical conditions are amenable to treatment and the cause of such conditions may also be prevented. If these clinical conditions culminating in aggressive behavior are not innate, the problem of their control is one of prevention or treatment rather than of social restraint.

Conceptually, the physiological considerations pertaining to aggression would best be encompassed by Rousseau's notion of a malleable organism molded by its environment. But, even a malleable organism has a definite morphology, so that certain structures will function according to their constitutional propensity unless modified by environmental conditions. Therefore, although males appear to be more aggressive than females and this higher level of aggression is probably correlated with level of testosterone, the manifestation of aggression is subject to environmental controls. Thus, rather than restraint or a garrison society to suppress or control aggressiveness which, according to the Hobbesian view is innate, the attempt to prevent or ameliorate those conditions that produce clinical aberrations in structure leading to aggressive behavior would seem to be both more humane and productive.

FRUSTRATION AND AGGRESSION

So far we have examined theories purporting that aggression is either innate or the result of aberrant physiological conditions or due to higher levels of androgen in the male sex. Another theory advanced about 35 years ago held that all aggressive behavior resulted from aggressive drive produced by frustration. When goal-directed activity is blocked, an aggressive drive is induced. Behavior intended to injure a person against whom it is directed is energized by this drive. Upon infliction of the injury, the aggressive drive is reduced. This frustration-aggression hypothesis, developed by Dollard, Doob, Miller, Mowrer, and Sears (1939), states that "the occurrence of aggressive behavior always presupposes the existence of frustration and, contrariwise, that the existence of frustration always leads to some form of aggression." Frustration and aggression are causally related and aggression is defined independently as "an act whose goal response is injury to an organism (or organism surrogate)." The authors state that "the strength of instigation to aggression should vary directly with: 1) the strength of instigation to the frustrated response; 2) the degree of interference with the frustrated response; 3) the number of frustrated response sequences" (p. 28). To illustrate the first principle, a 12-year-old boy would be more aggravated by finding a crucial page missing from a detective story as compared to a page from his history textbook. As an illustration of the second proposition, a child digging in the sand with two shovels would be less annoyed if one rather than both shovels were taken away from him. Implied by the third hypothesis is a cumulative effect of frustration, so that an individual encountering a series of setbacks in his office during the day will have less tolerance for an ill-prepared dinner upon arrival at home in the evening.

The assertion that aggression is always a result of frustration encountered almost immediate criticism and the Yale group (Miller et al., 1941) undertook the task of reformulating the hypothesis. The initial proposition was only one-half defensible, specifically the first part. Inasmuch as the second part suggests that frustration can have no other consequences but aggression, it is unfortunately open to misinterpretation. An instigation to some form of aggression is only one of a number of different responses possible to frustration. Thus, in a hierarchy of responses produced by a specific frustrating situation, if aggression is the strongest component, it will be the first response to occur. Other responses incompatible with aggression may also be instigated; if these responses are stronger than the instigation to aggression, they will occur first. The hypothesis was rephrased (Miller *et al.* 1941) to state "frustration produces instigations to a number of different types of response, one of which is an instigation to some form of aggression" (p. 338). In their reformulation, they also emphasized two qualifications of the hypothesis. The first qualification stated the uncertainty of how early in infancy the frustration-aggression hypothesis was applicable. The second, concerning the origin of the frustration-aggression relation, signified that no assumptions were made as to whether this relation was innate or learned.

A major criticism of the frustration-aggression hypothesis is that it tends to be tautological (Kaufmann, 1970). In the years since the hypothesis has been advanced, the terms "frustration" and "aggression" have become protean so that any antecedent situation can be interpreted as frustrating. Similarly, given the wide latitude for demarcating the aggressive response as direct or indirect or in the modes of catharsis or displacement, the interpretation of an aggressive act has become vague and ambiguous. Since frustration is an inner state presumably occurring when the organism is thwarted, there is no reliable way to measure this condition independent of some overt response such as aggression. However, if in order to demonstrate the existence of frustration we have to demonstrate in each instance an act of aggression or some other act in a hierarchy of responses, then we have gained little knowledge or predictive accuracy from such *post facto* reasoning.

Perhaps the antecedents of aggression might more readily be conceptualized as a class of aversive stimuli of which frustration is but one member. Therefore, the bond is between aversive stimuli and aggression rather than frustration and aggression. As an example of this model, the animal data on punishment show that painful stimuli will produce what Azrin and Holz (1966) term "operant aggression." The deliverer of the painful stimulus is destroyed or immobilized and the rewarding consequences of pain reduction maintain the aggressive response to pain. More likely, frustration, when it is amenable to objective measurement, is classified along with pain as an aversive stimulus.

Another major criticism voiced by Kaufmann (1970) is that "we find that there is no one-to-one relationship between these two alleged intervening variables at all. Aggression may often occur without any visible or detectable antecedent to frustration, and, conversely, as far as the hypothesized state called 'frustration' may be reasonably inferred, other responses are quite effectively learned" (p. 33). Kaufmann would assert that no reliable way of establishing a relation between these antecedent and consequent events has been devised.

It would seem equally (or perhaps more) economical to assume that aggressive behavior is a function of its consequences as well as of such antecedents as frustration. Aggression pays off in a multitude of ways (Buss, 1971), most often instrumentally in achieving a goal by removing an obstacle or in self-enhancement or self-defense. Thus, when aggressive behavior occurs, it is as important to search the environment for the reinforcing stimulus supporting the behavior as it is to look for a frustrating stimulus which, presumably, has elicited the aggressive response.

THE SOCIAL LEARNING OF AGGRESSION

Compared with theories holding that aggression is innate or the result of an aggressive drive, social learning theory seeks the external rather than the internal impellers to aggression. Bandura (1973a), a leading exponent, states: "In predicting the occurrence of aggression, one should be concerned with predisposing conditions than with predisposed individuals" (p. 5). This theory of aggression is based on a model comprised of three essential components (Bandura, 1973b). The first is concerned with the origins of aggression, specifically how our aggressive behavior patterns are acquired or developed. The second component deals with instigators of aggression and examines how aggressive behavior is activated or provoked. The third component deals with reinforcers of aggression and attempts to answer the question of how aggressive behavior is maintained once it occurs.

Most behaviors are acquired through imitation (observational learning). Such learning is either deliberate or inadvertent and is based on the influence of the example. In the case of aggression, three prominent sources of observational learning are afforded to the child: (1) familial influences, (2) subcultural influences, and (3) symbolic modeling. Youngsters who display antisocial aggression and assaultive behavior tend much more frequently to come from families where there is a much greater incidence of aggressive modeling than nondelinquent youngsters (McCord et al., 1959).

Although most assaultive youngsters do not come from a background where parents are criminally violent, the attitude of such parents is such that they tend to favor aggressive solutions to problems. Particularly as concerns disciplinary practices, children in these homes are furnished with an aggressive model when parents employ physical punishment (Lefkowitz *et al.*, 1963).

Subcultural influences include those situations where status is gained primarily through fighting and other physically aggressive solutions to problems. Thus, individuals who are successful in aggression are the prestigious models whose behavior is copied.

Symbolic modeling occurs largely through the pictures and words provided by mass media, particularly the omnipresent television set. Limitless opportunities are provided by these media for the child to view "stabbings, beatings, stompings, stranglings, muggings, and less graphic but equally destructive forms of cruelty before he has reached kindergarten age" (Bandura, 1973a, p. 8). That children acquire patterns of aggressive behavior through symbolic modeling is supported by a substantial body of research literature. (See, for example, Bandura, 1973b; Bandura, Ross, and Ross, 1961; Bandura and Walters, 1963). The social contagion of aggressive styles propagated through the influence of symbolic modeling is dramatic. One or two salient examples are enough to spread a new behavior among populations. Airline hijackings are one kind of model. Airline hijackings in conjunction with obtaining large sums of money and parachuting from the airplane is another variation. Campus protests, at Berkeley, served as a model for other universities throughout the country. Abductions of prominent individuals for political and/or monetary objectives in one part of the world serve as models for such events in other parts.

Another avenue for acquiring new modes of aggressive behavior is through direct experience in which the behavior is followed by rewarding or punishing contingencies. Successful acts or patterns of behavior are culled from general exploratory behavior and are differentially reinforced. Unsuccessful behaviors are eventually extinguished through lack of positive reinforcement or through the application of aversive consequences.

In a study of repeatedly victimized, passive children (Patterson *et al.*, 1967), counteraggression was effective in diminishing attacks upon them. Moreover, not only did their defensive responses increase in frequency but eventually these passive children themselves began to attack their aggressors. However, passive children who were seldom maltreated (because they tended to avoid other children) tended to remain passive along with those passive children whose counteraggressive responses were unsuccessful.

The second major component of the social learning theory model of aggression pertains to the instigation of aggressive behavior. Such activation occurs from learning experiences rather than innate mechanisms. Accordingly, Bandura describes five major instigators of aggression: modeling influences, aversive treatment, incentive inducements, instructional control, and bizarre symbolic control.

Numerous laboratory studies have shown that when children and adults have witnessed others acting in an aggressive manner, they will also behave more aggressively (Bandura and Walters, 1963). As will be illustrated in the forthcoming chapters, which deal with a field study concerning the influence on children of violent modeling on television, a similar effect occurs. Social learning theory delineates four processes that govern the modeling of aggressive behavior: (1) When the modeled acts serve as prompts or informative cues through association with past reinforcement, aggressive behavior in the observer is facilitated. (2) When aggressors receive approval or are even treated indifferently for their aggression, the observer receives the impression that such behavior is not only acceptable but even expected in certain situations. Modeled behavior of this kind serves to disinhibit the observer from his reluctance to perform in an aggressive manner. (3) Observing others aggressing generates emotional arousal in the observer and, according to a general arousal model, aggressive responding in the observer is enhanced. (4) This process pertains to the stimulus-enhancing effect of particular implements being used by the model. Specifically, the observer tends to use the same implements as the model, not necessarily in an imitative way although imitation may occur.

Physical assaults, verbal threats and insults, reductions in reinforcement which result in adversity, and thwarting are all frustrators and comprise aversive treatment — Bandura's second major category of instigators. In the context of social learning theory, frustration does not produce an aggressive drive that can be reduced only through aggressive behavior, but rather produces a generalized state of emotional arousal. This state can then eventuate in a variety of acts depending upon the individual's past learning history and the effectiveness with which various responses were used in coping with stress. For example, the prepotent response that occurs when the individual is faced with the stress of aversive treatment may be intensification of constructive efforts to overcome stress, withdrawal, the use of drugs including alcohol, or aggression.

The third major category of instigators in social learning theory is incentive inducements. This instigator produces aggression by means of man's capacity to anticipate events cognitively. Thus, instigation to aggression occurs from the expectation of positive consequences of an aggressive act rather than from the thrust of pain-producing stimuli.

Instructional control, a fourth major instigator, serves to activate aggression by using the results obtained from the socialization process in which people are trained to follow instructions. Legitimate authorities can successfully command aggression from others. The studies of obedience by Milgram (1963) dramatically illustrate that subjects will often act against their own values and hurt other people on the command of an authority.

Bizarre symbolic control, a fifth instigator, serves to provoke aggression when the individual is unable to test successfully his contact with experience or reality. In these cases, delusions (such as divine inner voices, paranoid suspicions, or grandiose convictions) result in tragic aggressive episodes such as murder and assassinations.

The third component in the social learning analysis model deals with the maintenance of aggressive behavior — the reinforcers of aggression. Bandura (1973b) delineates three major categories of reinforcement: external, vicarious, and self-reinforcement. In the case of external reinforcement, tangible rewards as well as those less tangible, such as social and status rewards that are contingently received, increase the likelihood for aggressive responding. Alleviation of aversive treatment is reinforcing because it is associated with pain reduction and tends to maintain such behaviors as coercive action or counteraggression. When humiliating or painful treatment can be mitigated by aggressive behavior, albeit defensive, such behavior is reinforced. The expression of pain cues or indications of injury by the target also tend to reinforce aggression. However, why this occurs is not clear. Pain cues may be associated with tension relief and thus may become reinforcing (Feshbach, 1970). Alternatively, pain and signs of suffering usually serve to inhibit rather than positively reinforce aggressive behavior. The results seem to be ambiguous in that in certain cases the infliction of pain on self and others may be reinforcing. On the other hand, ruthless aggression is learned, through the process of socialization, to be morally reprehensible. Consequently, elicitation of pain or cues of injury from a victim produce self-condemnatory feelings in the aggressor which should, and often do, inhibit aggressive behavior.

Aggressive behavior can be maintained through vicarious reinforcement when such behavior is observed as rewarded. In this case, it is emulated by the observer. When aggressive behavior is punished, the observer is less likely to behave aggressively.

Self-reinforcement is the third major contingency for maintaining aggressive behavior. In this respect social learning theory departs from traditional theories of reinforcement (Skinner, 1966a; 1966b) in that, in addition to external rewards and punishments, it attempts to embrace the regulation of behavior by self-produced consequences. Thus, in general, human beings behave in a way that produces self-satisfaction and feelings of self-worth; they avoid behaving in a manner that results in self-condemnatory behavior or harsh self-criticism. Aggressors must contend with their own reactions when they behave aggressively — so-called aggression anxiety — as well as with the reactions of others. Self-reward and self-punishment are ways of regulating aggressive behavior. In the former, aggressive behavior is a source of personal pride and self-esteem, and fighting prowess is equated with self-worth and manliness. In the latter, self-contempt is an antipodal feeling which serves to restrain aggressive behavior, most likely for the anxiety it produces in behaving in ways contrary to early socialization training. However, individuals have developed various ways of circumventing these feelings by neutralizing self-contempt or self-punishment. One technique is to dehumanize one's victims. A naturalistic observation of such dehumanization was made by an anthropologist (Fried, 1969) on a trip to Asia.

As a student of the Far East I have been making two or three trips a year to East Asia for the past several years. Quite frequently my seat mates, during tedious flights over the Pacific, have been members of the U.S. armed forces returning from leave or "rest and recreation." On a number of such occasions, during conversation, officers and men, particularly those returning to units in Vietnam, expressed the most horrifying opinions of the Asians among whom they were serving. To put it quite mildly, they did not regard Asians, whether friend or foe, as quite human.

I was given the impression that, if such attitudes were not consciously implanted at military indoctrination sessions, they were certainly reinforced there. In any event, the presence of such attitudes helps one understand the incredible; to realize that what took place at Songmy was not a matter of individual pathology of a company commander and many of his men, but the result of the corrupting influences of an intolerable situation.

Still another method for neutralizing self-punishment is to attribute blame to one's victims, making them culpable for the aggressor's behavior. Furthermore, by displacing responsibility for aggression to others and by diffusing responsibility for aggression to numbers of people, self-punishment may be either mitigated or entirely avoided.

"THE CULTURAL ENVELOPE"

Returning to our earlier discussion of social philosophy and the essential nature of man, we could formulate an analogy which states that the social learning of aggression is to Rousseau as innate aggression is to Hobbes. Man's essential nature is neither aggressive nor virtuous as the respective claims of Hobbes and Locke would have it. Rather, we maintain that man is born with a genotype and concomitant morphology. What he becomes is contingent upon the interaction of these species specific components with, as Eisenberg (1972) terms it, "the cultural envelope." In the broad sense, we feel that a socioeducational model would provide the best fit for a description of man's behavior. In the narrow sense, man learns to be aggressive through the agency of contingent reinforcement provided by the environment. These contingencies may be inadvertent, scheduled, or both. Because this socioeducational model allows for the malleability of the human organism, it more closely approximates the thinking of Rousseau than of Hobbes. Consequently, if aggressive behavior is learned and deemed to be maladaptive, it can also be unlearned or it need not be learned (taught?) at all.

In propounding a socioeducational model to account for aggressive behavior it would be inaccurate to conclude that we do not recognize the importance of human neurophysiology. Phenotypic considerations (such as primary and secondary sex characteristics, stature, and morphology) undoubtedly play a major role in the organism-environment interaction and the consequent learning of aggression. Endocrinological factors, particularly the level of gonadotropic hormones, are important for their effect on phenotype as well as levels of aggressive behavior. Moyer (1968) postulates the presence of six classes of aggressive behavior and adduces convincing evidence from the animal literature to show that each class has a particular neural and endocrine basis. For example, testosterone is an important variable in inter-male aggression but relatively unimportant in predatory aggression. And, as we noted earlier in this chapter, neurophysiological aberrations (such as limbic brain lesions) have been shown to potentiate and to be antecedents of aggressive behavior. Consequently, although our model for the development of aggressive behavior is largely derived from social learning theory, an important qualification is that environmental variables interact with widely varying biological organisms.

While we can demonstrate that manipulation of environmental variables will produce changes in aggressive behavior, we also believe that part of the variation in aggressive behavior is attributable to individual variation in genotype and phenotype. The present study focuses largely, but not exclusively, on the environmental side of the issue. Two reasons would explain this emphasis. When the study was conceived almost 20 years ago, the orientation and concern of the investigators with respect to aggression was psychosocial and epidemiological. Secondly, although the demarcation and measurement of environmental variables was no easy task, obtaining endocrine measures, karyotypes, and evidence of central nervous system insult for the countywide population of third-grade schoolchildren and their parents would have been beyond anyone's resources.

We began this chapter with a somewhat rhetorical question about the roots of aggression and violence in young adulthood. Our study of the major theories of the origins of aggressive behavior persuaded us that the question could best be answered within a socioeducational model provided by learning theory. Consequently, we formulated a design for a longitudinal field study for the psychosocial development of aggressive behavior (Eron *et al.*, 1971). Continuing over a ten-year span of time, the study focuses on aggressive behavior as a dependent (or outcome) measure and on four major classes of environmental conditions as the independent (predictor) variables. In the ten-year span between the two waves of the study, our thinking was influenced by the research findings on the physiological components in aggressive behavior. But the major assumption of our model still remains that aggression is a socially learned phenomenon. Accordingly, we selected for exploration the following classes of measures for their influence on the development of aggression: contingent responses to aggression, instigators, identification variables, and sociocultural variables. This longitudinal field study of aggressive behavior is presented in the remainder of this book.

SUMMARY

This chapter has focused on the three major theories concerned with the origins of aggressive behavior in humans: instinct theory, the frustration-aggression hypothesis, and social learning theory. Prior to an examination of these positions, definitions of aggression and certain semantic considerations were discussed. Philosophical theories of the nature of man, propounded in the 17th and 18th centuries by Hobbes, Locke, and Rousseau, were presented to illustrate their influence on the social contract by which men are governed and by which, presumably, aggression is controlled. These earlier theories of man's nature, which were developed by the social philosophers, were then related to 19th- and 20th-century theories of aggression. Freudian and ethological theories based on an instinct model and aggressive drive were analyzed and critiqued. Physiological theories and the frustration-aggression hypothesis were considered in a context in which aggressive acts are triggered by situational or clinical conditions. Social learning theory was examined from the perspective of the origins or learning of aggression, the instigation of the behavior once learned, and the maintenance or reinforcement of such behavior. Where germane, considerations of the research findings on the biology and physiology of aggression on human and infrahuman organisms were presented.

2
The Design of the Longitudinal Study

For the psychologist interested in establishing a causal model for a particular behavior, the laboratory is the ideal setting. Independent variables can be manipulated, and their effect on the dependent variables of interest can be measured. However, the causal basis for the development of aggression, popularity, leadership, psychopathology, and similar personality characteristics cannot be adequately studied in the laboratory. The child must be viewed in his natural environment over the course of his development to gain an understanding of how the complex stimuli in his environment interact to affect his personality development. Such an approach is known as a longitudinal study.

Unfortunately, in trading the highly stylized laboratory environment for the natural field setting, one also gives up the ability to manipulate independent variables. Cause and effect become much harder to separate in a field study; in fact, they are virtually impossible to separate unless the study is longitudinal. Is a child's delinquency a product of his parent's disharmony, or does his parent's disharmony stem from the child's delinquency? Even in a longitudinal field study, it is impossible to separate cause and effect with certainty. However, as we shall see, the psychologist can use a longitudinal field study to measure the relative plausibility of rival causal hypotheses.

It may seem as if we are dismissing laboratory experiments rather lightly. This is not the case. Most of the evidence reported in Chapter

1 was derived in laboratory experiments. Any theory of personality development should build upon both the manipulative experiments conducted in laboratories and data collected in natural settings. In particular, any causal model should be supported by laboratory experiments since causation is tested more easily there. On the other hand, we cannot be impressed by laboratory data unsupported by naturalistic evidence.

Given the wealth of laboratory studies, clinical investigations, and armchair theorizing on personality development, what seems most important to the emergence of more comprehensive theories would be the compilation of longitudinal data on children in their natural environments. The rest of this book will focus on one such study.

THE COLUMBIA COUNTY STUDY

Typically, longitudinal research tantalizes the social scientist with the promise of immeasurable gains and then presents him with insurmountable obstacles to achieving those gains. Longitudinal field studies are seldom planned in their entirety at their conception, and the one upon which this book is based was no exception. However, it was intended to be a longitudinal study from its conception. The initial goal of the study was to select a representative sample of American children, seven to nine years old, and to investigate the factors that might influence the development of aggression over a period of time. The dominant issues in selecting the sample were cost, geographical proximity, availability, representativeness, and low mobility. Bearing these factors in mind, we selected as our sample the entire third-grade population of one geographical area in the year 1959-1960. The area selected was Columbia County, New York. The details and conclusions of the 1960 study have previously been published (Eron et al., 1971); but the 1960 data alone were not sufficient for drawing formal causal conclusions about the development of aggression or other personality variables. Hence, in 1970 we tracked down as many of the original subjects as could be found, and restudied them about one year after most of them graduated from high school. It is the integration of the 1960 and 1970 findings that forms the basis for the causal models in this book.

The Setting

The extent to which our results can be generalized to the population of the United States depends in part upon the representativeness of our sample and the area from which it was drawn. However, Columbia County, New York, is hard to classify in a few words. Its county seat, Hudson, is a riverbank city about 120 miles north of New York City on the east bank of the Hudson. The rest of the county consists of rolling farmland between the Hudson River and the Berkshires. In general, Columbia County is semi-rural with only a few heavy industries. Of its 43,000 residents, 12,000 live in Hudson and 10,000 more in incorporated villages of less than 2,500 each. The remainder live in unincorporated areas. The population has sizable proportions of most major ethnic groups including Black, Irish, Italian, Jewish, and Slavic inhabitants. In 1960 there were 38 public and private third-grade classrooms in the county, with class sizes ranging from a small handful to 40 children.

The 1960 Sample

Each of the 875 children who were in the third grade in Columbia County in 1960 was studied intensively by our research group. The children were questioned and tested in their classrooms. Eighty-five percent of their mothers were interviewed and 71 percent of their fathers. The basic demographic information on this sample seems to be representative of what one would expect to find for third graders across much of the United States. The modal age was eight; the predominant socioeconomic environment was middle class, and the mean IQ at that time for the children in the sample was 104.4 ± 14.

The Learning of Aggression

The analysis of the 1960 data yielded a large amount of information about the characteristics of an aggressive child, his family, and his environment (Eron *et al.*, 1971). It is fair to say that all the major findings of that analysis were consistent with the hypothesis that aggression may be learned by a child from his interactions with his environment. For example, it was found that punishment of the child at home was correlated with the aggressiveness of the child at school. However, there were contrasting effects of punishment for two types of children — low-aggressive children who had close identification with their parents and high-aggressive children who identified only moderately with their parents. Punishment seemed to inhibit aggression in the former group and facilitate it in the latter group.

The difficulty with such a one-time field study is that one cannot tease apart causation from correlation. In the example above, was punishment correlated with aggression because an aggressive child is punished more, or because many children imitate the punishments they receive, or both? In order to separate causation and correlation, one needs to obtain repeated measurements on a child during his development. With such longitudinal data one can perhaps go beyond correlational theories and distinguish between the plausibility of rival causal theories. With this in mind, the 1970 reinvestigation of our 875 subjects was undertaken.

The 1970 Sample

The residential mobility of the American population makes any longitudinal study extremely difficult. From school records, we discovered that approximately 52 percent of the original sample had graduated from high school in June 1969 in Columbia County. To locate as many of the subjects in the original sample as possible, we queried school officials, examined high school yearbooks, telephone directories, voter lists, tax lists, and county directory. In addition, each subject who did appear was asked about the whereabouts of any of the missing subjects. In this way we finally obtained addresses for 735 of the 875 original subjects.

Obtaining addresses was only part of the problem, however. Getting subjects to come to an interview as an equally imposing task. Letters were sent to each of the 735 subjects asking them to come. As lures, we appealed to their sense of responsibility and offered each of them $20 for appearing. Of the 735 subjects to whom letters were sent, 460 indicated willingness to be interviewed. The remaining 275 subjects were categorized as shown in Table 2.1.* Of the 460 subjects who agreed to be interviewed 436 actually appeared. Of the 436 who appeared, 427 completed the procedure and contributed usable data.

It is judicious to ask how representative of the United States population these 427 subjects are, and how representative of the original 875 subjects they are. The 427 subjects had a modal age of 19 years. While 211 were boys, 216 were girls. On the average they had completed 12.6 years of school (in addition to kindergarten). Based on the 25 percent for which current IQ scores could be obtained (we have no reason to believe this is a biased sample), the mean 12th-grade IQ was 109.1 ± 11.6. Using father's occupation as a measure of social status (Warner *et al.*, 1960), the sample could still be described as predominantly middle class. It seems fair to say that

*Editors' Note: All tables and figures appear at the end of chapters.

our longitudinal sample of 427 children was not too different from what one would find in similar localities across the country.

On the other hand, the 427 subjects who were reinterviewed were not a completely representative sample of the original 875. In particular, the 13th-grade sample included more of the original low-aggression subjects and less of the original high-aggression subjects than one would have expected by chance. Of the boys in the lower quartile of aggression in the third grade, 57 percent were reinterviewed. However, of the boys who had been in the upper quartile in the third grade, only 27 percent were reinterviewed. The corresponding figures for girls were 63 percent and 33 percent, respectively. Why would almost double the number of low-aggressive subjects as high-aggressive subjects appear for the reinterview ten years later? The most compelling single explanation we can offer is based on a relationship we discovered between a family's residential mobility and its children's aggressiveness. We found these factors to be significantly positively correlated within our reinterview sample ($r = .17$ for boys); so it seems possible that the families of high-aggressive children were more likely to have moved between the times of the two interviews than the families of low-aggressive subjects.

Measurement Procedures

The procedures used in the third grade to interview the children and parents and the procedures used in the 13th grade to reinterview the children were carefully designed and pretested to avoid introducing experimenter bias (Eron *et al.*, 1971; Lefkowitz *et al.*, 1972). For the third grade, the instructions along with the parent interview and child self-report measures are presented in their entirety elsewhere (Eron *et al.*, 1971, pp. 184-268). For the 13th grade, the instructions and self-report questionnaire were published in the Surgeon General's Report (Lefkowitz *et al.*, 1972) but several parts are reprinted in Table 2.2.

MEASURING THE DEVELOPMENT OF PERSONALITY

Aggression

Before one can study aggressive behavior scientifically, one must have a reasonable operational definition of aggression. As argued in

Chapter 1, aggression is a behavior with many facets, some of which may aid an individual to cope with his environment. What we wish to investigate is the development of those facets of aggression that are desirable neither for the individual nor society.

Basically, we have employed four different techniques to evaluate the aggressiveness of our subjects: peer ratings, parent ratings, a personality test, and a self-report questionnaire. In the third grade only the peer ratings and parent ratings were obtained, while in the 13th grade all but parent ratings were used. These variables constitute our operational definition of aggression.

Peer-rated Aggression

To obtain peer ratings of aggression, we had each subject in the sample name all the subjects he knew who displayed specific aggressive behaviors. For example, each subject was asked to identify anyone "who starts a fight over nothing." In the third grade there were ten such questions interspersed with other items and in the 13th grade nine such questions as shown in Table 2.3.

These questions were selected after intensive pretesting and were subject to rigorous validation procedures.[1] In the third grade each child performed this peer-nomination task in a classroom setting, while in the 13th grade it was in a face-to-face interview. In either case a child's raw aggression rating was computed by adding up the number of times he was named by his peers on the aggression items and dividing by the total number of questions. To correct for the fact that a well-known subject might be named more often than another subject even though both were equally aggressive, we divided a subject's raw aggression rating by an estimate of the number of people who could have named him and multiplied the result by 100 to obtain a percentage. In the third grade this was the number of children present in the classroom on the day of testing, but in the 13th grade one could name any subject. Consequently, a subject's raw aggression score was divided by the number of times he was nominated by all others on the question, "who do you know?" This peer-rating procedure for measuring aggression has been employed successfully by other researchers including Feshbach and Singer (1971), Milavsky and Pekowsky (1973), Parton (1964), and Peterson (1971).

From Table 2.3 one can see that the questions for the aggression ratings were phrased in the past tense in the 13th grade. This suggests the possibility that 13th-grade ratings might simply be a remeasure of third-grade aggression ratings; however, the available evidence argues strongly against this interpretation. First, only those subjects who reappeared for an interview were used as raters in the 13th grade. It seems likely that most of them had known each other in recent years. Second, as part of the instructions, subjects were told to "base your answers on what you *last* knew of each person from personal observation and contact." Finally, and most importantly, the 13th-grade peer ratings closely agree with the other 13th-grade measures of aggression to be discussed below, but the third-grade peer ratings do not correlate nearly as well with these other 13th-grade measures (Table 2.4). Of course, the nominations made in the 13th grade were undoubtedly influenced to some extent by behaviors prior to that time, but the resulting 13th-grade aggression scores are clearly measures of more recent behaviors than were the third-grade scores.

Aggression Anxiety

In addition to a direct peer rating of aggression for each subject, we obtained a peer rating of each subject's concern with avoiding aggressive encounters. We labeled this measure *"aggression anxiety."* A person with a high score on this variable would have been nominated by many of his peers as one who "said 'excuse me' even when he had not done anything bad," and who "would never fight even when picked on."[2]

Parent-rated Aggression

During the reinterview in the 13th grade, each subject was administered the Minnesota Multiphasic Personality Inventory (Dahlstrom *et al.*, 1972). As Hathaway and Monachesi (1963) have reported, elevations on scales 4 and 9 of this inventory are indicative of delinquency. Hence, we added together each subject's scores (T-scores) on scales 4 and 9 of the MMPI to get an aggressiveness score. This measure correlated highly with the 13th-grade peer-nominated aggression score (Table 2.4).

Personality Assessment Inventory

During reinterview in the 13th grade, each subject was administered the Minnesota Multiphasic Personality Inventory (Dahlstrom *et al*, 1972). As Hathaway and Monachesi (1963) have reported, elevations on scales 4 and 9 of this inventory are indicative of delinquency. Hence, we added together each subject's scores (T-scores) on scales 4 and 9 of the MMPI to get an aggressiveness score. This measure correlated highly with the 13th-grade peer-nominated aggression score (Table 2.4).

Self-report Questionnaire

In order to secure self-reports of aggression from our subjects in the 13th grade, we included two sets of questions in the interview. One set was designed to have face validity as a measure of a subject's propensity for antisocial behavior and the other set was designed to measure the intensity of a subject's aggressive habits. The questions in both these sets had been derived through pretesting and are denoted in Table 2.2, by the mnemonic BEH and RAG. A *Total Aggressive Habit* score was derived by summing the scores on all the questions from both sets. That score correlates highly with 13th-grade peer-rated aggression (Table 2.4).

Each of the above measures of aggression possesses reasonable face validity. In addition, their demonstrated statistical interrelatedness supports their validity. With regard to reliability, however, we only have information on the MMPI and peer-rated measures, both of which are highly reliable (Walder *et al.*, 1961).

Do these aggression variables measure the type of aggression in which we are interested: "an act which injures or irritates another person?" To answer this question, we asked the Division of Criminal Justice of the State of New York to determine the number of arrests of male subjects who were low, medium, and high on aggression.[3] The results of the survey shown in Table 2.5, support the contention that our aggression measures are valid. Subjects high on the peer-rated aggression measure were more likely to be arrested for a violent crime.

Psychopathology

While our attention in this book is focused primarily upon the development of aggression, several other personality characteristics were assessed in the 13th grade. It is enlightening to trace the development of these personality traits and their relation to aggression.

Aggression, as defined in this book, could be interpreted as a pathological bahavior; yet other pathological behaviors may occur that have little relation to aggression. It would be of interest to have a general measure of *psychopathology*. The MMPI (Minnesota Multiphasic Personality Inventory) provides such a measure in the form of four scales called the psychotic tetrad — scales 6, 7, 8, and 9. High scores on these scales are suggestive of psychosis. Scale 6 measures paranoia; scale 7, psychasthenia (obsessive-compulsive habits); scale 8, schizophrenia; and scale 9, hypomania (manic behaviors). We added together each subject's scores on these four scales to get a single variable called *psychopathology*.

Popularity and Leadership

Each subject's popularity and leadership were evaluated through a peer-rating procedure identical to the aggression-rating procedure.[4] Peer nominations on two items were used to assess popularity: "who did you like to sit next to in class," and "who were the students who you would have liked to have had for your best friends?" To assess leadership, peer nominations on "who was a leader of a club or group" were used. While the popularity ratings were derived in both grades, the leadership ratings were only obtained for the 13th grade. Again, the questions on these scales were selected after extensive pretesting and validation (Walder *et al.*, 1961). For example, all have interjudge reliabilities of above .70.

While a few other personality characteristics were recorded, these four variables — aggression, psychopathology, popularity, and leadership — are the ones we selected for investigation.

POTENTIAL PREDICTORS OF AGGRESSION

A scientist always begins an investigation with preconceptions about what may be found. The background for our preconceptions about the development of aggression was given in Chapter 1. The most important role that these preconceptions played was to guide our choice of which potential predictors of aggression we would study — that is, what our independent variables would be. Yet the hypotheses we hold which guided these choices are based on reasonable scientific evidence.

We view the maze of environmental variables to which a child is exposed as consisting of four distinct types: instigators, contingent responses, identification variables, and sociocultural variables. We hypothesize that exposure to each type of variable affects the development of personality differently. This classification system emerged out of our view that the nature and extent of a child's future behaviors are influenced by the learning conditions attendent upon his early behavior.

Instigators

An instigator to a behavior is a stimulus that usually elicits the behavior in question as a response. For example, frustration is probably an important instigator to aggression. Since instigation is only one of many factors affecting the occurrence of a behavior, the relation between an instigator and its response may not be one to one. For each subject in the third grade we measured four major characteristics, which we considered potential instigators of aggression: *parental rejection of the child, parental disharmony, lack of nurturance of the child by the parents*, and the *child's IQ*. This last variable, measured by the California Test of Mental Maturity (Sullivan *et al.*, 1957), was obtained as a control measure, but upon reflection we hypothesized that low IQ might act as a frustrator and instigator to aggression. The other three instigation variables were scored through the interviews with the parents. Each parent's responses to questions about rejection, disharmony, and nurturance were summed. The questions employed were selected and validated with a procedure described elsewhere (Eron *et al.*, 1971). A very high score on the rejection scale would represent a parent who complains that his child is too forgetful, has bad manners, does not read as well as he should, does not take care of his things, does not follow directions, wastes too much time, and has poor taste in what he buys for himself. A high score on the disharmony. scale would represent parents who disagreed with each other about their choice of friends and social life, who spend little of their time together, who can think of nothing they like to do together, who have serious arguments in front of their children about how to raise them, who have left home during arguments, and who are disinterested in each other's work. Finally, a very low score on nurturance would be achieved by a parent who does not know why his child cries, what upsets his child, or what his child dreams about, who seldom tries to figure out what his child fears, who does·not have time to talk to his child, and who cannot say how he shows his child that "he is on his side." In the 13th grade *IQ* scores and *achievement test* scores were obtained from the schools on small subsamples of subjects.

Besides the instigators to aggression measured in the third grade, we collected data on one other potential instigator to aggression during the 13th-grade interview of the subject. We asked each subject several questions that assessed how many times he had been the *victim of an aggressive act* (see Table 2.2, items VAG 39-43). Of course, we were hypothesizing that being victimized would be an instigation to aggression. Further, it has been demonstrated in laboratory studies with children that highly aggressive subjects seek out situations in which they will be likely targets for aggression (Parton, 1964; Patterson *et al.*, 1967; Peterson, 1971).

Contingent Responses to Aggression

While instigators may trigger aggressive acts, the development of more enduring aggressive habits should be influenced by how a subject's environment responds to his aggressiveness. Among the most important reinforcing agents for an eight-year-old or younger child are undoubtedly his parents; so in the third grade we selected the parents' use of *punishment* as a measure of how a child's aggressive acts are reinforced. An assumption underlying this choice was that those parents who employ less punishment resort to positive reinforcement to control the child's behavior. However, looking back, we see that it was a mistake not to assess the extent of the positive reinforcement of nonaggressive behavior on the part of the child by the parent. In any case, punishment scores were computed separately for each parent on 24 items and averaged to obtain an overall score. The higher the score, the more punishment a parent said he used in controlling his child.

In an attempt to obtain a comparable measure of the subject's own proclivity to use punishment ten years later, we asked each subject during his 13th grade reinterview how he would punish an eight-year-old child of his own sex for committing identical offenses. The responses to these questions formed the basis for a *"potential for punishment"* score for each subject. The 24 punishment items, identical to those administered to the parents of our subjects ten years earlier, are presented in Table 2.2, identified by the mnemonic "PUN."

Identification

The importance of modeling and observational learning in the acquisition of behavior has become increasingly clear in recent years. The child does what he sees being done, especially if he sees it being reinforced (Bandura and Walters, 1963; Bandura *et al.*, 1963). While various characteristics of the model and the situation influence the likelihood of observational learning (Bandura, 1969), observational learning would seem to have great potential as a determiner of life-long patterns of behavior.

A second type of identification relevant to the development of personality is the psychoanalytic concept of internalization of parents' values, desires, and standards (Freud, 1923). The child who successfully internalizes his parents' standards finds it easy to control his own behavior in line with his parents' proscriptions.

Identification by modeling

Both types of identification variables — modeling and internalization — were measured in the third grade. The modeling category included the child's copying of parental behaviors, his sex-role modeling, and his potential for modeling aggressive behaviors observed on television. To measure *the child's identification with each parent*, we calculated an Expressive Behavior Profile for both parents and for the child. In this procedure, a variation of the Semantic Differential Technique (Osgood *et al.*, 1957), the subject rated several of his own expressive behaviors — e.g., walking, talking — on 18 five-point scales with bipolar adjectives as anchors — e.g., fast-slow (see Table 2.2, items PID). Since parents were also asked to rate themselves on the behaviors, a measure of discrepancy between the child and each of his parents could be obtained.[5] The sign of this variable was then reversed to make it a direct measure of identification.

The child's *sex-role identification* was measured by the Games and Activities Preference List and is presented elsewhere (Eron *et al.*, 1971). Each third-grade child was presented with a list of questions requiring a choice between two activities. For example, "Would you rather go shooting or go bowling?" or "Would you rather use lipstick and powder or use a razor and shaving cream?" The hypothesis which led to the development and use of this measure of identification was that preference for masculine activities would be positively related to aggression. (Lefkowitz, 1962).

Television violence

With the increasing prominence of violence in our society, television programming (with its heavy emphasis on interpersonal violence and acquisitive lawlessness) is proposed as a model that teaches the child aggressive habits. In Chapter 4 we will review the important laboratory studies indicating the short-term effects of exposing a child to violent television. With this longitudinal field study we hoped to test the effects of a steady exposure to violent television upon the development of a child's aggressiveness.

The child's exposure to aggressive models on television was measured in the third grade by asking the mother to name the child's three favorite television programs. All programs mentioned were then categorized as violent or nonviolent by two independent raters with 94 percent agreement in their ratings. A program was scored 2 for violent, 0 for nonviolent, and 1 when the raters disagreed. Each subject's TV violence score was the mean rating for his three favorite programs.

Ten years later, each subject was asked for his/her four favorite current television programs. Again all programs then categorized for presence or absence of violence by two independent raters who were only a few years older than the subject. Scores, assigned to each program on the basis of agreement between the raters, ranged from 0 when both raters said nonviolent, to 1 when they disagreed, to 2 when both said violent. Here again there was good agreement between the two raters. They agreed on 81 percent of the 125 programs mentioned by the subjects. The score given a subject was the mean of the violence ratings for the four programs mentioned. The programs from both years and their classifications are in Tables 2.6 and 2.7.

The designation by these raters of violent and nonviolent programs agreed very well with the assignment of programs by Feshbach and Singer (1971) to aggressive and nonaggressive diets of programs in their field experiment. Furthermore, the judgments of our raters were in close agreement with the results obtained by Greenberg and Gordon (1970), who did an extensive rating study in which they used as raters both established television critics and 300 persons randomly selected from the Detroit telephone directory. We recomputed our subjects' 13th-grade television violence scores on the basis of Greenberg and Gordon's ratings and found a high correlation ($r = .94$) between the resulting scores and our own.

One might argue that mothers would not be very knowledgeable about their eight-year-old's viewing habits, or might lie about them, and, hence, that the third- and 13th-grade violence scores cannot be compared. While we will see that third-grade scores based on mother's report do not correlate well with 13th-grade scores based on subject's report, it seems most appropriate to attribute this finding to the long time lag. For example, we found that for a small subsample of third-grade subjects, the TV violence scores based on mothers' information significantly correlated with scores obtained only five years later from the subject's informaton ($r = .16$) (Huesmann et al., 1973). Furthermore, the mother did not need to know all that her child watched to give us adequate responses. She only needed to know her child's favorite programs. Thus, we find the argument against the use of mothers' ratings to be unconvincing.

Another criticism that might be leveled at our method of assessing a child's exposure to television violence is that "preference" is not "watching." Perhaps, but preference for a program certainly indicates some watching. Besides, to model behaviors seen on TV, the child must attend to the TV; so we would argue that preference is a better measure of potential for modeling aggression than is watching. If a child likes a program, he attends to it and can model the actors' behaviors.

Three other aspects of our subjects' television viewing habits were assayed in this study. We had the mothers (in the third grade) and the subjects themselves (in the 13th grade) estimate how many *hours of television the subject watched* each week. In addition, we had the subjects in the 13th grade report on their *sports viewing habits* and their feelings about *how realistic television seems to be.*

In the 13th grade we also asked the subject to report on one type of experience which might indicate a potential for identification with aggressive models. We asked each subject (through a set of questions given in Table 2.2, items WAG 44-48) how many times he/she had *witnessed aggressive acts being* performed.

Identification by internalization

Identification with parents through internalization of values was assessed by the amount of *confessing* of transgressions to parents that the child performed and the amount of *guilt* the child expressed to his/her parents. Both of these behaviors were reported by each parent. A child low on confessing would be one who, according to the parents, always denies doing "naughty" acts. A child low on guilt would be one who, according to his/her parents, feels that his/her punishments are not justified, doesn't worry about lies, tries to get away with things he/she shouldn't do when no one seems to be watching, and who does not feel sorry when he/she disobeys.

Sociocultural Variables

Sociocultural variables could be hypothesized to affect the development of personality in a variety of ways ranging from genetic predispositions to nutrition to learning. In choosing the variables to represent a subject's sociocultural environment, we entertained no particular hypotheses about the processes underlying their effect; rather we tried to be exhaustive in our coverage of potential sociocultural predictors of aggression. In both the third and 13th grade we rated the *status of the father's occupation.* In the third grade the 1960 Census scale (United States Bureau of Census, 1960) was used with low numbers representing high status, while in the 13th grade the Warner scale (1960) was used with low numbers again representing high status. Similarly, during the third-grade interview, we measured *the educational levels achieved by the mother and father.* Seven levels[6] were coded as follows:

1 = graduate or professional training
2 = college graduate
3 = 1-3 years of college
4 = high school graduate
5 = 10-11 years
6 = 7-9 years
7 = under 7 years

Besides educational and occupational status, we evaluated the parents' (in the third grade) and subject's (in the 13th grade) general *mobility orientation.* A parent high on mobility orientation would be very willing to learn new skills, leave friends, move, take on more responsibility, and give up spare time to get ahead. The *ethnic background* of the family was also assessed during the third-grade interview. A highly ethnic family would be one in which one or all the grandparents were born in another country.[7] The *frequency of church attendance* as reported by the parents in the third grade and the subject in the 13th grade was also recorded. Finally, the subjects' educational and occupational *aspirations* were assessed in the 13th grade.

DATA ANALYSIS TECHNIQUES

The mean scores of our 427 subjects on these variables are shown in Table 2.8. However, in a field study such as this, where variables were not manipulated, other statistics besides means provide crucial information. The most important statistic is probably the correlation coefficient.

The *correlation* (r) between two variables measures how well one could predict a person's score on one of the variables from his score on the other variable. A correlation can range from -1 to 0 to +1. A correlation of zero means that the variables are unrelated (unrelated linearly, to be precise); a correlation of +1 means a perfect direct relation; and a correlation of -1 means a perfect inverse relation. Of course, in the real world no two variables are ever correlated +1 or -1 because of noise in data — e.g., measurement or other error. The squared correlation coefficient between two variables, which can range from 0 to 1, measures the percentage of variation in one variable that can be explained by the variation in the other variable.

For example, in the next chapter we will see that a child's IQ correlates about -.3 with his aggressiveness at age 8. The negative sign indicates that IQ and aggression are inversely related — the higher the IQ, the lower the aggression. The .3 means that $(.3)^2 = .09 = 9$ percent of the variation in a child's aggressiveness can be explained by his IQ *or* that nine percent of the variation in his IQ can be explained by his aggressiveness. It is important to realize that correlation does not imply causation. A correlation between two variables might be due to causation in either direction or might be due to a third variable that causes them both.

One can also measure how strongly one variable is related to a whole set of predictor variables by computing the *multiple correlation* between the variable of interest and the set of predictor variables. Like a correlation between two variables, a squared multiple correlation (R^2) ranges from 0 to 1 and measures the percentage of the variation in the one variable explained by the set of predictors.

Associated with every correlation or multiple correlation is an equation describing the line that best relates the predictor or predictors to the dependent variable of interest. This line is called the *regression line* and the coefficient of each predictor variable in the equation of the line is called a *regression coefficient.* The standardized regression coefficient for a variable measures the importance of that variable in determining the value of the dependent variable of interest when other predictor variables are contolled. Therefore, regression coefficients provide a way to evaluate how each of a set of variables independently affects a dependent variable of interest. It is primarily through the extensive use of correlation and regression analyses that we derive a model of the development of aggression from our longitudinal data.

When one computes a set of correlations, regression coefficients, or means from a sample of data, one is obligated to test how likely it is that the value of the statistic is representative of the population from which the sample was drawn. For example, could the -.30 correlation between IQ and aggression have been obtained by chance, or can we be reasonably certain that it represents a real relationship between IQ and aggression in the population? This question can be answered by computing the probability of obtaining an observed statistic by chance. If the probability of getting the observed statistic by chance is found to be less than .05 (five chances in 100), the statistic is said to be significant. In the following chapters we will report the significance of most statistics we compute. For example, in our sample the probability of finding a correlation of -.30 between IQ and aggression purely by chance is less than .001 (one chance in 1000); so we can be reasonably sure that it reflects a real relationship. We would note this probability in the text by writing "p <.001" in parentheses after the correlation, meaning "the probability is less than .001." The smaller the probability, the more significant is the result.

The probability of obtaining an observed statistic by chance is computed in a variety of ways (t-tests, F-tests, Chi-squared tests), which some readers may not understand. However, the reader should be aware that these probabilities are influenced by sample size. In this research we have studied a reasonably large sample. Therefore, our statistics are reasonably good estimates of population characteristics.

SUMMARY

In this chapter we have described the several measures of aggression we selected as our primary dependent variables and the measures of psychopathology, popularity, and leadership we studied. We suggested that the variables affecting the development of aggression fall into four fairly distinct classes: instigators, contingent responses to aggression, identification variables, and sociocultural variables. In the next chapter we will describe how these variables interact to determine the aggressive habits that a child develops between age eight and age 19.

NOTES

[1] A factor analysis indicated that they all weighted highly on a single factor of aggressiveness, and they were found to have high test-retest reliabilities — i.e., .85 to .95 (Walder *et al.*, 1961).

[2] Unlike the aggression variable, the raw number of nominations was not divided by "who knows you?"

[3] Only aggregate statistics were provided so that the anonymity of each subject was protected.

[4] Unlike the aggression measure, the raw peer-nomination scores were not divided by "who knows you?"

[5] The total discrepancy between a parent and child was the square root of the sum of the squared discrepancies on each adjective for each behavior.

[6] Since a high educational level was denoted by a lower number, the signs were reversed before analyses. Thus, throughout this book a lower number means a lower educational level.

[7] This variable actually measured the number of generations born in America so the sign was reversed to make it a direct measure of ethnicity.

Table 2.1 The Reasons Why Subjects in the Original Sample Were Not Reinterviewed

Reasons	Number of Subjects	%
Successfully reinterviewed	427	48.8
Appeared for interview, but did not finish	9	1.0
Agreed to interview, but did not appear	24	2.7
Located address, but		
(a) subject refused	81	9.3
(b) subject in military service	38	4.4
(c) subject deceased	4	.5
(d) subject in prison	2	.2
(e) subject did not reply	105	12.0
(f) post office returns	45	5.1
No address located	140	16.0
	875	100.0

Table 2.2 Pertinent Parts of the 13th-Grade Self-Report Questionnaire

HAND THIS AND NEXT PAGE TO *S*.

BEH   Here are a number of things which you might do that could
get you into trouble. Please tell us how many times you have
done these things in the last three years. For each question,
put a check in the box next to the answer that is true.

<table>
<tr><td></td><td colspan="6">Number of times</td></tr>
<tr><td>In the last three years
how many times have
you done this?</td><td>5 or
more</td><td>4</td><td>3</td><td>2</td><td>1</td><td>0</td></tr>
</table>

.01 Stayed out later than
parents said you should

.02 Got into a serious fight
with a student in school

.03 Run away from home

.04 Taken something not
belonging to you worth
under $50

.05 Went onto someone's land
or into some house or
building when you weren't
supposed to be there

.06 Set fire to someone else's
property on purpose

.07 Been suspended or
expelled from school

.08 Got something by telling
a person something bad
would happen to him if
you did not get what
you wanted

Table 2.2 Pertinent Parts of the 13th-Grade Self-Report Questionnaire (Cont'd.)

In the last three years how many times have you done this?	5 or more	4	3	2	1	0

.09 Argued or had a fight with either of your parents

.10 Got into trouble with the police because of something you did

.11 Hurt someone badly enough to need bandages or a doctor

.12 Damaged school property on purpose

.13 Taken something from a store without paying for it

.14 Hit a teacher

.15 Drunk beer or liquor without parent's permission

.16 Smoked in school (against the rules)

.17 Hit your father

.18 Taken a car that didn't belong to someone in your family without permission of the owner

.19 Taken an expensive part of a car without the permission of the owner

Table 2.2 Pertinent Parts of the 13th-Grade Self-Report Questionnaire (Cont'd.)

In the last three years how many times have you done this?	5 or more	4	3	2	1	0

.20 Taken part in a fight
where a bunch of your
friends are against
another bunch

.21 Hit your mother

.22 Taken something not
belonging to you worth
over $50

.23 Had to bring your parents
to school because of something
you did

.24 Taken an inexpensive part
of a car without permission
of the owner

.25 Skipped a day of school
without a real excuse

.26 Used a knife or gun or
some other thing (like a
club) to get something
from a person

Table 2.2 Pertinent Parts of the 13th-Grade Self-Report Questionnaire (Cont'd.)

Please put a checkmark for each statement in the box which best describes how you act.

	4 Almost Always true	3 Often true	2 Some-times true	1 Seldom true	0 Never true
RAG 52. I get angry and smash things					
RAG 53. I am a little rude to people					
RAG 54. I lose my temper at people					

RAG 55.   Have you ever spanked a child?   0. No or not sure

IF YES: How many times would 1. once
you estimate that you have   2. twice
done this?   3. three times
                               4. four or more times
                            98. not sure

RAG 56.   Have you ever slapped or
kicked another person?   0. No or not sure

IF YES: How many times   1. once
would you estimate that   2. twice
you have done this?   3. three times
                               4. four or more times
                            98. not sure

Table 2.2 Pertinent Parts of the 13th-Grade Self-Report Questionnaire (Cont'd.)

RAG 57.   Have you ever punched or
beaten another person?   0. No or not sure

               IF YES: How many times   1. once
would you estimate that   2. twice
you have done this?   3. three times
                                       4. four or more times
                                  98. not sure

VAG. 39   Have you ever been slapped
or kicked by another person?   0. No or not sure

               IF YES: How many times   1. once
would you estimate that   2. twice
this has happened to you?   3. three times
                                       4. four or more times
                                  98. not sure

VAG. 40   Have you ever been punched
or beaten by another person?   0. No or not sure

               IF YES: How many times   1. once
would you estimate that   2. twice
this has happened to you?   3. three times
                                       4. four or more times
                                  98. not sure

VAG 41.   Have you ever been choked
by another person?   0. No or not sure

               IF YES: How many times   1. once
would you estimate that   2. twice
this has happened to you?   3. three times
                                       4. four or more times
                                  98. not sure

Table 2.2 Pertinent Parts of the 13th-Grade Self-Report Questionnaire (Cont'd.)

VAG 42. Have you ever been
threatened or actually cut by
somebody using a knife?   0. No or not sure

IF YES: How many times   1. once
would you estimate that   2. twice
this has happened to you? 3. three times
            4. four or more times
          98. not sure

VAG 43. Have you ever been
threatened with a gun or
shot at?   0. No or not sure

IF YES: How many times   1. once
would you estimate that   2. twice
this has happened to you? 3. three times
            4. four or more times
          98. not sure

IN PUN ITEMS SEX OF ADULT AND OF CHILD IS SAME AS
SEX OF *S*.

"We would like to learn something about your ideas for raising
children. Imagine that you are the father (mother) of an eight-
year-old boy (girl) and try to answer the following questions
accordingly."

PUN 21. If you saw your son (daughter) grab 0. no
things from another child, would you 1. yes
tell him (her) that young men (ladies) 98. DK
don't do this sort of thing?

PUN 22. If you saw your son (daughter) grab 0. no
things from another child, would you 1. yes
say, "I would like to be proud of you"? 98. DK

Table 2.2 Pertinent Parts of the 13th-Grade Self-Report Questionnaire (Cont'd.)

PUN 23.   Would you make your son (daughter)   0. no
           apologize if he (she) grabbed things   1. yes
           from another child?   98. DK

PUN 24.   Would you tell your son (daughter)   0. no
           you don't love him (her) for grabbing   1. yes
           things from another child?   98. DK

PUN 25.   Would you point out how some close   0. no
           friend of his (hers) behaves better   1. yes
           than your son (daughter) does, if he   98. DK
           (she) grabbed things from another child?

PUN 26.   If you saw your son (daughter) grab   0. no
           things from another child, would you   1. yes
           not let him (her) play with his (her)   98. DK
           friends for two days?

IN PUN ITEMS SEX OF ADULT AND OF CHILD IS SAME AS
SEX OF *S*.

"Imagine again that you are the father (mother) of an eight-year-old
boy (girl) and try to answer the following questions accordingly."

PUN 49.   If you heard your son (daughter) say   0. no
           mean things to another child, would you   1. yes
           tell him (her) in a nice way to act   98. DK
           differently?

PUN 50.   If you heard your son (daughter) say   0. no
           mean things to another child, would you   1. yes
           say, "Get on that chair and don't move   98. DK
           until you apologize."?

PUN 51.   Would you *not* let your son (daughter)   0. no
           play with his (her) friends for two days   1. yes
           if you heard him (her) say mean things   98. DK
           to another child?

Table 2.2 Pertinent Parts of the 13th-Grade Self-Report Questionnaire (Cont'd.)

PUN 52.	If you heard your son (daughter) say mean things to another child, would you point out how some close friends of his (her) behave better than he (she) does?	0. 1. 98.	no yes DK
PUN 53.	If you heard your son (daughter) say mean things to another child, would you wash out his (her) mouth with soap?	0. 1. 98.	no yes DK
PUN 54.	If you heard your son (daughter) say mean things to another child, would you say, "I would like to be proud of you."?	0. 1. 98.	no yes DK

IN PUN ITEMS SEX OF ADULT AND OF CHILD IS SAME AS SEX OF *S*.

"Imagine again that you are the father (mother) of an eight-year-old boy (girl) and try to answer the following questions accordingly."

PUN 63.	If your son (daughter) were rude to you, would you tell him (her), "I will give you something you like if you act differently."?	0. 1. 98.	no yes DK
PUN 64.	If your son (daughter) were rude to you, would you wash out his (her) mouth with soap?	0. 1. 98.	no yes DK
PUN 65.	Would you remind your son (daughter) of what others will think of him (her) if he (she) were rude to you?	0. 1. 98.	no yes DK
PUN 66.	If your son (daughter) were rude to you, would you say, "Get on that chair and don't move until you apologize."?	0. 1. 98.	no yes DK
PUN 67.	Would you tell your son (daughter) that young men (ladies) don't do this sort of thing—if he (she) were rude to you?	0. 1. 98	no yes DK

Table 2.2 Pertinent Parts of the 13th-Grade Self-Report Questionnaire (Cont'd.)

PUN 68.   Would you spank your son (daughter)   0. no
           until he (she) cries—if he (she) were rude   1. yes
           to you?   98. DK

IN PUN ITEMS SEX OF ADULT AND OF CHILD IS SAME AS
SEX OF *S*.

"Imagine again that you are the father (mother) of an eight-year-old
boy (girl) and try to answer the following questions accordingly."

PUN 99.   If your son (daughter) got very mad at   0. no
           you, would you get angry with him (her)?   1. yes
                                                         98. DK

PUN 100.   If your son (daughter) got very mad at   0. no
           you, would you slap him (her) in the   1. yes
           face?   98. DK

PUN 101.   Would you say, "That isn't a nice thing   0. no
           to do," if your son (daughter) got very   1. yes
           mad at you?   98. DK

PUN 102.   Would you tell your son (daughter) you   0. no
           don't love him (her) for getting very   1. yes
           mad at you?   98. DK

PUN 103.   Would you tell your son (daughter) in a   0. no
           nice way how to act differently if he   1. yes
           (she) got very mad at you?   98. DK

PUN 104.   If your son (daughter) got very mad at   0. no
           you, would you send him (her) to   1. yes
           another room where he (she) would be   98. DK
           alone and without toys?

Table 2.2 Pertinent Parts of the 13th-Grade Self-Report Questionnaire (Cont'd.)

PROFILE IDENTIFICATION — PID — INSTRUCTIONS

REMOVE THIS PAGE AND HAND QUESTIONNAIRE TO S.

We are interested in finding out how you do certain things such as walking, talking, and so forth. On the sheet of paper before you is a list of things described by sets of opposite words. Between each pair of words are five steps, or grades, ranging from one way of doing something to its opposite. I would like you to rate yourself for each type of activity, such as walking, talking, etc., by placing a check mark on one of the steps on each line. Notice that the closer you place your check mark to either of the opposite words, the more it means you act the way the word says.

Please try the example. If I were to ask you how you like your coffee, how would you place your check marks?

IF S GIVES ONLY EXTREME RESPONSES ON EXAMPLES, SAY:

You showed that you liked your coffee very hot/cold. How would you place your check mark if you wanted your coffee just a little less hot/cold?

(*AFTER EXAMPLE IS COMPLETED*) Thank you, would you please complete the list.

SCAN PID FOR COMPLETION OF EACH ITEM AND THEN RETRIEVE QUESTIONNAIRE.

PID   I like coffee

hot   ____ ____ ____ ____ ____   cold

light   ____ ____ ____ ____ ____   dark

sweet   ____ ____ ____ ____ ____   not sweet

Table 2.2 Pertinent Parts of the 13th-Grade Self-Report Questionnaire (Cont'd.)

PID

I walk

fast	_____ _____ _____ _____ _____	slow
loud	_____ _____ _____ _____ _____	soft
often	_____ _____ _____ _____ _____	not often

I talk

slow	_____ _____ _____ _____ _____	fast
soft	_____ _____ _____ _____ _____	loud
not often	_____ _____ _____ _____ _____	often

I stand

| straight | _____ _____ _____ _____ _____ | lean forward |
| at ease | _____ _____ _____ _____ _____ | firm |

I eat

| much | _____ _____ _____ _____ _____ | little |
| fast | _____ _____ _____ _____ _____ | slow |

I write

slow	_____ _____ _____ _____ _____	fast
small	_____ _____ _____ _____ _____	large
heavy	_____ _____ _____ _____ _____	light

Table 2.2 Pertinent Parts of the 13th-Grade Self-Report Questionnaire (Cont'd.)

My body is

light	_____ _____ _____ _____ _____	dark
tall	_____ _____ _____ _____ _____	short
thick	_____ _____ _____ _____ _____	thin
hard	_____ _____ _____ _____ _____	soft
strong	_____ _____ _____ _____ _____	weak

WAG 44.   Have you ever seen another
person slapped or kicked?   0. No or not sure

IF YES: How many times   1. once
would you estimate that you   2. twice
have seen another person   3. three times
slapped or kicked?   4. four or more times
                                98. not sure

WAG 45.   Have you ever seen another
person punched or beaten?   0. No or not sure

IF YES: How many times   1. once
would you estimate that you   2. twice
have seen another person   3. three times
punched or beaten?   4. four or more times
                                98. not sure

WAG 46.   Have you ever seen
another person choked?   0. No or not sure

IF YES: How many times   1. once
would you estimate that you   2. twice
have seen another person   3. three times
choked?   4. four or more times
                                98. not sure

Table 2.2 Pertinent Parts of the 13th-Grade Self-Report Questionnaire (Cont'd.)

WAG 47.   Have you ever seen
another person threatened
or actually cut with a
knife?   0. No or not sure

IF YES: How many times   1. once
would you estimate that you   2. twice
have seen another threatened   3. three times
or actually cut with a knife?   4. four or more times
                                             98. not sure

WAG 48.   Have you ever seen
another person threatened
with a gun or shot at?   0. No or not sure

IF YES: How many times   1. once
would you estimate that you   2. twice
have seen another person   3. three times
threatened by a gun or   4. four or more times
shot at?   98. not sure

Table 2.3 The Peer Rating Items Used in the Third and 13th Grades

	Third Grade	13th Grade
Aggression Items:	1. Who does not obey the teacher?	Who did not listen to the teacher?
	2. Who often says, "Give me that"?	--------OMITTED--------
	3. Who gives dirty looks or sticks out their tongue at other children?	Who gave dirty looks or made unfriendly gestures to other students?
	4. Who makes up stories and lies to get other children into trouble?	Who made up stories and lies to get other students into trouble?
	5. Who does things that bother others?	Who did things that bothered others?
	6. Who starts a fight over nothing?	Who started fights over nothing?
	7. Who pushes or shoves children?	Who pushed or shoved students?
	8. Who is always getting into trouble?	Who was always getting into trouble?
	9. Who says mean things?	Who used to say mean things?
	10. Who takes other children's things without asking?	Who took other students' things without asking?
Popularity Items:	1. Whom would you like to sit next to in class?	Whom did you like to sit next to in class?
	2. Who are the children that you would like to have for your best friend?	Who were the students that you would like to have had for your best friend?

Table 2.3 The Peer Rating Items Used in the Third and 13th Grades (Cont'd.)

	Third Grade	13th Grade
Leadership Item:	1. ------------OMITTED------------	Who was a leader of a club or a group?
Aggression Anxiety Items:	1. Who says "Excuse me" even when they have not done anything bad?	Who used to say "excuse me" even when they did not do anything bad?
	2. Who will never fight even when picked on?	Who would never fight even when picked on?
Who Knows You Item?	1. ------------OMITTED------------	Whom do you know?

Table 2.4 The Correlations Between the Peer Ratings of Aggression and the 13th-Grade Self-Ratings of Aggression

13th-Grade Self-Ratings of Aggression	Third-Grade Peer Ratings of Aggression	13th-Grade Peer Ratings of Aggression
Total Aggressive Habit	.18	.50
MMPI Sum of Scales 4 and 9	.19	.35

Table 2.5 The Percentage of Male Subjects Arrested in New York State
Before 1973 as a Function of Their Third- and 13th-Grade Aggressiveness

13th-Grade Peer-Rated Aggression	N	Arrested at Least Once	Never Arrested
Low (< 26 percentile)	51	1	50
High (> 75 percentile)	53	6	47

Third-Grade Peer-Rated Aggression	N	Arrested at Least Once	Never Arrested
Low (< 26 percentile)	55	2	53
High (> 75 percentile)	54	5	49

Table 2.6 3rd-Grade Violent and Nonviolent Television Programs

Violent

Alaskans
Badge 714
Bat Masterson
Black Saddle
Bronco
Bugs Bunny
Cheyenne
Colt 45
Fighting
Gunsmoke
Have Gun, Will Travel
Hawaiian Eye
Highway Patrol
John Slaughter
Jungle Jim
Kit Carson
Laramie
Law Man
Lock Up
M-Squad
Maverick
Murders

Mystery Stories
Overland Trail
Peter Gunn
Rawhide
Rebel
Rifleman
Sea Hunt
77 Sunset Strip
Sheena
Shotgun Slade
Sugarfoot
Superman
The Thin Man
The Three Stooges
Tightrope
Trouble Shooters
Twilight Zone
Wagon Train
Wells Fargo
Wyatt Earp
Vikings
Yancy Derringer

Nonviolent

Adventure Stories
American Bandstand (Dick Clark)
Amos'n Andy
Bachelor Father
Betty Hutton Show
Big Top
Bonanza
Bozo the Clown
Breakfast Carnival
Breakfast with Happy
Bringing Up Father
Captain Kangaroo
Cartoon Capers
Cinderalla

Circus Boy
Cisco Kid
Concentration
Crazy Bear
Dance Party (Arthur Murray)
Danny Thomas
Dave Garroway
Death Valley Days
Dennis the Menace
Dinah Shore
Ding Dong School
Dobie Gillis
Doggie Daddy
Donald Duck

Table 2.6 3rd-Grade Violent and Nonviolent Television Programs (Cont'd.)

Nonviolent (Cont'd.)

Donna Reed	Mighty Mouse
Ed Sullivan	Mr. Wizard
Ernie Ford	Oh Susannah!
Exploring the Sea	Ozzie & Harriet
Father Knows Best	People Are Funny
Fibber McGee and Molly	Perry Como
Flicka	Perry Mason
Freddy Freihofer	Peter Pan
Funday Funnies	Play Your Hunch
Fury	Popeye
Gene Autry	Porthole
Honeymooners	Price is Right
Hopalong Caddidy	Queen for a Day
Howdy Doody	Real McCoys
Huckleberry Hound, Yogi Bear,	Rescue 8
Quick Draw McGraw	Red Skelton
Huckleberry Finn	Rin Tin Tin
I Love Lucy (Lucy Show)	Rocky
Jerry Mahoney	Roy Rogers
John Gnagy	Ruff and Ready
John Gunther	Satellite Six (Glendora)
Johnny Reed	Science Fiction
Lassie	Shirley Temple
Late Show or Dinner Theater	Sky King
or Early Show	Space
Lawrence Welk	Sports
Leave It to Beaver	Steve Allen
Life of Riley	Talent Shows
Life with Father	Teenage Barn
Little Lenny	Telephone Hour
Little Lulu	Topper
Little Rascals	Walt Disney
Lone Ranger	War Pictures
Loretta Young	Winter Olympics
Love That Bob	Woody Woodpecker
Man and The Challenge	Zorro
Mickey Mouse	

Table 2.7 13th-Grade Violent and Nonviolent Television Programs

Violent

Avengers	It Takes a Thief
Bold Ones	Lancer
Bonanza	Land of the Giants
Daniel Boone	Man from Uncle
Dark Shadows	Mannix
Dragnet	Mission: Impossible
FBI	Mod Squad
Get Smart	Name of the Game
Gunsmoke	Prisoner
Hawaii Five-O	Superman
High Chapparal	Then Came Bronson
I Spy	Three Stooges
Invaders	Virginian
Ironsides	Wild, Wild West

Nonviolent

Adam 12	David Frost
Adams Family	David Susskind
American Bandstand	Days of Our Lives
Andy Williams	Dean Martin
Another World	Debbie Reynolds
Art Linkletter	Dick Cavett
Auto Racing	Doris Day
Banana Splits	Ed Sullivan
Basketball	Engelbert Humperdinck
Beverly Hillbillies	Evening with the Pops
Bewitched	Family Affair
Big Valley	First Tuesday
Bill Cosby	Football
Bracken's World	Fugitive
Brady Bunch	Galloping Gourmet
Bullwinkle	Ghost and Mrs. Muir
Burke's Law	Glen Campbell
Cartoons	Gomer Pyle, U.S.M.C.
Carol Burnett	Governor and J.J.
Comedy Shows	Green Acres
Comedy Tonight	Hullaballoo
Courtship of Eddie's Father	He and She

Table 2.7 13th-Grade Violent and Nonviolent Television Programs (Cont'd.)

Nonviolent (Cont'd.)

Hee Haw	My Three Sons
Here Come the Brides	N.E.T. Playhouse
Hogan's Heroes	News Programs
Honeymooners	Pat Paulsen Show
Huntley-Brinkley	Perry Mason
I Dream of Jeannie	Petticoat Junction
I Love Lucy	Quiz Shows
Jack Benny	Ray Stevens
Jeopardy	Red Skelton
Jim Nabors	Room 222
Johnny Carson	Science Shows
Johnny Cash	Sesame Street
Julia	Sixty Minutes
Kraft Music Hall	Soap Operas
Lassie	Smothers Brothers
Laugh-In	Star Trek
Leonard Bernstein	Stock Car Races
Let's Make a Deal	That Girl
Love, American Style	The Doctors
Love Is a Many Splendored Thing	The Show
Love Stories	To Rome with Love
Marcus Welby, M.D.	Today
Mayberry, R.F.D.	Tom Jones
Medical Center	Undersea World of Jacques Cousteau
Meet the Press	Walt Disney
Merv Griffin	Walter Cronkite
Mike Douglas	White Paper
Monkeys	Wide World of Sports
My Favorite Martian	

Table 2.8 The Means and Standard Deviations of the Variables Studied in the Third and 13th Grades for Boys and Girls

Type	Variable	Boys			Girls		
		N	Mean	S.D.	N	Mean	S.D.
	THIRD GRADE						
Dependent Measures							
Aggression	Peer-nominated aggression	211	12.12	12.73	216	7.51	9.87
Aggression	Peer-nominated aggression anxiety	211	16.70	12.33	216	20.36	13.69
Aggression	Father-rated recency of home aggression	144	20.11	4.99	157	19.79	5.12
Aggression	Mother-rated recency of home aggression	186	21.23	5.00	184	20.38	5.51
Popularity	Peer-nominated popularity	211	25.29	16.63	216	25.03	14.81
Potential Predictors							
Instigator	Parental rejection of child	128	13.42	1.89	120	12.57	1.87
Instigator	Parental disharmony	128	9.51	2.19	120	9.67	2.19
Instigator	Child's IQ	205	108.21	13.42	207	106.00	13.83
Instigator	Parental nurturance of child	128	12.80	2.01	120	12.38	2.35
Contingent Responses	Parental punishment of child	128	15.18	6.16	120	15.51	5.63
Identification	Child's identification with father	132	-6.25	1.72	125	-6.66	1.76
Identification	Child's identification with mother	167	-6.44	1.81	146	-6.51	1.94
Identification	Father's aggressiveness	144	15.28	2.03	157	15.24	2.16
Identification	Mother's aggressiveness	186	15.36	1.90	184	15.22	1.69
Identification	Child's preference for violent television	184	7.15	5.05	175	5.29	4.73
Identification	Child's preference for boys' games	132	17.71	.60	125	11.06	1.59
Identification	Child's preference for girls' games	185	6.77	.61	171	11.79	.71
Identification	Child's guilt as judged by parents	128	9.36	1.09	120	9.61	1.14
Identification	Child's confessing to parents	186	6.09	1.60	184	6.42	1.64
Identification	Child's hours of television viewing per week	186	11.87	3.84	184	11.63	4.04
Sociocultural	Father's current occupational status	144	7.38	4.42	157	7.76	4.57
Sociocultural	Parents' mobility orientation	128	14.72	2.44	120	14.91	2.23
Sociocultural	Parents' frequency of church attendance	128	2.64	1.19	120	2.54	1.28
Sociocultural	Parents' educational level	128	-3.99	1.26	120	-4.21	1.19
Sociocultural	Ethnicity of family	144	-2.69	1.20	157	-2.76	1.22

Table 2.8 The Means and Standard Deviations of the Variables Studied in the Third and 13th Grades for Boys and Girls (Cont'd.)

Type	Variable	Boys			Girls		
		N	Mean	S.D.	N	Mean	S.D.
	THIRTEENTH GRADE						
Dependent Measures							
Aggression	Peer-nominated aggression	211	8.05	9.70	216	2.65	3.77
Aggression	Sum of scales 4 + 9 on MMPI	211	123.70	19.68	215	119.65	18.50
Aggression	Self-reported total aggressive habit	211	31.19	15.66	216	21.85	10.36
Aggression	Peer-nominated aggression anxiety	211	19.69	24.49	216	23.98	29.03
Popularity	Peer-nominated popularity	211	58.77	49.10	216	61.13	50.18
Leadership	Peer-nominated leadership	211	3.69	6.48	216	3.88	6.63
Psycho-pathology	Sum of scales 6, 7, 8, and 9 on MMPI	211	244.01	39.34	215	230.81	32.02
Potential Predictors							
Instigator	Subject as a victim of aggression	211	4.75	3.46	216	2.62	2.55
Instigator	Subject's IQ	53	107.72	12.59	50	110.60	10.30
Instigator	Subject's achievement test score	58	649.83	267.59	62	745.08	207.72
Contingent Responses	Subject's potential for punishment	210	11.86	6.28	213	11.42	6.35
Identification	Subject's preference for violent television	211	6.39	6.09	216	5.07	4.71
Identification	Subject's hours of television viewing	210	11.41	10.26	216	11.13	8.80
Identification	Subject's preference for sports on television	211	7.27	2.34	216	5.71	1.66
Identification	Subject's judgment of how realistic TV is	211	16.52	6.53	216	15.39	7.12
Identification	Subject's witnessing of aggression	209	7.21	4.20	193	4.22	2.99
Sociocultural	Subject's current educational level	211	12.58	.80	216	12.56	.84
Sociocultural	Subject's mobility orientation	211	15.60	2.49	216	16.02	2.35
Sociocultural	Subject's frequency of church attendance	211	2.05	1.60	215	2.47	1.55
Sociocultural	Subject's educational and occupational aspirations	174	8.36	2.77	154	8.90	2.22
Sociocultural	Father's current occupational status	209	3.86	1.69	210	3.87	1.68

3
The Roots of Aggression

The question with which we began this book was: "What are the roots of aggression and violence in young adulthood?" In this chapter we answer that question by showing which variables in a child's environment are important in determining his aggressive behavior as a young adult.

Already described in the previous chapter in terms of rationale and formulation, these predictor variables consist of environmental events which impinged on or presumably affected the child during his development. Needing qualification, the term "environment" is employed liberally to encompass those conditions that affect a child's behavior and are concomitant with a child's development but in all likelihood are not genetically determined. To recapitulate, these four classes of predictor or independent variables are: (1) instigation variables, (2) contingent responses to aggression, (3) identification variables, and (4) sociocultural variables. These are the roots of aggression we uncovered which led to eight-year-olds behaving aggressively as judged by their peers. Do these roots still, metaphorically speaking, feed aggression ten years later? The provenance, various connotations, and definition of aggression as used in this study were discussed in the first two chapters. Here we shall state how the four classes of predictor variables relate not only to the variables formulated to measure aggression in the third grade but especially to additional dependent measures of aggression formulated in the follow-up phase of the study.

In addition to these four classes of environmental variables, the child's peer-nomination score for aggression in the third grade will be used to predict to various measures of his behavior obtained ten years later.

As described in Chapter 2, the measures of aggressive behavior obtained in the 13th grade were: (1) peer nominations obtained from our subjects, (2) various self-ratings of aggressiveness and the pro-clivity for behaving aggressively, (3) scores on MMPI scales 4 and 9 (Hathaway and Monachesi, 1963), and (4) data on arrest of our male subjects obtained from the New York State Division of Criminal Justice Services. The aggregate data on arrests in New York State were used as a measure of validation of the peer nominations. The findings have already been discussed in Chapter 2.

Conceptually, these four measures may be assigned to two groups: direct and indirect. In the direct group are the peer nominations, the self-ratings comprising the measure of total aggressive habit, and the aggregate data on arrests. Because scales 4 and 9 are embedded in the total 399 Form R MMPI items (Hathaway and McKinley, 1969) and are not obvious measures of aggressive behavior, we termed the sum of these scales our indirect measure of aggression.

Preliminary analysis indicated that the measures of aggression distinguished the males from the females. There were statistically significant differences between males' and females' mean scores on every measure of aggression in both grades. The differences were more pronounced in the 13th grade. In addition, a principal compo-nents factor analysis of subjects' sex and the variables that were used in the study yielded a first principal factor whose largest loadings were for the measures of aggression and whose next largest loading was for subject's sex. (See section on sex differences below).

Finally, a comparison of girls in the highest quartile of aggression with those in the lowest quartile revealed a difference in profiles on the Minnesota Multiphasic Personality Inventory: the high-aggressive girls were significantly more masculine in their interests and atti-tudes. Because of these findings, the data for males and females were analyzed separately.

How do the third-grade predictors fare in their ability to presage aggression in our 13th-grade subjects? We obtained our answer to this question from multiple correlation analyses and our conclusions are based upon multiple regression equations computed to predict both synchronous and later aggression from the independent variables. The overall theme suggested by these analyses and forming the basis for the remainder of this chapter is the following: While the occurrence of instigators to aggression is a good predictor of a child's immediate or synchronous aggression, the best predictors of aggression longitudinally are the identification variables and the socio-cultural variables.

RELATION OF EARLY TO LATER AGGRESSION

Before we present the results and implications of the regression analyses of third- and 13th-grade predictors to third- and 13th-grade outcomes, it would be instructive to study how aggression in our eight-year-olds related to aggression when they were 19. Methodologically, therefore, peer nominations of aggression in the third grade, which at that period served as the dependent measure, may now be viewed as an independent variable for predicting 13th-grade aggression. Consequently, the direction of prediction is from the third-grade measure of aggression to the three dependent measures of aggressive behavior which were obtained for the same subjects ten years later. These 13th-grade dependent variables have been enumerated above and also described in Chapter 2.

These analyses (see Tables 3.1 and 3.2) reveal that peer nominations of aggression in the third grade relate very well to peer nominations of aggression ten years later for both boys and girls ($r = .38$, $r = .47$, $p < .001$). Aggression in the third grade is also predictive of potential for delinquent behavior — as measured by scales 4 and 9 of the MMPI — for both sexes ten years later. For boys, aggression at age eight was also correlated over time in a statistically significant fashion to self-rated aggression in the 13th grade. For each sex group, the highest correlations were between the peer-nomination aggression scores at the third and 13th grades.

The relation of early aggression to aggression ten years later may appear to be a test reliability index rather than an index of stability of behavior. The evidence available supports a stability of behavior interpretation of the correlation. The scores each time were derived from overlapping but different sets of raters who based their nominations upon different observations. There were some raters who were rating the same classmates on both occasions. Perhaps they were indeed influenced by their own memory of how they answered the questions on a single day ten years before or perhaps their nominations stem from descriptive labels about each child which were learned by each classmate from his social group. The latter notion, reminiscent of reputation, seems more substantial than the former. However, our data from earlier studies of this peer-nominaton measure (Eron *et al.*, 1971; Walder *et al.*, 1961) suggest that, while reputation is a factor, the raters were responding to the rated child's behaviors in addition to any response to other people's descriptions of that child. Furthermore, the 13th-grade peer-rating measure of aggression was correlated more highly with the 13th-grade self-rating measures of aggression than were the third-grade peer ratings (see Table 2.4). The consistency of aggression over time and in a wide variety of situations strongly suggests that aggression is a stable behavior which conforms to the definition of a trait. We do not mean to imply any necessary underlying biological correlates but only that a child early on learns a manner of responding to certain situations which is distinctive for him/her and is perpetuated probably because of the success it brings. The consistency of aggressive behavior over time and on different measures is illustrated clearly in Table 3.3 for males and females. This table shows that, as the peer-rating classification of aggression in the third grade increases from low to high, mean scores on three different measures of aggression obtained from the same individuals ten years later also increases in the same direction. Moreover, this phenomenon occurs for both males and females.

It is interesting (returning to Tables 3.1 and 3.2) that we were able to get such high correlations between self- and peer ratings in the 13th grade although there had been no such correlation in the third grade. Perhaps at age 19 subjects can describe themselves better; or they feel it is less incriminating to admit these behaviors to an interviewer who is a stranger and whom they will probably never see again than when they were in a classroom in third grade and had no real assurance that the teacher would not see their answers. Or perhaps it might even be the difference in the times — in 1960 it was not the "in thing" for young people to engage in or admit to certain antisocial behaviors which now are acceptable at least to a number of persons in this age group. "Ripping off" is the term currently used to legitimize stealing and to make it socially acceptable. In 1960 there was no such euphemism.

FOUR CLASSES OF ENVIRONMENTAL VARIABLES AND AGGRESSION

Having established that aggression is not a transient characteristic, let us now consider the role of each of the four classes of independent variables: instigators to aggression, contingent responses to aggression, identification, and sociocultural variables in predicting aggression. The depiction of these relationships statistically is presented in Table 3.4 for boys and 3.5 for girls.

Instigators

Within the class of variables termed instigators, rejection was the most prominent predictor of synchronous aggression, predicting well for both boys and girls. Also, low nurturance and low IQ were strong predictors of synchronous aggression for boys. Low IQ for girls and nurturance for boys and are only weak predictors of aggression longitudinally. It seems fair to say that when considered in conjunction with the predictors none of the instigator variables are powerful determiners of later aggression. Instigators are perhaps necessary antecedents to comtemporaneous aggression, but apparently their effect is short-lived and other variables are more important in predicting later aggression.

IQ was included in the class of instigators on the hypothesis that the frustrations of coping with a low IQ would lead to higher aggression. Regression analyses showed that IQ did not predict later aggression independently of other child-rearing variables. However, low IQ was consistently correlated with high aggression for both males and females within our sample. Furthermore, IQ was highly correlated with other variables that did not enter into these regression equations — e.g., identification with mother ($r = .35$) and identification with father ($r = .26$). This suggests that IQ and other of the child-rearing variables might be explaining the same portion of the variance in a child's aggression. Thus, a general incompetency factor could be one cause of aggression as illustrated by the relative inability of the low-IQ child to imitate his/her parents' behavior. Since IQ and identification variables are not orthogonal, only one — identification — would enter the regression equation. Another interpretation of low IQ is not as an instigator but rather as a condition that limits a child's ability to learn a variety of socially acceptable behaviors. Such a child's repertoire of behavior may be constricted in comparison with that of a child of average or high IQ. The low-IQ child simply has more difficulty learning to behave in a nonaggressive manner. Such a child finds it easier to learn the direct and salient behaviors such as aggressiveness. The child with a higher IQ has more learning options open to him/her so he/she is able to learn a wider variety of social behaviors.

Perhaps a better measure of instigation to aggression associated with low IQ is school achievement. In support of this observation we found a -.39 correlation (p < .01) between achievement test scores in high school and synchronous aggression for girls and -.36 (p < .01) for boys. Indeed Semler and Eron (1967) found that among third-grade boys, achievement explained the major portion of the variance in the relationship between IQ and aggression.

Contingent Responses to Aggression (Punishment)

Punishment for aggression which, when studied in the third grade with a much larger sample (Eron *et al.*, 1963) seemed to be a very important variable in determining aggressive behavior of boys at that time, does not seem so important when examined in the longitudinal context of the multiple regression analysis. With the attenuated sample (only those who were reinterviewed) punishment does not serve as a significant longitudinal predictor to aggression. However, the correlation between punishment and contemporaneous aggression (Tables 3.6 and 3.7) is significant in the third grade for the peer-rating measure of aggression and approaches significance in the 13th grade for this measure. Indeed, early parental punishment for aggression is significantly correlated for boys, across the ten-year span, with the 13th grade measure of aggressive habit. Furthermore, when the subjects are partitioned into groups having high- medium- and low-punishing parents as illustrated in Table 3.8, an interesting pattern of relations among mean scores emerges which the correlation coefficient may actually be masking. This is likely to happen when the variables are skewed, or nonlinear effects otherwise exist. It can be seen in Table 3.8 that the least aggressive boys are those whose parents are moderately punitive toward aggressive behavior. When parents are either very permissive or harshly punitive toward aggression by their sons, these boys in late adolescence tend to be more aggressive. It should be emphasized that this is not a statistically significant effect but only a suggestive trend.

It will be recalled that at age eight there were opposite findings for highly identified and moderately identified boys in regard to punishment by father. The analysis was repeated in the 13th grade with the attenuated sample. The previous results were not replicated, indicating that the moderating influence of identification on the effect of punishment does not persist to age 19. We shall have more to say, in our discussion of implications in Chapter 6, about the effects of early punishment for aggression on later aggression.

Identification

As can be seen from the regression analyses (Tables 3.4 and 3.5) and the correlations (Tables 3.6 and 3.7), the identification variables are much more successful than punishment in predicting aggression both synchronously and longitudinally. Two of the identification measures — children's confessing and guilt as reported by parents — are often viewed as indications of the child's internalization of parental interdictions; when viewed in a dynamic model of behavior, they are presumed indications of conscience, which develops through identification with parents.

It is instructive to consider the child behaviors that are associated with high amounts of confessing and with guilt. These behaviors are a form of communication from the child — a self-disclosure about some negative or undesirable action on his or her part. The fact that a child admits a transgression to a parent suggests that that parent has supported such communications and is probably a positively reinforcing agent for the child. If so, a child with high scores on our measures of identification might well have a parent who uses a child-management system that includes positive aspects. Such systems are much more effective in building behavior controls that are mediated by the child himself/herself and not as situationally or time bound as predominantly negative control systems. This might explain why identification variables are effective across time and why externally imposed conditions such as punishment are less so. It has been demonstrated (Azrin, 1958; Chasdi and Lawrence, 1955) that punishment has an effect only when the punishing agent is likely to be there, while positive reinforcement has a more pervasive effect on behavior.

In confirmation of our hypothesis concerning identification and aggression, identification as measured by confessing behavior was negatively correlated with aggression for both boys and girls at both time periods. The measure of guilt behaves in the same fashion in its negative relationship to aggressive behavior but less consistently, especially for boys. For girls, the regression equations show that confessing behavior is a predictor of low aggression synchronously, while guilt behavior predicts low aggression later in life. Perhaps the most consistent relationships between identification and aggression occurred as a function of a child's identification with his parents in expressive behavior. Low identification with the mother is a highly significant predictor of later aggression in boys. On the other hand, for girls, low identification with the father was a significant predictor of later aggression. Examination of the aggression scores of high-, medium-, and low-identification subjects (Table 3.9) revealed that low identification with both parents was the most potent predictor of aggression, irrespective of the subject's sex. Thus, the hypothesis that identification with parents in certain motor behaviors (such as walking, eating, and talking) and in perceptions of body image would be related to aggressive behavior was substantiated. As seen in the tables of correlations (Tables 3.6 and 3.7), these measures obtained from both parents independently and from children in the third-grade classroom were correlated significantly to aggression synchronously in the third grade and longitudinally to aggression in the 13th grade. These findings lend support to the idea that what is termed conscience or internalization of parental proscriptions not only is copying of moral precepts and guilt for transgressions but is also copying of manifest motor behavior of the socializing agent. As will be seen, this behavior parallels the effect of imitating television models.

The measure of sex-typed behavior, comprised of empirically determined sex preferences for games and activities, was included to test the hypothesis that identification with a particular sex role is related to aggression. The data supported this hypothesis. A boy's preference for girls' games and activities was an indicator of low aggression both synchronously and in later years. Boys' preference for girls' games and activities was inversely correlated with peer nominations of aggression both in the third and 13th grades. Although not statistically significant, preference by boys for boys' games and activities was also in the hypothesized direction: the greater the preference, the more the aggression both in the third and 13th grades. For girls, no statistically significant relationships occurred.

The present data indicate at least a portion of the variance accounting for sex differences in aggression is probably culturally determined. Masculine or feminine preferences made as early as eight years of age influence aggressive behavior at that time and also ten years later. What emerges from these findings is that when boys opt for feminine games and activities, the choice in itself seems to act as a suppressor of early and later aggression. Preference for feminine activities may simply be incompatible with aggressive responses. Further evidence bearing on these relationships will be presented below, where it is shown that when adult females prefer stereotyped masculine activities, such behavior is positively related to aggression.

Further support of the hypothesis that childhood preferences for stereotyped masculine and feminine games and activities is a predictor of aggression is derived from the principal components factor analysis computed for our 427 subjects after the longitudinal data were collected. Boys' games and activities correlated .504 with factor one, which appears to be an aggression factor, and girls' games and activities correlated -.579 with this same factor.

Sociocultural Variables

While generally the sociocultural variables were good predictors of a child's aggression in the third and 13th grades, several were inconsistent. However, one consistent predictor of aggression was socioeconomic status as measured by the father's occupation. High-status occupations were designated by a low number so the multiple regressions (Tables 3.4 and 3.5) indicate that a child's aggressiveness increases as father's occupational status increases. This effect is highly significant for daughters at both the third and 13th grades but only at the third grade for sons. Furthermore, the best single predictor of later aggression in boys was found to be upward social mobility orientation. Parental mobility orientation was also a good predictor to aggressive behavior at age 19 for girls. Social mobility as measured in the present was contingent upon movement, change, and continuing demands for adjustments to new situations. These kinds of behaviors are similar to instigators of aggression in that they characterize a fluid and unstable situation, which is conceivably frustrating to children. In addition, socially mobile parents have less time to spend with their child, which may also serve as a frustrating situation.

The conventional view that aggression is a positive trait associated with ambition, the entrepreneurial spirit, and such events as discovery and the technological advancement of a society are actually supported by these findings. If the child's aspirations and achievements were correlated with those of his parents, then aggressive behavior might be positively associated with high occupational aspirations, achievement of high occupational status, and upward social mobility. Data from the longitudinal phase of the present study tend to support such an hypothesis. A total self-aspiration score comprised of educational, financial, and occupational aspirations was computed for each of the 13th-grade subjects. For both sexes, the correlations between 13th-grade peer-rated aggression and this total aspiration score were positive and in the hypothesized direction (males: r - .36, p < .01; females: r = .14, p < .10). Thus, not only is parents' striving for material accomplishments related to their children's aggression, but, as these children mature, their own desire for material success is positively associated with aggressiveness.

While higher occupational status of her father was found to be predictive of higher aggression in a girl, higher parental educational status was associated with lower aggression in girls both in the third grade and ten years later. This finding appears to repeat our earlier discovery in which significant negative correlations were obtained between achievement test scores in high school and 13th-grade aggression. Low school achievement was interpreted to be an instigator of aggression. In the same manner, low education of parents may be viewed as an instigator of aggression in their daughters. It may simply be the case that poorly educated parents are unaware of those child-rearing techniques that serve to mitigate aggressiveness and so create an environment which contains more frustrating situations for their daughters than that of better educated parents.

Parents' frequency of church attendance appears to have a differential effect upon their sons' and daughters' aggressiveness. The more the parents reported they attended church when the subjects were eight years old, the less was the aggressiveness of their daughters ten years later. For boys, however, there was no relationship. These results may be indicative of differential socialization practices. Parents may attempt to inculcate church teachings to "love your enemies" and "turn the other cheek" in training their daughters to respond to aggression. Since nonaggression is "ladylike" and an expectation of girls, such training is consonant with church doctrine. For boys, just the opposite in socialization practices is often the case. For boys to respond to aggression with counteraggression is seen as manly; in effect, to "turn the other cheek" is viewed as craven. Recall that these subjects were raised in the period of the early 1950s when the notion of unisex and women's liberation were not widely known. Expectations of boys were that they behave like men and, if anything, training in the direct expression of aggression was the rule. Thus, if nonaggression as a principle was promulgated by the church, it may have had less relevance to the socialization of boys than of girls.

It is noteworthy that in Western, Christian countries a close association exists between soldiering and masculinity. Women may enlist or be drafted for noncombatant positions — in the main, clerical and nursing — but Christian societies would view with opprobrium the suggestion that women directly "man" the weapons of death and destruction. Whereas, the opposite is true for men.

Opposition to the Equal Rights Amendment in the United States was in part based on the argument that, if passed, women might be used in combat positions.

However, there are indications that socilization of young girls may be changing. Current research with nine-year-old boys and girls (Chiswick, 1973) indicates that girls now for the first time over the past 15 years are obtaining scores just as high as boys in an experimental situation in which overt aggressive behavior is measured. Concurrently, we note that in the last five or six years, while these nine-year-old girls have been increasingly exposed to television, there have been increasingly more aggressive females whose behavior could be copied, e.g., "Mod Squad," "Ironsides," and "Girl from UNCLE." This is not to say that one is causing the other. Both may be a function of the rapidly changing role of women in our society (Mulvihill and Tumin, 1969).

In summary, the data collected on the four classes of independent variables have shown a variety of important relationships to aggression. The patterning of the relationships indicates that certain socialization practices called instigators (such as rejection) have their greatest effect on aggressive behavior during the period of childhood but that the effect does not extend into young adulthood. Other variables, however (such as modeling and sociocultural factors), influence aggressive behavior synchronously and also across time. Sex of subject was another dimension in which patterning differences occurred. Preference for viewing televised contact sports was positively associated with 13th-grade aggression, but only for females, and, as noted, parents' church attendance was related to girls' aggression but not to boys' aggression.

The aggression measures themselves were substantially correlated across time, indicating that aggression as measured in childhood is a good predictor of aggression in young adulthood and that it is a fairly stable characteristic. In addition, the peer-nomination measure of aggression was significantly correlated with other measures of aggression obtained in the 13th grade.

THIRD-GRADE PREDICTORS AND OTHER 13th-GRADE MEASURES

In Tables 3.6 and 3.7, the correlations are shown between the four classes of third-grade predictors and two measures of 13th-grade aggression in addition to peer nominations. As stated earlier, one of these measures, *total aggressive habit*, was considered to be one of the direct measures of aggression, while the other, *MMPI scales 4 + 9*, was categorized as an indirect measure.

Certain consistencies are evident in these bivariate data, particularly for boys. If a variable predicts in a statistically significant manner to aggression synchronously, then it also tends to predict significantly to one or more of the longitudinal measures. Conversely, if a variable does not correlate with aggression synchronously, it tends not to do so across the time span. Thus, 14 of the 19 predictor variables in Table 3.6 or 74 percent, conform to this pattern. The predictive consistency of several of these variables is more salient than others. Both in childhood and young adulthood, aggression in males is predictable from parental rejection, low IQ of the child, poor identification of the boy with either father or mother, preference for a diet of violent television during childhood, and the boy's willingness to confess transgressions to his parents.

Table 3.7 illustrates that the same pattern occurs for females: when a third-grade predictor variable correlates significantly with synchronous peer nominations of aggression, it also tends to be significantly correlated with aggressiveness ten years later. Similarly, if no significant relation occurs at the third grade, the absence of a relation at the 13th grade increases in likelihood. Numerically, these relations occur at about the same frequency for girls as for boys with 13 of the 19 (74 percent) third-grade predictors conforming to this pattern.

Inspection of the first two columns of coefficients in Tables 3.6 and 3.7 permits a comparison to be drawn of the number of statistically significant correlations emerging between the classes of predictor variables and the synchronous and longitudinal measures of aggression derived from peer nominations. For the class of instigators, the ratio of significant coefficients between synchronous and longitudinal, respectively, was 2:1 for boys and 3:1 for girls. Clearly, the proposition is upheld that the variables we termed instigators are better predictors of aggressive behavior measured at eight years of age than of aggressive behavior measured ten years later. The same examination of the identification variables produces ratios of 4:5 for boys and 4:3 for girls. These third-grade variables appear to be as effective predictors of aggression in young adulthood as in childhood. For the sociocultural variables, the ratio of significant intercorrelations from synchronous to longitudinal measures is 1:1 for boys and 2:1 for girls.

CONTROLLING FOR THIRD VARIABLES

Previously we showed that third- and 13th-grade aggression were substantially correlated. The correlations among these early and later aggression scores need to be examined for their dependence upon some third variable such as IQ, social status, or aggressive milieu. When the effects of fathers' occupational status or fathers' aggressiveness on the relationships between early and later aggression are nullified, no appreciable change in these relationships occurs for either sex (see Tables 3.1 and 3.2). When the effect of IQ on the relationships between third- and 13th-grade aggression is controlled, a trivial decrease in several of the correlations becomes evident. In most cases statistical significance levels are not affected except for the relationship between third-grade aggression and scales 4 + 9 of the MMPI. For both males and females, this diminution of the correlations as a result of controlling for the effects of IQ suggests that IQ explains some of the variance in the longitudinal relationship of these aggression measures. That IQ as measured in the third grade is negatively related to this MMPI measure of potential for antisocial behavior is demonstrated by the significant negative correlation between these variables for all subjects ($r = -.14$, $p < .01$). A negative relationship between IQ and the clinical scales of the MMPI — except for scale 5 — has been reported in the literature addressed to this topic (see, e.g., Dahlstrom and Welsh, 1960). The consistency with which a negative relationship occurs between IQ and the MMPI clinical scales may be viewed as one more datum in support of the hypothesis that low IQ is a stable predictor of psychopathology.

SYNCHRONOUS PREDICTORS OF AGGRESSION IN THE 13th GRADE

The longitudinal relationships between predictor variables of aggression obtained when our subjects were eight years of age and the criterion behaviors of aggression obtained ten years later are probably the most trenchant findings of this study. However, the relationships between certain variables measured in the 13th grade and measures of aggression acquired at the same time have import for the consideration of the causes of aggressive behavior. The 13th-grade criterion measures, *peer nominations, total aggressive habit,* and *MMPI scales 4 + 9,* have been discussed earlier in this chapter and were described fully in Chapter 2. The variables germane to the topic of aggression measured at the same time as the criterion variables and correlating significantly with them are *witness of aggression, victim of aggression, IQ, school achievement,* and *fathers' occupational status.* These relationships are shown in Tables 3.10 and 3.11. Youths who admit to being bystanders during the commission of aggressive acts or who state that they are victims of aggressive acts are themselves aggressive according to both the direct and indirect criterion measures obtained in the 13th grade.

Also found in these tables is validation for our hypothesis that lowered intellectual functioning, particularly in the area of school achievement, is so frustrating that this condition serves as an instigator to aggression. This implication of lowered intellectual functioning in the etiology of aggressive behavior occurring at age 19, may be construed as a cross-validation of our longitudinal finding that intellectual functioning measured as early as age eight is negatively associated with aggressive behavior at age 19.

Fathers' occupational status as reported by their children in the 13th grade is inversely related to their children's aggressive behavior — i.e., low occupational status was associated with high aggression in their children ($r = .13$). This finding — more evident for males than females — is diametrically opposed to the results of the multiple regression analyses (see Tables 3.1 and 3.2) in which high occupational status was associated with high aggression when the subjects were age eight. In the third grade, information concerning fathers' occupational status was obtained directly from the parent, whereas in the 13th grade it was obtained from his/her child. Nevertheless, a moderate correlation between measures is evinced over the ten-year span for the total sample ($r = .57, p < .001$).

Why should the results be reversed from the third to the 13th grades? One plausible theory to explain this phenomenon is that low occupational status and its accompanying economic and cultural impoverishment is fundamentally an instigator to aggression because of the day-to-day frustrations produced by these conditions. However, the effects of lower social class status may be cumulative and only reach threshold value during adolescence and early adulthood. Consequently, during the childhood years, children from lower class homes receive lower aggression scores because they are not yet frustrated by socioeconomic conditions to the point of behaving aggressively and because of the absence of upward mobile, high-achievement models for emulation which are present in middle- and upper-class homes. Children from the latter homes are more aggressive in their younger years, perhaps due to imitation and modeling, but their aggressive behavior tends to be mitigated as they reach adolescence and young adulthood when they become cognizant of the fact that aggressive behavior produces negative consequences. This contingency is counterproductive for the attainment of upward social mobility and higher social class status, which is based on educational and occupational achievement.

SEX DIFFERENCES IN AGGRESSION

The literature on aggression is monotonous in the consistency with which it reports sex differences in aggression both in animal and human subjects. Males are more aggressive than females and the reasons for this sex difference have been attributed to the learning of sex-role stereotypes, to biological-hormonal variables, or both (Bronson and Desjardins, 1968; Feshbach, 1970; Maccoby and Jacklin, 1971; Mark and Ervin, 1970; Mischel, 1970; Young et al., 1964). The present data concerning sex-role learning and aggression are not at all in harmony with the position of biological determinism as an explanation of more aggression in the human male. Rather, the present findings lend support to the position of cultural anthropologists (Alland, 1972; Montagu, 1968) that, although the capacity to acquire culture may be biologically determined, the manifestation of a particular behavior is contingent upon its being learned in that culture. The hypothesis that phenotype is produced by genotype and environment has weathered the test of time rather well. Eisenberg (1972) states the case for such interaction eloquently when he asks,

> Would it not be far more parsimonious to begin with the assumption that men are by nature neither aggressive nor peaceful, but rather are fashioned into one or another as the result of a complex interaction between a widely, but not infinitely, modifiable set of biological givens and the shaping influences of the biological environment, the cultural envelope, and individual experience? (p. 126)

How do data from the present study bear on sex differences in aggression? In the principal component factor analysis sex of subject correlates highly (r = .60) with the first factor, which is clearly an aggression factor. The interpretation of this finding is that sex of subject is associated with aggression and for this study it is specifically the male sex. Continuing with the analysis, Table 3.12 shows that irrespective of the aggression measure used, males had significantly higher mean scores than females. The consistency with which these differences occur is even more noteworthy when the range in the types of measures is taken into consideration. In one case aggression was judged by peers at two different time periods on the basis of school behavior; the two sets of judgments were made ten years apart. In the other cases the aggression measures are comprised of self-reports of aggressive and delinquent behavior including scales 4 + 9 from the MMPI. In still another case the measures assayed how frequently the subjects were victims of an aggressive act and how frequently they witnessed such acts being committed. Notwithstanding the diversity of these measures, females were found to be significantly less aggressive than males.

One compelling hypothesis to account for sex differences in aggression is that girls are trained not to express aggression in a direct manner while boys are. The data we have collected on television contact sports help demonstrate the tenability of such an hypothesis (Lefkowitz *et al.*, 1973). The mean amount of television contact sports viewed by boys was greater than for girls (see Table 2.8). However, no significant correlation occurred between aggressiveness and viewing of contact sports for boys, whereas this correlation was quite significant ($r = .33$, $p < .01$) for girls. In addition, TV viewing of contact sports for girls was positively correlated with scores on scale 5 of the MMPI. For a girl, a high score on this scale is indicative of masculine attitudes and a preference for masculine interests.

As shown in Table 3.13, the peer-nomination measures of aggression for girls at both the third and 13th grades are significantly, positively correlated with the measure of masculine interests. Neither of these correlations is statistically significant for boys.

The effects for girls of MMPI scale 5 on the correlation between viewing television contact sports and aggression were controlled by means of partial correlation. These data are shown in Table 3.14. This control reduced only one of the correlations — contact sports and MMPI scales 4 + 9 — just below the level of statistical significance.

The hypothesis that preference for viewing contact sports is positively associated with the manifestation of aggressive behavior was substantiated, but only for girls. Peer nominations of aggression at ages eight and 19, both of the paper-and-pencil self-ratings, and responses to MMPI scales 4 + 9 collected at age 19 related to this preference for TV sports in the predicted direction. The way in which these variables were measured makes it unlikely that method variance could account for the obtained relationships. Certainly the peer nominations and subjects' responses to certain viewing preferences are methodologically independent.

A more likely explanation of events lies in the subjects' conditioning history. In the process of socialization, girls are trained not to express aggression in a direct or overt manner and nonaggressive behaviors are reinforced. The stimuli for aggressive behaviors are as relevant for females as for males, but the avenues for the expression of aggression are far more constricted for females by social expectations. Consequently, females may learn other socially acceptable ways of expressing aggressive responses. One of these ways could be through vicarious identification with aggressive models (Bandura, 1969, p. 130).

Viewing contact sports is a socially sanctioned activity in which more aggressive girls may express aggressive behavior vicariously. Two opposing theoretical positions — learning and psychoanalytic — suggest that participation in vicarious aggressive activities will, respectively, either increase the probability that the participant or observer will behave in an aggressive fashion (Bandura, 1965; 1969; Berkowitz, 1969c) or will decrease this probability according to the principle of catharsis (Dollard et al., 1939; Feshbach and Singer, 1971). The pronounced synchronous relationship for girls between peer-nominated aggression and contact sports may be the cumulative result of such vicarious participation. This interpretation of the results would lend support to the learning theory model. Furthermore, the witness of aggression measure may be construed to be another indication of vicarious participation in aggression in that the subject states how frequently he has been the observer of certain aggressive acts.

Why viewing contact sports is not correlated with aggression for boys again may inhere in socialization practices and peer expectations. Less restraint is placed on boys who are often socially reinforced by adults and peers for the straightforward expression of aggression (Eron et al., 1971; Feshbach, 1970). Direct avenues for the expression of aggressive behavior (such as fighting, wrestling, pummeling, war games, etc.) are open to boys and discouraged for girls. Moreover, both peer and adult cultures encourage and reinforce direct rather than vicarious participation for boys in contact sports but make little provision for the participation of girls. Thus, for boys, knowledge of these sports is virtually peer-mandated and required for peer acceptance and popularity.

Although girls' preference for masculine interests and activities is related to peer nominations of aggression (Table 3.13) and also to viewing contact sports as demonstrated in Table 3.15, MMPI scale 5 appears to account for only a small part of the relationship between this variable and aggression. When the effects of MMPI scale 5 on sports and aggression are controlled by partial correlation (Table 3.14), the correlations between viewing contact sports and aggression are not diminished significantly. Based on manifest behavior, results of the present study indicate that when females are aggressive, some of their interest and activities are deviant from that of their sex group and are similar to behavior of the male sex group.

The vicarious conditioning of emotional responses has been treated in depth by Bandura (1969) who suggests that vicarious emotional conditioning can occur by observing others experiencing positive or negative emotional effects in the presence of certain stimulus contingencies. Associative learning is the principle Bandura invokes to explain the process of vicarious conditioning, which, of course, may also be used to explain direct conditioning. However, a basic difference obtains between direct and vicarious conditioning: in the former, the learner is the recipient of the stimulus contingency, whereas, in the latter, a model or some other person is the recipient of the pain- or pleasure-producing stimulation. Yet significant learning also occurs in this indirect or modeling context. When this principle is related to viewing television contact sports, males and females respond differently because of their different conditioning histories associated with variation in socialization practices. Males, because aggression is permitted and even encouraged as a mark of masculinity, accept and tend to model themselves after aggressive actors — particularly when the behavior is positively socially sanctioned such as contact sports. Females, because aggression is unlady-like and believed to produce negative consequences (such as a tomboy reputation, which may result in alienation of the opposite sex), are taught by their parents to eschew identification with aggressive models. In the next chapter we will see how this model is supported by data pertaining to the differential effects of TV violence on the aggressive behavior of males and females.

Theories relating gender to aggression were expounded in Chapter 1. Although the data of the present study cannot refute the possible contribution of biological and hormonal components in the causation of aggressive behavior, they can and do support the theory that the different socialization practices used in rearing male and female children contribute to at least some of the differences in aggressive behavior attributable to gender.

Pertinent at this point is the discussion by Mulvihill and Tumin (1969) concerning the differences in criminality between males and females. These authors cite certain cultural and socialization factors which affect the female and presumably contribute to these differences in criminal behavior. The female child is not permitted by her parents to roam the streets and is more closely supervised than males. Also girls are taught that softness and gentleness are virtues, whereas males learn to eschew these characteristics and to value physical prowess and aggressiveness. Economically, women are not required to achieve success in the marketplace, although the changing status of females is undoubtedly altering this expectation. A woman's social status or rank in society has been derived vicariously through association with males by marriage. Marriage and family rather than economic competition have been set forth by child-rearing agents as proper goals for women. Finally, women have had fewer models for criminal acts than men; even when they commit such an act, the courts treat them with greater leniency than men. For example, although one out of seven arrests for serious crimes is a woman, only one woman for 22 men is confined in state and federal prisons.

These cultural factors, in large measure, serve to account for the differential rate of criminal behavior between males and females. The fact that aggressive behavior is shaped by learning through socialization practices and varies by sex within conspecifics detracts from the theories of Ardrey (1966), Lorenz (1966), and Morris (1967), who argue that aggression in man is innately determined. If females of the human species are less aggressive than males (as they seem at present to be) then a theory to explain away the absence of female aggression, such as sublimation or other second-order assumptions, is required. Scientifically cumbersome, however, this manner of explanation violates the principle of parsimony because the phenomenon of aggressive behavior could be explained on a simpler level requiring fewer assumptions. Lifestyles that expose individuals differentially to stimuli culminating in aggressive behavior would be a more parsimonious explanation of sex differences in aggression. Differential socialization practices in child rearing, upon which later lifestyles are contingent, are part of this explanation. Where cultural roles of women and men become congruent, the criminal rates of these groups become comparable (Mulvihill and Tumin, 1969). Similarly, data from our subjects show that as females' interests and attitudes become more masculine, their behavior becomes more aggressive. In this context a prominent feminist, Susan Brownmiller, (1973), believes that the time has come to reject the ideal of femininity in which nonaggression is apotheosized if for no other reason than self-defense necessary for survival on urban streets. Consequently, she recommends training in physical aggression for women and she herself is being tutored in such aggression by a Japanese male instructor. She notes that the Japanese are well-suited to give such training because they have learned to compensate for their smaller stature as compared to Western males. Smaller in stature and musculature, women in this sense, Ms. Brownmiller argues, are in the analogous position of Japanese males.

Some interesting data germane to the topic of changing roles for females are provided in a report by Kirchner (1974), who studied the interaction of age and sex effects for 246 three-, four-, and five-year-olds on the fight question of the Wechsler Preschool and Primary Scale of Intelligence (Wechsler, 1967). This question asks: "What is the thing to do if a boy (girl) much smaller than yourself starts to fight with you?" Analyzing sex differences by age, she found that "hit back" responses decreased for boys and increased for girls. For example, about twice as many boys as girls gave this response at age three, whereas boys and girls were approximately equal at age five. Because the "hit back" response is presumably socially proscribed and because girls, presumably, are taught not to aggress physically, Kirchner raises the question about possible recent changes in socialization practices and expectations for girls.

PERINATAL COMPLICATIONS AND AGGRESSION

In Chapter 1 we noted that some aggressive behavior may result from brain damage incurred from perinatal stress. Mark and Ervin (1970) argue that all violent behavior is the result of a lesion or lesions in the limbic system. The notion of a continuum of reproductive casualty (Pasamanick and Knobloch, 1966) suggests that aggressive behavior may be part of such a continuum. Other research (Mednick, 1970; White, 1974) suggests the presence of a direct link between disturbed behavior in children and central nervous system insult due to pregnancy and birth complications.

Subsequent to data collection in the 13th grade, we were afforded the opportunity of examining certain hypotheses concerning birth weight, mother's age at time of delivery, and later aggressive behavior of offspring (Lefkowitz et al., 1974). Our concern was with the question of whether certain complications of pregnancy and birth could be antecedents of aggressive behavior in childhood and young adulthood. Such complications are frequently associated with prematurity manifested by low birth weight and with an insufficient intrauterine environment related to mother's age. Because of the unequivocal relationship between low birth weight — 2500 grams or less — and central nervous system insult (see e.g., Birch and Gussow, 1970; Winick, 1974), we hypothesized that aggressive behavior in our subjects would be inversely related to their birth weight. In addition, we hypothesized that children born of mothers whose age at time of delivery was less than 18 or more than 35 years, would be more aggressive than children born of mothers between the ages of 18 and 35.

Birth record information was obtained from the Division of Biostatistics of the New York State Department of Health for 333 (78 percent) of our subjects — 166 girls and 167 boys. The missing data fell chiefly in the categories of *no known birth record* (16 percent), *out of state birth* (four percent), and *information not recorded* (one percent).

The first hypothesis, that low birth weight would be positively related to later aggressive behavior, was not substantiated for either boys or girls. Rather, Fig. 3.1 shows a tendency for birth weight and third grade peer nominations of aggression to be curvilinearly related. For both boys and girls, low and high birth weights are associated with lower aggression scores, whereas birth weights in the middle range are related to the higher aggression scores. A one-way analysis of variance of these data proved to be statistically significant for boys ($F = 2.503$, $p = .04$).

This tendency for birth weights and aggression to be related in a curvilinear manner is an empirical finding; any interpretation of it can only be speculative and, of course, *post hoc*. In this and other research (Harper and Wiener, 1965) birth weight and stature have been found to be positively correlated. From our subjects, the following correlations between birth weight and height at age 19 were obtained: boys, $r = .17$, $p = .025$; girls, $r = .31$, $p = .001$. Thus, it may be that our smaller subjects, because of the consequences, have learned not to behave aggressively, and the larger children — more popular and leaders — are reinforced for prosocial behavior and find aggression superfluous in their behavior repertoire. Children of medium stature are in an ambiguous status and may have received intermittent reinforcement for behaving aggressively. If so, this response mode would become more probable in further interaction with peers. This interpretation suggests that stature — a concomitant of birth weight — rather than neurological dysfunction is related to aggressive behavior. For both sexes, birth weight was unrelated to any of the measures of aggression obtained in the 13th grade.

The second hypothesis, that mother's age at time of delivery is related to aggressive behavior of offspring, was supported in part but only for boys. Table 3.16 shows that in a three-way classification of mother's age (less than 18 years, between 18 and 35, and more than 35 years) the greatest increase in aggressive behavior occurred in the offspring of mothers who were older than 35. A one-way analysis of variance of these scores was statistically significant ($F = 2.970$, $p = .05$). Similarly, mean scores on MMPI scales $4 + 9$, a measure of the propensity for antisocial behavior, also increased in this age category as did peer nominations of aggressive behavior in the 13th grade. For the latter two measures, however, only a tendency is indicated inasmuch as the probability levels were marginal at the .09 level. This hypothesis was proposed to examine two aspects of complications of pregnancy associated with a continuum of repro-ductive casualty. On the one hand, the occurrence of pregnancy during the mother's growth years would put her in competition with the fetus for essential nutrients, where loss to the fetus could produce central nervous system damage ultimately manifested in aggressive behavior. On the other hand, pregnancy in women over the age of 35 subjects the fetus to a potentially insufficient intrauterine environment, resulting in damage to the central nervous system. For example, cerebral palsy is known to occur with greater frequency when mothers are this age group. Although the present findings tend to support the latter part of the hypothesis, certain reservations should be noted. The age category, over 35, contains only 17 cases as compared to 139 in the middle group and ten in the group less than 18 years of age. Thus, the results could be an artifact of improper sampling. In addition, two of the three findings only approach statistical significance. Furthermore, the possibility of uncontrolled third variables such as different child-rearing practices employed by older mothers could have contributed systematic but extraneous variance to this relationship. Given these qualifications, however, the occurrence of the highest aggression scores in the extreme age group and the absence of significant correlations between mother's age and the subject's aggression scores, places the effect largely in the age category where complications of pregnancy are expected.

No unequivocal evidence was adduced to place the aggressive behavior of our subjects on the continuum of reproductive casualty. Stature, rather than central nervous system dysfunction, would best explain the obtained relationship between birth weight and aggression. However, aggressive behavior might be an aspect of this continuum in the case of boys born of mothers past 35 years of age. It is in this age group that a defective intrauterine environment is most likely to occur.

The cultural variables play a strong role in shaping aggressive behavior seems evident. However, these data do not resolve the question of whether or not man potentially — in the genetic sense — is aggressive. The validity of biological theories treating aggression as an instinct is subject to scientific scrutiny at the level of infrahuman organisms. When applied to humans, however, instinct theory tends to become metaphysical and teleological. For ethical considerations, experimental research with humans is proscribed and data pertaining to an aggressive instinct are usually in the form of extrapolation from animal research or the result of reasoning by analogy. It would seem prudent in this respect to adopt the credo of logical positivism — if a thing exists, it should ultimately be measurable; if not measurable, then the most parsimonious view is that the thing does not exist. Thus, with regard to an instinct of aggression in man, the best hypothesis at this time would be the null hypothesis.

SUMMARY

In this chapter we have attempted to delineate those environmental conditions that are relevant to the formation of aggressive behavior. Furthermore, we tried to show the effect of these conditions on the development of aggressive behavior at two moments in time. One was at the modal age of eight years when the subjects of the study were children in the third grade, and the other was when these same subjects were at the modal age of 19 and were young adults at the close of their high school years.

Four classes of variables were shown to be associated synchronously and longitudinally with aggressive behavior of our subjects. Termed predictor or independent variables, they were instigators, contingent responses to aggression, identification, and sociocultural variables. The dependent measures were peer nominations of aggression obtained during childhood and young adulthood, various self-ratings of aggressiveness, scores on certain scales of the Minnesota Multiphasic Personality Inventory (which have been used to assess the potential for delinquent behavior), and aggregate information from the New York State Division of Criminal Justice Services on arrests of our male subjects.

Our hypotheses relating environmental conditions to early and later aggressiveness were tested statistically by the technique of multiple regression analysis. The data collected on the four classes of independent variables entered into a variety of important relationships with the measures of aggression obtained at both age periods. Certain socialization practices termed instigators (for example, rejection) exert their greatest effect on aggressive behavior during childhood. Prolongation of the effect into adulthood was either nonexistent or minimal. On the other hand, the identification and sociocultural categories of variables tended to be better predictors of aggression in young adulthood, although certain variables within these classes (for example, television violence viewing) were related to aggression at both ages. In this chapter we also attempted to explore the possible contribution of such variables as low birth weight and mothers' age at time of delivery to aggressive behavior. We assumed that these conditions were indexes of central nervous system insult. Some evidence emerged suggesting that aggressive behavior of our male subjects was associated with mothers' parturition at or past age 35.

The analyses were performed separately for males and females because of the sex difference in aggression found in this and most other studies. With respect to the general finding that males are significantly more aggressive than females, the results of the present study suggest that an alternative hypothesis to that proposed by the instinctualists might be considered. This hypothesis states that females are less aggressive due to training not to express aggression in a direct manner because of the aversive contingencies. Indeed, we found that the aggressive females tended to be more like males at least insofar as their interests and attitudes were concerned.

Finally, we performed two cross validations of the findings that emerged from our multivariate analyses. The original multivariate analysis had been based on data from 128 boys and 120 girls. These included all subjects for whom there were complete data (i.e., a score on every independent and dependent variable). In the first cross validation, all 427 subjects were included whether or not they had a score on each variable. The second cross validation used a 50 percent random sample of those subjects in the first cross validation. Those variables that appeared on the original regression analysis and held up on both cross validations are termed to be of excellent validity; those that held up only on one cross validation are termed fair; and those that appeared on neither cross validation are termed to be of poor validity. For boys, TV violence and nurturance are of excellent validity; identification with mother, preference for girls' games, and mobility orientation of parents are of fair validity; while ethnicity is of poor validity. For girls, parents' religiosity and child's guilt are of excellent validity; TV violence, identification with father, and father's occupation, education, and mobility orientation are of fair validity; IQ is of poor validity.

Table 3.1 Correlation[a] for Boys between Early and Later Aggression with Selected Controls

			Control Variables for Partialed rs		
				Father's	
			Child's	occupational	Father's
Predictor	Outcome	r	IQ	status	aggressiveness
Third-grade aggression	13th-grade aggression	.38**	.34	.39	.38
	Victim of aggression	.17*	.16	.18	.17
	Witness of aggression	.06			
	Total aggressive habit	.16*	.13	.18	.16
	MMPI scales 4 + 9	.21**	.17	.22	.21

[a]The correlation coefficients were computed using the largest number of subjects available. Thus, in some cases the Ns are greater than those in the multivariate analyses.

*p < .05 for a two-tailed test   **p < .01 for a two tailed test

Table 3.2 Correlation[a] for Girls between Early and Later Aggression with Selected Controls

| | | | | Control Variables for Partialed rs | |
| | | | Child's | Father's occupational | Father's |
Predictor	Outcome	r	IQ	status	aggressiveness
Third-grade aggression	13th-grade aggression	.47[**]	.44	.46	.47
	Victim of aggression	.11			
	Witness of aggression	.09			
	Total aggressive habit	.07			
	MMPI scales 4 + 9	.13[*]	.09	.12	.13

[a]The correlation coefficients were computed using the largest number of subjects available. Thus, in some cases the Ns are greater than those in the multivariate analyses.

[*]$p < .05$ for a two-tailed test   [**]$p < .01$ for a two-tailed test

Table 3.3 Consistency of Aggression Through Time and Across Measures

Third-Grade Aggression	N	Males 13th-Grade Aggression	MMPI 4 + 9	Aggressive Habit
Low	44	24.61	116.00	22.07
Medium	139	83.10	124.32	33.44
High	28	155.07	132.71	34.39
		Females		
Low	29	9.21	112.24	18.66
Medium	165	22.78	120.12	22.27
High	22	77.27	125.91	22.96

Table 3.4 Multiple Regression Analyses for Boys*

Third-Grade Predictor Variable	Type	Predicting Third-Grade Aggression		Predicting 13th-Grade Aggression	
		Standardized Coefficient	Significance	Standardized Coefficient	Significance
Parental rejection of child	Instigator	.248	p < .004		
Parental disharmony	Instigator				
Child's IQ	Instigator	-.230	p < .005		
Parental nurturance of child	Instigator	-.304	p < .001	-.166	p < .041
Parental punishment of child	Contingent				
Child's identification with father	Identification				
Father's aggressiveness	Identification				
Child's identification with mother	Identification			-.191	p < .020
Mother's aggressiveness	Identification				
Television violence	Identification	.166	p < .038	.251	p < .003
Child's guilt	Identification				
Child's confessing to parents	Identification				
Child's preference for boys' games	Identification				
Child's preference for girls' games	Identification	-.141	p < .075	-.189	p < .023
Father's occupational status	Sociocultural	-.203	p < .011		
Parents' mobility orientation	Sociocultural			.271	p < .002
Parents' religiosity (frequency of church attendance)	Sociocultural				
Parents' educational level	Sociocultural				
Ethnicity of family	Sociocultural			.137	p < .095
		R = .535, p < .001		R = .499, p < .001	

*The regressions were computed in a stepwise manner. Stepping was stopped when no variable could be entered which would explain at least 2% of the variance in the criterion aggression variable.

Table 3.5 Multiple Regression Analyses for Girls*

Third-Grade Predictor Variable	Type	Predicting Third-Grade Aggression		Predicting 13th-Grade Aggression	
		Standardized Coefficient	Significance	Standardized Coefficient	Significance
Parental rejection of child	Instigator	.322	$p < .001$		
Parental disharmony	Instigator				
Child's IQ	Instigator			-.119	$p < .186$
Parental nurturance of child	Instigator				
Parental punishment of child	Contingent				
Child's identification with father	Identification			-.175	$p < .05$
Father's aggressiveness	Identification				
Child's identification with mother	Identification	-.289	$p < .001$		
Mother's aggressiveness	Identification				
Television violence	Identification			-.172	$p < .04$
Child's guilt	Identification			-.143	$p < .100$
Child's confessing to parents	Identification	-.202	$p < .012$		
Child's preference for boys' games	Identification				
Child's preference for girls' games	Identification				
Father's occupational status	Sociocultural	-.293	$p < .002$	-.332	$p < .001$
Parents' mobility orientation	Sociocultural			.172	$p < .044$
Parents' religiosity (frequency of church attendance)	Sociocultural			-.192	$p < .025$
Parents' educational level	Sociocultural	-.152	$p < .103$	-.261	$p < .015$
Ethnicity of family	Sociocultural	-.165	$p < .033$		
		$R = .602, p < .001$		$R = .534, p < .001$	

*The regressions were computed in a stepwise manner. Stepping was stopped when no variable could be entered which would explain at least 2% of the variance in the criterion aggression variable.

Note on Elaboration of the Multiple Regressions in Tables 3.4 and 3.5

The multiple regressions were computed in a stepwise manner with only those independent variables being entered that could account for at least two percent of the variance in the criterion aggression variable.

As Darlington (1969) and others have pointed out, one can treat the standardized coefficients in a multiple regression equation as measures of the relative contributions of the independent variables in determining the dependent variable. This approach assumes that all causal variables not in the regression equation are uncorrelated with those that are and that the criterion variable is not "causing" any predictor variable. While it is probable that these assumptions are violated, it is still worthwhile to examine the coefficients as approximate measures of causal contributions. Hence, a multiple regression equation was computed by a stepwise method that entered the third-grade variables into the equation in order of their utility in predicting the criterion variables of third- and 13th-grade aggression. The regressions for 128 boys are shown in Table 3.4, while the regressions for 120 girls are shown in Table 3.5. These multiple regression equations differ slightly from comparable regression equations published previously (Eron *et al.*, 1972) for two reasons. First, certain additional independent variables were considered in the present analyses. Second, only those subjects for whom data on *every* independent variable were available entered into the current analyses. Thus, the number of subjects used is‌ substantially less than the total number of subjects.

Table 3.6 Correlations for Boys between Third-Grade Predictor Variables and Aggression in the Third and 13th Grades

Third-Grade Predictor Variables	Third Grade	13th Grade		
	Aggression Third	Aggression 13th	Aggressive Habit	MMPI 4 + 9
Parental punishment of child	.18*	.13	.21*	.08
Parental rejection of child	.28**	.10	.08	.19*
Parental disharmony	-.08	.07	.07	.01
Child's IQ	-.29**	-.18**	-.14*	-.16*
Parental nurturance of child	-.16	-.15	-.05	.01
Child's identification with father	-.25**	-.16*	-.13	-.12
Father's aggressiveness	.01	.11	.10	.00
Child's identification with mother	-.23**	-.17*	-.13	-.03
Mother's aggressiveness	.01	.03	.15*	.02
Television violence	.21**	.31**	.11	.12
Child's guilt	-.14	-.05	-.05	-.06
Child's confessing to parents	-.19**	-.18*	-.10	-.19**
Child's preference for boys' games	.11	.11	.09	.10
Child's preference for girls' games	-.16	-.17*	-.10	-.14
Father's occupational status	-.16*	.03	.10	.09
Parents' mobility orientation	.15	.25**	.11	.03
Parents' frequency of church attendance	.04	.09	.07	.14
Parents' educational level	-.05	-.07	-.15	-.03
Ethnicity of family	.13	.07	.22**	.14

*p < .05 for a two-tailed test.   **p < .01 for a two-tailed test.

Table 3.7 Correlations for Girls between Third-Grade Predictor Variables and Aggression in the Third and 13th Grades

Third Grade Predictor Variables	Third Grade Aggression Third	Aggression 13th	13th Grade Aggressive Habit	MMPI 4 + 9
Parental punishment of child	.12	.04	.07	.15
Parental rejection of child	.35***	.04	.11	.07
Parental disharmony	.17*	.12	.05	-.02
Child's IQ	-.28**	-.19**	.04	.14*
Parental nurturance of child	.02	-.09	-.06	-.12
Child's identification with father	-.22*	-.22*	-.12	-.03
Father's aggressiveness	.02	.06	.17*	.17*
Child's identification with mother	-.30**	-.19*	-.02	-.06
Mother's aggressiveness	.12	.06	.03	.08
Television violence	-.02	-.13	-.03	-.06
Child's guilt	-.34***	-.20*	-.01	-.03
Child's confessing to parents	-.31**	-.14	-.01	-.07
Child's preference for boys' games	.04	.12	.05	.15
Child's preference for girls' games	-.04	-.01	.09	-.07
Father's occupational status	-.16*	-.14	.13	.04
Parents' mobility orientation	.02	.06	-.06	.06
Parents' frequency of church attendance	-.18*	-.20*	-.10	-.01
Parents' educational level	-.06	-.13	-.17*	-.19*
Ethnicity of family	-.07	-.08	-.14	-.02

*p < .05 for a two-tailed test.   **p < .01 for a two-tailed test.   ***p < .001 for a two-tailed test.

Table 3.8 Mean Aggression Scores of Boys at Age 19 According to Punishment by Parents at Age 8

| | Aggression Scores | |
Punishment	Unadjusted	Adjusted*
Low	87.4	89.4
Medium	67.4	66.5
High	89.2	88.1

*These scores have been adjusted for covariation with aggression score in the Third grade.

Table 3.9 The Prediction of Aggressive Behavior in Young Adulthood from Identification with Parents in Childhood

Males

| | | Mother | |
Father	High	Medium	Low
High	55.72	84.65	26.00
Medium	56.89	79.13	71.14
Low	2.50	165.22	93.37

Females

| | | Mother | |
Father	High	Medium	Low
High	11.89	22.80	1.00
Medium	32.33	18.81	15.91
Low	4.33	21.25	43.04

Table 3.10 Predictors of Aggression for Males in the 13th Grade

| | Criteria | | |
Predictors	Peer nominations 13th grade	Total aggressive habit	MMPI 4 + 9
Witness of aggression	.30**	.45**	.29**
Victim of aggression	.31**	.47**	.29**
IQ	−.16	−.20	−.01
School achievement	−.36**	−.29*	−.25*
Father's occupational status	.19*	.13*	.15*

*$p < .05$ for a two-tailed test   **$p < .01$ for a two-tailed test

Table 3.11 Predictors of Aggression for Females in the 13th Grade

	Criteria		
Predictors	Peer nominations 13th grade	Total aggressive habit	MMPI 4 + 9
Witness of aggression	.16*	.23**	.27**
Victim of aggression	.19**	.41**	.24**
IQ	-.05	.10	.06
School achievement	-.39**	-.08	-.20
Father's occupational status	.05	.13*	.07

*p < .05 for a two-tailed test   **p < .01 for a two-tailed test

Table 3.12 Sex Differences in Aggression

	Females		Males		
Variable	M	S.D.	M	S.D.	t
Third-grade aggression	7.51	9.87	12.12	12.73	-4.182**
13th-grade aggression	26.51	37.68	80.46	96.98	-7.610**
Victim of aggression	2.62	2.55	4.75	3.46	-7.278**
Witness of aggression	4.22	2.99	7.21	4.20	-8.145**
Total aggressive habit	21.85	10.36	31.19	15.66	-7.286**
MMPI 4 + 9	119.65	18.50	123.70	19.68	-2.192*

*p < .05 for a two-tailed test.   **p < .001 for a two-tailed test.

Table 3.13 Correlations Between MMPI Scale 5 and Measures of Aggression

| | Girls | | Boys | |
| | Scale | | Scale | |
Variable	5	N	5	N
Third-grade aggression	.18*	215	-.13	211
13th-grade aggression	18*	215	-.04	211
Total aggressive habit	.09	215	-.11	211
Victim of aggression	.07	215	-.07	211
Witness of aggression	.09	192	-.04	209
MMPI Scales 4 + 9	.10	215	.13	211

*p < .01 for a two-tailed test.

Table 3.14 Partial Correlations for Girls Between Amount of Contact Sports Viewed and Measures of Aggression with MMPI Scale 5 Controlled

Variable	N	TVSPT	TVSPT with Scale 5 Partialled
Third-grade aggression	215	.22**	.20**
13th-grade aggression	215	.33**	.31**
Total aggressive habit	216	.19**	.18**
Witness of aggression	216	.20**	.19**
MMPI scales 4 + 9	215	.14*	.13

*p < .05 for a two-tailed test.   **p < .01 for a two-tailed test.

Table 3.15 Correlations between Amount of Contact Sports Viewed and Other Variables

Variable	Girls TVSPT	N	Boys TVSPT	N
Third-grade aggression	.22**	216	−.08	211
13th grade aggression	.33**	216	−.08	211
Total aggressive habit	.19**	216	.04	211
Witness of aggression	.20**	216	.01	209
MMPI scales 4 + 9	.14*	215	−.01	211
IQ	.01	50	.29*	53
Social class	.06	210	−.00	209
Hours watched	.09	216	.24**	210
MMPI scale 5	.15*	215	−.20**+	211

*p < .05 for a two-tailed test.   **p < .01 for a two-tailed test.
+A high score represents deviation from the norms of one's own sex.

Table 3.16 One-Way Analyses of Variance of 13th-Grade Measures of Aggression and Mother's Age at Time of Boy's Birth

Mother's Age	N	Mean Aggression Scores Total Aggressive Habit	MMPI 4 + 9	13th-Grade Peer Nomination
< 18	10	28.00	123.70	43.70
18-35	139	30.12	122.50	72.76
> 35	17	39.29	133.29	116.65
df		2/163	2/163	2/163
F		2.970	2.412	2.379
p		.05	.09	.09

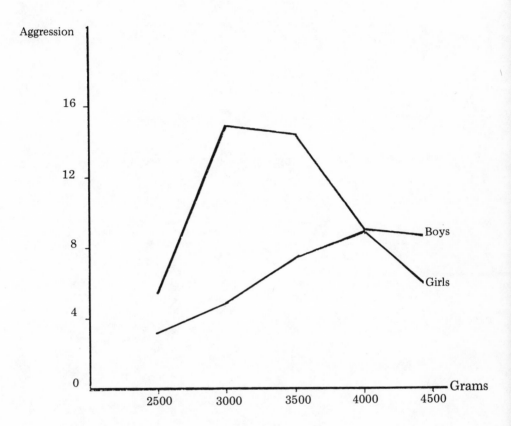

Fig. 3.1. Birth weight and third-grade aggression.

4
Television and the Development of Aggression

The available information about the effect of television violence on children has been drawn either from laboratory experiments in artificial settings or field studies in which cause and effect could not be separated. The results of both types of investigation have led many to assign television programming, with its heavy emphasis on interpersonal violence and acquisitive lawlessness, a role both in inciting aggression and teaching viewers specific techniques of aggressive behavior. The manipulative laboratory experiments have demonstrated that observing an aggressive display on film or television increases the immediate aggressiveness of a child viewer (Bandura, 1974; Bandura et al., 1961; 1963a; 1963b; Berkowitz et al., 1963; Goranson, 1970; Liebert et al., 1973). This suggests that the child is learning to be aggressive by imitating the actors on film or TV much as he learns cognitive and social skills by imitating parents, siblings, and peers (Bandura and Walters, 1963). Furthermore, it has been shown that children can be desensitized to have less emotional arousal to violence by exposing them to violence on TV (Cline et al., 1973). Thus, a child exposed excessively to media violence might be less frightened by real violence.

However, these laboratory experiments can be criticized for not duplicating real-life situations and possibly not accounting for anything more than a transient effect on the viewer. Therefore, it is valuable to look at the results of field studies on the relation between television violence and aggression. While these studies have not provided data about cause and effect, they have consistently found a significant positive correlation between aggression and TV violence viewing on the order of r = .25 (Bailyn, 1959; Chaffee, 1972; Eron, 1963; Schram *et al.*, 1961). Two other field experiments deserve special mention.

Feshbach and Singer (1971), in a bold attempt to compromise between laboratory manipulation and a field setting, regulated the amount of violent television teenage boys in a number of private residential schools and homes for neglected children were allowed to watch. They found some evidence that boys who watched more violent TV behaved less aggressively. However, several factors confounded the experiment and make their results, which are at odds with the other field studies, highly suspect. Many subjects resented being told that they could not watch programs they liked (usually violent programs) and they may have reacted aggressively against the control. In a few cases boys in the nonviolent viewing group were allowed to watch violent programs to retain their cooperation. Some boys guessed the purpose of the experiment. In any case, the subjects may well have been old enough that modeling of TV actors was no longer likely. Finally, the sample of subjects used was hardly representative of any population.

Milgram (1973) has also conducted a large and remarkable field experiment with essentially negative   results about the effect of TV violence on adults. Again, however, the procedures contained many flaws that might account for the results (Comstock, 1972). Without their knowing that they were in an experiment, a large number of adult subjects were shown an unusual antisocial act on TV. They were then observed to see if they would engage in the same act when provoked. The major problems with the experiment were that the antisocial act was a serious all-or-none act and that the subjects were adults who would hardly be expected to model actors' behaviors for more than a very transient period.

In summary, the evidence prior to our study indicated that TV violence viewing and aggression were correlated in the real world and that exposure to TV violence in the laboratory would increase the aggressiveness of young viewers for short periods. With our longitudinal field study in which the same variables were measured on the same people at two different times, it is possible to test causal theories more rigorously. By comparing the television violence and aggression scores obtained in the third grade with those obtained in the 13th grade, we can account more clearly for the antecedent-consequent relation between television violence and aggression.

It seems appropriate to analyze the effects of television violence upon boys and girls separately. We saw in the last chapter that boys, on the average, are substantially more aggressive than girls, and that, when girls are aggressive, they have more masculine attitudes, interests, and behaviors. We attributed these discrepancies primarily to differing socialization practices for male and female children, though biological differences may play a role as well. But more importantly, the hypothesized role of television violence in the development of aggression is as an identification variable — that is, the child may model what he sees on TV. Since the sex of a model is important in determining ease of identification (Bandura and Walters, 1963), and more aggressive males than females could be seen on TV in 1960, one should not expect to find the same effects for boys and girls.

BOYS WATCH MORE VIOLENCE

As explained in Chapter 2, we measured the child's exposure to television violence by determining his favorite television programs and adding up ratings of their violence content. For example, the favorite programs of an eight-year-old boy with a very high television violence score might have been "77 Sunset Strip," "Gunsmoke," and "Three Stooges." The favorite programs of a boy with a very low television violence score might have been "American Bandstand," "Death Valley Days," and "Ozzie and Harriet." The mean violence scores differed considerably by sex. In the third grade (eight-year-olds), subjects' scores could range from 1 for no violent programs to 4 for three violent programs. The mean score for boys was 2.14, but for girls it was only 1.59. Similarly, in the 13th grade, where subjects' scores could range from 0 to 8, the mean violence score for boys was 6.39 and for girls was 5.07. In other words, boys watched more violent television than girls at both eight and 19 years of age.[1]

THE EFFECTS OF TELEVISION VIOLENCE UPON BOYS

The relation between boys' preferences for violent television at age eight and their aggressiveness revealed itself *unequivocally in our study.* *The greater was a boy's preference for violent television* at age eight, *the greater was his aggressiveness* both at that time and *ten years later.*)A boy's preference for violent television correlated .21 (p < .01) with his concurrent peer-rated aggressiveness and .31 (p < .001) with his aggressiveness ten years later. We found that viewing was related to greater aggressiveness regardless of whether aggression was assessed by peer-ratings, self-ratings, or scales 4 + 9 of the MMPI (see Table 4.1).

Although the .31 correlation between third-grade preferences and 13th-grade peer-rated aggression means that only about ten percent of the variation in a boy's aggression is explained by his earlier TV preferences, ten percent is impressive when one considers the large number of variables affecting aggression and the small explanatory power of those other variables (see Chapter 2).[2] The extremely low likelihood of finding a relationship as strong as r = .31 by chance is a good indicator of the strength of the relation between eight-year-old boys' preference for violent TV programs and their aggressiveness ten years later.

While the TV viewing habits of an eight-year-old boy are related to his concurrent aggressiveness and predict his aggressiveness as a young adult, his TV viewing habits at age 19 no longer seem to be related to aggression. There is no relationship between a 19-year-old boy's current preference for TV violence and his current aggressiveness (Table 4.1). The programs a boy watches on TV by the time he is 19 do not seem to affect his aggressiveness. Perhaps modeling of behaviors seen on TV only occurs during a critical period in a boy's development, or perhaps the models presented on TV are no longer realistic to a 19-year-old.

In order to reveal clearly the relation between viewing television violence and later aggression, we partitioned the boys into groups who were low, medium, and high in their TV violence viewing habits in the third grade. The boys in the high-TV-violence group were more aggressive concurrently and *ten years later* regardless of how aggression was measured (Table 4.2). Oddly, the low-TV-violence viewers rated themselves higher on aggression than the medium-TV-violence viewers, even though they were rated least aggressive by their peers. Perhaps this is because the self-ratings include questions about the impulse to aggress. The low-violence viewers may have substantial impulses to aggress, but they do not act upon them.

Could initial differences in aggressiveness between children who like and don't like violent TV account for these results? Table 4.3 shows dramatically that it could not. Regardless of a child's initial level of aggressiveness, a preference for TV violence significantly increases his later aggressiveness. The initially low-aggressive boys who prefer violent television become more aggressive by age 19 than the initially high-aggressive boys who did not watch violent television.[3]

Causal Analysis

Having established that there exists a highly significant relationship between a preference for violent television in the third grade and aggressive habits as young adults, one can consider the alternative causal explanations for this phenomenon. Of course, one cannot demonstrate that a particular hypothesis is true. One can only reject untenable hypotheses and present evidence on the plausibility of the remaining hypotheses.

Cross-lagged Correlations

Consider the pattern of correlations diagramed in Fig. 4.1; the correlations on the diagonals are called *cross-lagged correlations*. The cross-lagged correlation between a preference for violent television in the third grade and aggression in the 13th grade was highly significant. However, the correlation between aggression in the third grade and a preference for violent television in the 13th grade was insignificant. When coupled together, these contrasting results lend considerable support to the hypothesis that preferring to watch violent television is a cause of aggressive behavior. This causal hypothesis is diagramed in Fig. 4.2a. However, a few rival hypotheses are seemingly consistent with the difference and deserve consideration.

One alternative hypothesis is that preference for violent television in the third grade stimulates concurrent aggression, and this aggression leads to 13th-grade aggression. The corresponding causal chain is diagramed in Fig. 4.2b. This interpretation can be rejected because, if it were true, the relation between the end points of the causal sequence would have been no stronger than the product of the relations between all adjacent intermediate points. But the correlation between the end points was .31, which was much higher than the product of the intermediate correlations.

For a similar reason, the causal chain diagramed in Fig. 4.2c can be eliminated as an alternative hypothesis. If early aggression caused a preference for violent television, which in turn contributed to later aggression, the correlation between early and later aggression would have been less than the product of the two intermediate correlations. It was not.

One cannot reject so easily the more realistic alternative hypothesis diagramed in Fig. 4.2d. This causal hypothesis asserts that early aggression causes both contemporaneous preferences for violent television and later aggression. Part of this hypothesis, that early aggression contributes to later aggression, is undoubtedly true, as shown in Chapter 3. What is of interest here, though, is whether or not the relation between early television preferences and later aggression can be explained as an artifact of early aggression can be explained as an artifact of early aggression. The pattern of means shown in Table 4.3 strongly contradicts this theory. One can also obtain evidence to refute this idea by computing the partial correlation between third-grade television violence (TVVL3) and 13th-grade aggression (AGG13) while controlling for third-grade aggression (AGG3). A partial correlation between two variables with a third variable control measures the amount of the relationship between the two variables which is *not* due to the third variable. If the hypothesis diagramed in Fig. 4.2d were the complete explanation of the correlation between early television preferences and later aggression, then the partial correlation would have been zero. But it was not. It was .25, or only .06 below the original correlation between a preference for television violence in the third-grade and 13-grade aggression. Hence, the hypothesis diagramed in Fig. 4.2d is implausible as a complete causal explanation.

The final plausible alternative to be considered is that early aggression causes a diminished preference for violent television. This theory is diagramed in Fig. 4.2e. If one views the cross-lagged correlations as deviations from the initial cross-correlation, then the zero correlation between early aggression and later television preferences might indicate that early aggression had reduced a preference for violent television. One can analyze this probability with a technique developed by Rozelle and Campbell (1969).[4] Applying their technique, we found the hypothesis that aggression diminishes a preference for violent television to be untenable.

As Rozelle and Campbell (1969), Kenny (1972), and others have pointed out, the validity of cross-lagged correlation inferences depends on the assumption that the underlying causal structure is stationary over time. If it is not, one must be careful about the inferences drawn. The large difference between the third-grade and 13th-grade synchronous correlations is indicative of lack of stationarity and necessitates consideration of some artifactual effects.

These artifactual effects are discussed in footnote to Fig. 4-1, and have been analyzed by others as well (Kenny, 1972; Neale, 1972).

The conclusions of all these analyses have been that while the effect may not be as strong as the cross-lagged correlations indicate, the single most plausible causal hypothesis is that a preference for watching violent television in the third grade contributes to the development of aggressive habits. This does not mean that other variables are not of equal or greater importance in stimulating aggression, but only that a preference for television violence and the viewing behavior that the preference indicates probably are independent and important causes of aggressive habits.[5]

Are Other Variables Responsible for the Relation?

None of the data presented up to this point sheds light on the possibility that another variable such as IQ, social class, parental punishment, or parental aggression might have stimulated both the child's preference for violent television and his aggressiveness. However, one can test some of these hypotheses by computing the partial correlations between television violence and aggression with such variables controlled. If the relation of TV violence to aggressiveness were an artifact of a third variable, the partial correlation should be significantly lower than the original correlation. But this was not the case for any of the potential third variables we measured (Table 4.4). Neither the child's aggression in the third grade, social class, mobility orientation of parents, IQ, parental punishment, nor parental aggression accounts for the relation between violence viewing and aggression. Nor can the relation be explained by the total number of hours of television watched by the subject in either the third or 13th grades.

The multiple regression analysis for predicting boys' 13th-grade aggressiveness from third-grade child-rearing variables also reveals the importance of early violence viewing to later aggression (see Table 3.1). A boy's preference for television violence at age eight was the second best predictor (second largest standardized coefficient, $p < .003$) of aggression at age 19 when considered in conjunction with the other child-rearing variables.[6] This means that violence viewing is making a substantial contribution to later aggressiveness independently of the other child-rearing variables. The significance of this finding is enchanced because the results held up excellently (cross-validated) on a 50 percent random subsample of our subjects and on the entire sample.

A more specialized technique for using multiple regression coefficients to estimate causal effects is path analysis (Heise, 1970). The path coefficients for television and aggression are shown in Fig. 4.3. These coefficients are standardized regression coefficients. In other words, the path coefficient from third-grade television to 13th-grade aggression represents the causal contribution of third-grade violence viewing to 13th-grade aggression under the assumptions of the path analysis model. The obtained pattern of path coefficients adds further credence to the argument that watching violent television contributes to the development of aggressive habits.

Interpretation of Analyses

The above results indicate that television habits established by age eight-nine years influence boys' aggressive behavior at that time and at least through late adolescence. The more violent are the programs preferred by boys in the third grade, the more aggressive is their behavior both at that time and ten years later. This relation between early television habits and later aggression prevails both for peer-rated aggression and for self-ratings of aggression. Actually, these early television habits seem to be more influential than current viewing patterns since a preference for violent television in the 13th grade is not at all related to concurrent aggressive behavior, nor are early television habits strongly related to later television habits.

It would be very difficult to explain these results as methodological artifacts. As explained in Chapter 2, both the peer-rated aggression measures and the ratings of the television programs for violence content possess demonstrated reliability. While only *preferences* for violent television were measured in both the third and 13th grades, as discussed in Chapter 2, it is reasonable to assume that a child's preference for a television program is very highly correlated with the length of time that he attends to that program.

These findings of a direct positive relation between the viewing of television violence and aggressive behavior on the part of the viewer corroborate in a long-term field study what has already been demonstrated as a short-term effect in the laboratory (Bandura and Walters, 1963; Berkowitz *et al.*, 1963; Goranson, 1970). Because the latter are manipulative studies in which systematically varied treatments were administered to randomly selected subjects under controlled conditions, statements about cause and effect relations based on their findings can be made with more confidence perhaps than those based on findings of field studies. In such studies, many uncontrolled variables are unaccounted for, and observation and measurement cannot be as precise. We feel that our findings relating television violence and aggressive behavior over a ten-year period strengthen the conviction that this is indeed a real relation. The causal direction indicated for the relation is that viewing violence regularly on television at age eight leads to more aggressive behavior on the part of the male viewer at that time and also in subsequent years than does viewing nonviolent programs. Thus, the significance of the laboratory studies is extended to indicate that the influence of television violence is not confined to short-term effects.

THE EFFECTS OF TELEVISION VIOLENCE UPON GIRLS

As was suggested at the beginning of this chapter, the differential socialization practices to which girls are exposed might limit the effect of television violence on girls. The correlations between girls' violence viewing and aggression show that there is virtually no direct relation between girls' preferences for violent television and aggressiveness at any time (Table 4.5). Girls' mean scores on the major aggression measures also did not vary with their preferences for violence in the third grade.

However, as pointed out previously, a multiple regression analysis can expose the causal contribution of each of several predictor variables to a dependent variable. If the effect of some predictor is being masked by other predictors, the regression analysis may expose it. The regression analysis for predicting girls' 13th-grade aggressiveness from third-grade child-rearing variables (Table 3.5) indicates that viewing television violence may lead to *lessened* aggressiveness for some girls. While the effect is not strong, it is significantly different from zero (p < .04).

Why would TV violence affect girls this way? First, one must recognize that there are other hypotheses that could explain the regression beside the one saying that viewing violent television reduces aggression in girls. Because there are no statistically significant correlations between girls' aggressiveness and their TV viewing habits, a cross-lagged analysis cannot be applied here to distinguish between rival hypotheses. However, a path analysis would be appropriate. The path analysis displayed in Fig. 4.4 weakly suggests both that early aggression leads to girls viewing less violent television and that the viewing of violent television leads to lessened aggression. This is a much weaker effect than that found for boys, and the lack of statistically significant correlations makes us somewhat skeptical about pushing this theorizing too far. Nevertheless, let us try to explain why the viewing of violent television, which clearly leads to heightened aggression in boys, might lead to lessened aggression in girls.

First, boys are encouraged and reinforced in the direct and overt expression of aggression. On the other hand, girls are trained not to behave aggressively in a direct manner and nonaggressive behaviors are reinforced. Thus, for girls, television violence viewing may actually be a positively sanctioned social activity in which aggressive girls may express aggression vicariously since they cannot express aggression directly in social interactions. The direct avenues for expression of aggressive behavior (such as fighting, wrestling, pummeling, war games, etc.) are open to boys and discouraged for girls. Moreover, both peer and adult cultures encourage and reinforce direct rather than vicarious participation for boys in contact sports but make little provision for the participation of girls.

Second, there were far fewer aggressive females on television in 1960 for a girl to imitate than there were aggressive males for a boy to imitate. Further, when girls did appear in violent sequences on television, they were usually victims of aggression or, at best, passive observers. So the more violent the programs that girls watched, the more they were exposed to female models as victims or passive observers, and the more they felt vicariously the aversive consequences of aggression. Therefore, the less likely they were to be aggressive. In summary, we propose that children watching television are exposed both to aggressive and nonaggressive models and they learn both aggressive and nonaggressive behaviors. It is suggested that the more the television characters resemble the child viewers, the more the children will model their behaviors after the actors. They will model both aggressive and nonaggressive characters. Hypothetically, the overt behavior that the children ultimately display will be the resultant of all the models they have observed weighted by the salience of each model for the particular child. Generally, female characters will be more salient for girls, and male characters for boys. Thus, the modeling effect will be larger when the sex of the model and observer are the same.

In addition to these explanations, one other factor may play a role in the differential effect of television violence on boys and girls. We have proposed that girls have been conditioned to express aggression only in a few acceptable forms. One of these would be fantasy. We now suggest that girls more clearly see television as fantasy and thus can express their aggressions through viewing television violence. Boys, on the other hand, see television as more realistic; so the modeling effect dominates for them.

What support can we marshal for this theory? It is well known that young girls have greater verbal fluency, read better, and are better able to fantasize than boys (Maccoby, 1966). Recent research by Singer (1972) has revealed that children do not learn aggression by viewing aggressive acts if they have been trained to distinguish reality from fantasy. Thus, if our theorizing is correct, one would expect girls to be able to distinguish reality from fantasy in television programs better than boys could. Data we collected in the 13th grade confirm just this. Girls think that television is significantly less realistic than do boys (t = 1.706, df = 425, p < .05). Given this finding, one can check some other implications of this theory. Assuming that girls who think that television is realistic would be poor fantasizers, one would expect to find such girls in the higher aggression groups. As one can see from Table 4.6, this is exactly the case. Finally, we note that girls who see themselves as masculine in the 13th grade — i.e., who obtain high scores on scale 5 of the MMPI—tend to perceive television as more realistic and tend to be more aggressive in situations where their peers can see them. The correlation between masculinity and perceiving television as realistic was .22 (p < .01), while the correlation between masculinity and aggression for girls was .18 (p < .05). In summary, while it is only weakly suggested by our data that a girl's viewing of television violence reduces her aggressiveness, there are plausible reasons why this might be the case. Even if it is true, though, the negative effect of television violence upon most boys would seem to be far more significant than the small positive effect it might have on some girls.

In this regard it is interesting to note recent changes in the behavior of little girls, changes that are perhaps related to the changing behavior of the models they are exposed to as well as to direct tuition in aggression. Current research (Chiswick, 1973) with nine-year-old boys and girls indicates that girls are now for the first time in our studies over the last 15 years getting aggression scores just as high as boys in an experimental situation in which overt aggressive behavior is measured. Concurrently, we note that in the last five or six years, while these nine-year-old subjects have been increasingly exposed to television, there have been increasingly more aggressive female models whose behavior could be copied — e.g., "Mod Squad," "Ironsides," "Get Christie Love," and "Girl from UNCLE." This is not to say that one is causing the other. They both may be a function of the rapidly changing role of women in our society (Mulvihill and Tumin, 1969).[7]

AMOUNT OF TV VIEWING AND PERSONALITY DEVELOPMENT

Our discussion thus far has been restricted to the effect of viewing TV violence upon later aggressiveness. Now we will consider the effects on a child of sheer amount of viewing.

Males

While the *amount of TV viewing* a boy engages in at age eight is not related to his later aggressiveness, it is negatively correlated with his concurrent peer-rated aggressiveness (r = -.19, p < .05). The more TV a boy watches, the less aggressive he is rated by his peers at age eight. One might hypothesize that boys who are nonaggressive stay home and watch TV, perhaps to avoid aggressive encounters. However, an alternative explanation that we find more tenable is that boys who stay home and watch TV are aggressive at home and are not seen being aggressive as frequently by their peers. We find this latter hypothesis more appealing because the aggression of the child as rated by the mother increased with increased TV watching (r = .24, p < .01) and also since aggression anxiety, which should be high if a boy is extremely *non*aggressive, was not high for the boys who watched a lot of TV.

The amount of TV boys watch is consistently related to their families' social status as the data in Fig. 4.5 demonstrate. Since high status (as measured by the father's occupation) was denoted with low numbers, these positive correlations mean that boys in low-status families watch more television than boys in high-status families. Since the difference between the correlations on the diagonals is small, we cannot make a causal inference of the basis of this cross-lagged analysis. However, the path analysis (also shown in Fig. 4.5) indicates that the more plausible causal hypothesis goes from lower social status to greater TV viewing.

The relation between a boy's IQ and the amount of TV he watches is more complicated. While there was no correlation between these two variables in the third grade, a negative relation had appeared by the 13th grade (r = -.22). Apparently, low-IQ teenage boys watch more TV than high-IQ boys. The data are not strong enough to permit us to make the type of causal statement we made about TV violence because of the small number of boys for whom 13th-grade IQ scores were available.

Third-grade IQ is also related to how realistic boys think TV is in the 13th grade (r = -.21, p < .01). Low-IQ subjects think that TV is more realistic. It is interesting in this regard that the more the subjects watch television at age 19 and the more violent the programs they prefer, the more likely they are to believe that situations depicted on television crime stories and Westerns are realistic representations of life.[8] (Thus, boys who watch television for many hours and prefer violent programs perhaps do not consider these aggressive behaviors as deviant but as appropriate ways of solving real-life problems. \

Females

The amount of television a girl watches is mostly unrelated to her aggressiveness. However, as with boys, social class is an important predictor of how much television a girl watches. The lower the status of the father's occupation, the more television his daughter watches. This pattern of correlations between the status of the father's occupation (low numbers mean high status) and the hours of TV his daughter watches is shown in Fig. 4.6. The significant differences between the two correlations on the diagonals suggest that low social status is an antecedent to high TV viewing. The path analysis (also shown in Fig. 4.6) supports this causal hypothesis very strongly. Possibly the cultural impoverishment of many low-status families and the ready availability of the television compared to other activities account for this effect.

The relation between girls' IQ and the amount of TV they watch is very similar to what was found for boys. Though there was no relation in the third grade, by the time these subjects were in the 13th grade, concurrent low IQ was a significant predictor of high TV viewing (r = -.18, p <.05). Since boys and girls display the same pattern of correlations between IQ and hours watched, we can combine their data to create a cross-lagged analysis with enough subjects to be valid.

The cross-lagged correlational analysis between IQ and hours of television watched by all children is shown in Fig. 4.7. The implication of this analysis is that *low IQ is a cause of children watching more television*. The associated path analysis confirms this interpretation.

Why would low-IQ subjects turn to more television viewing between the ages of eight and 19? Quite probably their interactions with their environment have led to many painful outcomes for them because of their low IQ. By retreating to the livingroom and watching TV, they enter a world where success may be vicariously experienced. In this world the content of most programs does not require even an average IQ to be understood. As a result, the low-IQ child may find television viewing a safe harbor where he can avoid the challenges of coping with the world. In fact, low IQ is correlated with the belief that television programs resemble real life.[9]

SUMMARY

In this chapter we have presented compelling evidence that there is a probable causative influence of watching violent television programs in early years on a boy's later aggressiveness. Of course, it is not claimed that television violence is the only cause of aggressive behavior. As we saw in the last chapter, many other variables are significant predictors of aggression. However, the effect of television violence on boys is relatively independent of any of these factors, including IQ.

The effect of television violence on girls was much less pronounced and went in the opposite direction. It is possible that the viewing of television violence reduces the aggressiveness of some girls. It was suggested that this was due to the lack of aggressive female models on TV and to the socialization practices that train most girls to be nonaggressive and express aggression in fantasy.

The amount of television a child watches was found to be inversely related both to IQ and social class. The most plausible hypotheses seemed to be that the low social class environment influences the child to watch more TV and that the low-IQ child retreats into the world of TV viewing. In Chapter 5 we will see that the social achievement of the subjects was also inversely related to the amount of TV watched.

NOTES

[1] The probability of obtaining these differences between boys' and girls' scores by chance are less than .001 in the third grade (t = 3.60, df = 359) and less than .01 in the 13th grade (t = 2.51, df = 425).

[2] In addition, the size of the correlation is probably restricted by the skewness of the distribution of aggression and violence scores and by the ten-year lag separating the measurement periods.

[3] A statistical technique which controls for third variables in analyzing mean differences (analysis of covariance) corroborated this conclusion. The one-way analysis of covariance tested the differences in 13th-grade aggression between the boys who were high-, medium-, and low-TV-violence watchers in the third grade. Third-grade aggression was the control variable. This analysis yielded an $F = 4.35$ with 2 and 179 degrees of freedom. The probability of such a result by chance is less than .015.

[4] Rozelle and Campbell (1969) propose that one should compare the cross-lagged correlations with a baseline cross correlation. They suggest that the most appropriate baseline is not the early contemporaneous correlation, but the average of the two contemporaneous correlations attenuated for the reliability of the variables. The higher the reliabilities, the less is the attenuation. With a conservative assumption of a very high temporal reliability of .70, the baseline for Fig. 4.1 would be $[(.21 + (-.05) \text{ X } .70 \text{ X } .70] /2 = .06$. Since the cross-lagged correlation from early aggression to later television preferences is very close to this baseline, one can reject the notion that early aggression reduces a preference for TV violence.

[5] The controversy over the interpretation of these results extends into statistical questions beyond the scope of this book. The interested reader should see Armour's (1975) paper and our reply (Huesmann, et al., 1975).

[6] This multiple regression equation differs slightly from a previous version published elsewhere (Eron et al., 1972) for two reasons. First, a few additional independent variables were considered in the present analysis. Second, only subjects for whom data were available on every independent variable were used.

[7] The authors are currently engaged in a three year study of 600 elementary school children that should more clearly elaborate the role of sex differences and fantasy-reality distinctions in the modeling of violence.

[8] $r = .28$ (p<.001) between judged realism of television programs and number of hours television is watched; $r = .36$ (p<.001) between judged realism and television violence.

[9] The correlation between third-grade IQ and a belief that TV is real (in the 13th grade) is -.16, p = .01, N - 427.

Table 4.1 The Correlations Between a Boy's Preference for Violent Television Programs and His Aggressiveness at Two Different Time Periods (based on 184 boys)

| | Third Grade | | 13th Grade | | | |
	TVVL3	AGG3	TVVH13	AGG13	TAH13	MMPI-49S13
Third Grade:						
TVVL3	1	.21**	.05	.31***	.11	.12
AGG3		1	.01	.38***	.16*	.21**
13th Grade:						
TVVL13			1	-.05	.04	.07
AGG13				1	.50***	.39***
TAH 13					1	.48***
MMPI-49S13						1

Note: Abbreviations: TVVL = preference for violent television programs; AGG = peer-rated aggression; TAH = total aggressive habit—a self-rating of frequency of aggressive behavior; MMPI-49S = sum of T scores on scales 4 and 9 of the Minnesota Multiphasic Personality Invertory.

*p < .05   **p < .01   ***p < .001

Table 4.2 Mean Aggression Scores as a Function of a Boy's Preference for Violent Television Programs in the Third Grade

TVVL3	n	AGG3		AGG13		TAH13		MMPI-49S13	
		M	SD	M	SD	M	SD	M	SD
Low	31	9.06	9.91	5.14	5.05	34.35	14.17	121.97	20.50
Medium	139	11.19	11.54	8.14	9.88	29.05	13.71	122.50	19.33
High	14	21.00	13.79	16.46	13.30	36.53	18.83	135.86	18.14
TOTAL	184	11.58	11.75	8.27	9.86			123.42	19.67
		$F = 5.43$**		$F = 6.82$***		$F = 2.92$		$F = 3.11$*	
				$t^a = 4.1$**					

Note: Abbreviations: TVVL = preference for violent television programs; AGG = peer-rated aggression; TAH = total aggressive habit—a self-rating of frequency of aggressive behavior; MMPI-49S = sum of T scores on scales 4 and 9 of the Minnesota Multiphasic Personality Inventory.

*$p < .05$.   **$p < .01$.   ***$p < .001$.

[a]Because of heterogeneity of variance, a t-test between the two most discrepant means for AGG13 was also performed. The t was conservatively evaluated by using degrees of freedom equal to the df for the smallest group—that is, 13.

Table 4.3 Mean Aggression Scores for Boys in the 13th Grade as a Function of Third-Grade Aggression and Preference for Violent Television

Level of Peer-Rated Aggression in the Third Grade	Preference for Television Violence in the Third Grade			
	High	Med	Low	
High	16.58 n = 13	11.69 n = 27	6.06 n = 5	11.44 n = 45
Med	10.33 n = 15	8.95 n = 59	5.87 n = 17	8.38 n = 91
Low	11.08 n = 8	1.90 n = 31	3.24 n = 9	5.41 n = 48
	12.66 n = 36	7.51 n = 117	5.06 n = 31	8.41 n = 184

Test of effect of preference for television violence: $F_{2, 175} = 6.63$, $p < .005$

Table 4.4 Partial Correlations Between a Boy's Preference for Violent Television and His Aggressiveness Ten Years Later

Controlled Variable	n	Partial correlation between TVVL3 and AGG13
None	184	.31
Third-grade variables		
Peer-rated aggression	184	.25
Father's occupational status	140	.31
Child's IQ	179	.28
Father's aggressiveness	140	.30
Mother's aggressiveness	184	.31
Parental punishment of the child	184	.31
Parents' mobility orientation	140	.31
Hours of television watched	184	.30
13th grade variables		
Father's occupational status	182	.28
Subject's aspirations	149	.28
Subject's hours of television watching	183	.30

Note—Abbreviations: TVVL3 = a measure of preference for television violence in the third grade; AGG13 = peer-rated aggression in the 13th grade.

Table 4.5 The Correlations Between a Girl's Preference for Violent Television Programs and Her Aggressiveness at Two Different Time Periods (based on 175 Girls)

	Third Grade		13th Grade			
	TVVL3	AGG3	TVVL13	AGG13	TAH13	MMPI-49S13
Third Grade:						
TVVL3	1	.02	.08	-.13	-.03	-.05
AGG3		1	-.08	.47***	.07	.13
13th Grade:						
TVVL13			1	-.05	.14	.01
AGG13				1	.24***	.28***
TAH13					1	.45***
MMPI-49S13						1

Note: Abbreviations: TVVL = preference for violent television programs; AGG = peer-rated aggression; TAH = total aggressive habit—a self-rating of frequency of aggressive behavior; MMPI-49S = sum of T scores on scales 4 and 9 of the Minnesota Multiphasic Personality Inventory.

*p < .05   **p < .01   ***p < .001

Table 4.6 Means Scores for Girls on "Realism of Television Programs"
as a Function of Girls' Aggressiveness

Third Grade Aggression	Realism
Low	12.65
Med	15.58
High	17.50

$F_{2, 213} = 2.33, p < .041$

13th Grade Aggression	Realism
Low	13.77
Med	15.91
High	19.10

$F_{2, 213} = 4.07, p < .018$

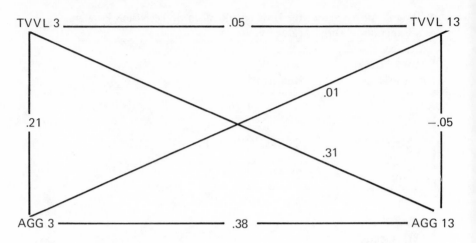

Fig. 4.1. The correlations between preference for violent television (TVVL) and peer-rated aggression (AGG) for 184 boys over a ten-year lag. The difference between the cross-lagged correlations (.31 and .01) is highly significant (z = 2.95, p < .003)

Testing Artifactual Causes of the Relation Between a Boy's Preference for Violent Television and His Later Aggression

One possible interpretation of the cross-lagged correlations in Fig. 4.1 is that the aggression measure increased in reliability between the third and 13th grades. Such an increase would have allowed the measured correlation between third-grade television violence and 13th-grade aggression to increase even though the true correlation did not change. However, the reliability of the peer-rated aggression variable in the third grade was measured by a variety of methods and consistently found to be between .85 and .95 (Walder *et al.*, 1961). Hence, an increase in reliability of the aggression measure is not a plausible explanation of the pattern.

Similarly, a decrease in the reliability of the television violence ratings between the third and 13th grade could have caused the decrease in the longitudinal correlation between third-grade aggression and 13th-grade television violence over the synchronous correlation. Low reliability for 13th-grade television violence is in fact plausible since 13th-grade television violence correlates poorly with most other variables. However, there is little evidence that third-grade television violence had much higher reliability. Furthermore, the reliability of 13th-grade television violence could not affect the cross-lagged correlation from television violence to aggression. Hence, a decrease in the reliability of the television violence variable is not sufficient to explain the pattern of cross-lagged correlations.

Basing the causality argument on the finding that the cross-lagged correlation is greater than the initial synchronous correlation raises another question. Was the increase significant? It is not appropriate to compare the cross-lagged correlation directly with the third-grade synchronous correlation, since that correlation should erode over time. Using Kenny's (1972) method for estimating erosion rates yields a rate of .605 for the correlation between television violence and aggression. Thus, one should compare the cross-lagged correlation of .31 with .605 (.21) = .127. For N=184, this comparison yields a z of 2.33, which is significant at the .02 level.

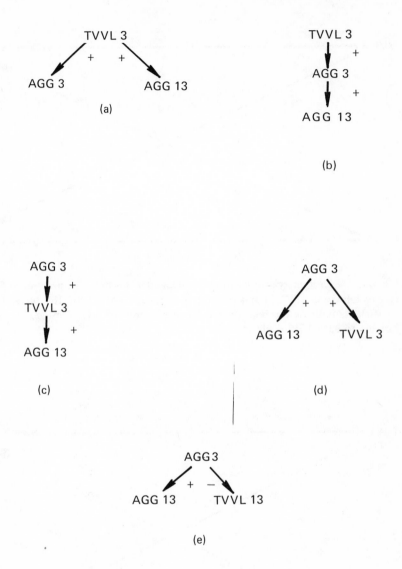

Fig. 4.2. Five feasible causal hypotheses for the correlations presented in Fig. 4.1.

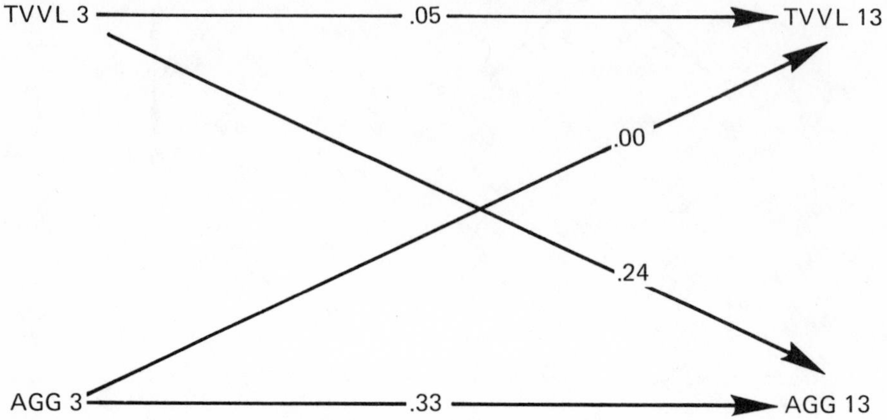

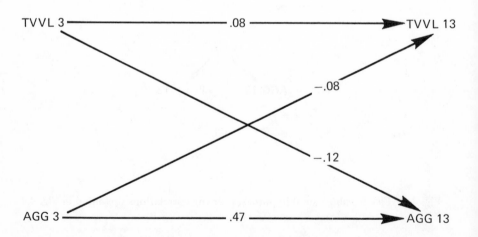

Fig. 4.3. A path analysis indicating the dependencies between preference for
violent television (TVVL) and peer-rated aggression (AGG) for 184 boys. The
coefficients indicate the relative causal contributions of each third-grade
variable to each 13th-grade variable.

Fig. 4.4. A path analysis indicating the dependencies between preference for
violent television (TVVL) and peer-rated aggression (AGG) for 175 girls. The
coefficients indicate the relative causal contributions of each third-grade
variable to each 13th-grade variable.

Correlations:

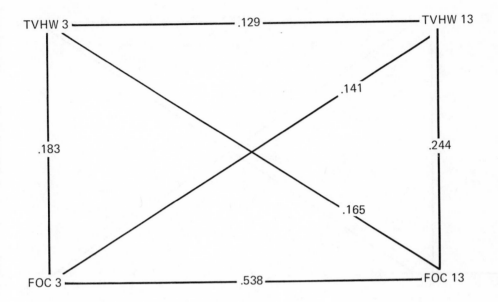

Path Analysis:

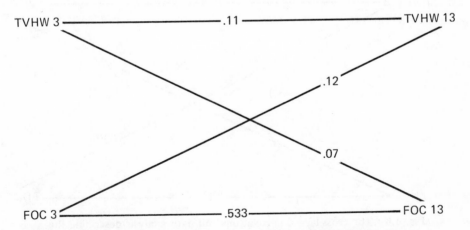

Fig. 4.5. The cross-lagged correlations and path analysis describing the dependencies between a father's occupational status (FOC) and the amount of television his son watches (TVHW). Since low-status occupations were given high numbers, the positive correlations indicate that low status correlates with greater amounts of TV viewing.

Correlations:

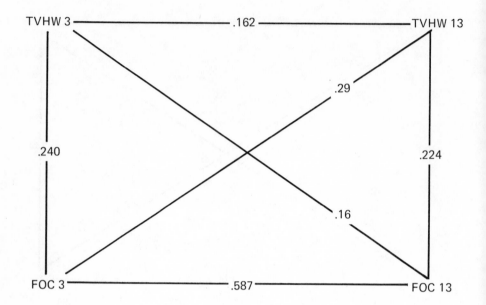

Path Analysis:

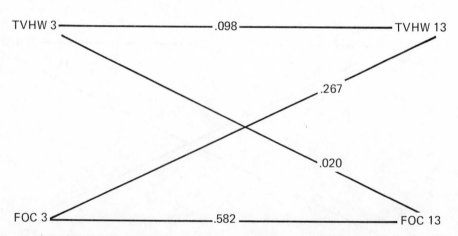

Fig. 4.6. The cross-lagged correlations and path analysis describing the
dependencies between a father's occupational status (FOC) and the amount of
television his daughter watches (TVHW). Since low-status occupations were
given high numbers, the positive correlations indicate that low-status correlates
with greater amounts of TV viewing.

Correlations:

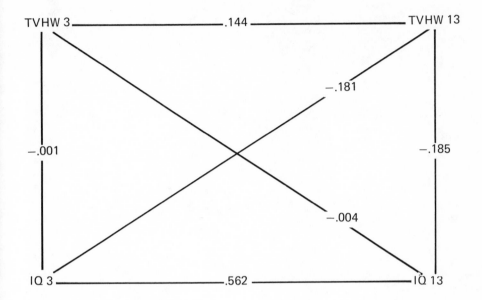

Path Analysis:

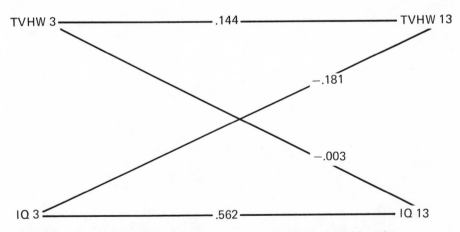

Fig. 4.7. The cross-lagged correlations and path analysis describing the dependencies between a child's IQ and the amount of television he or she watches (TVHW). These patterns suggest that low IQ is causing increased viewing of television.

5

Correlates of Aggression:
Psychopathology and Social Attainment

PSYCHOPATHOLOGY

In the original formulation of this research program it was assumed that aggression was one aspect of emotional health and the learning conditions that were precursory to the appearance of hostile behavior would be similar to the antecedents of other types of maladaptive behavior. Unfortunately, there were no direct measures of emotional disturbance or psychopathology included for the subjects when they were eight years old, making causal analysis of the data difficult. One index to emotional disturbance that was used was admission of subjects to state hospitals in New York. However, only three of 427 subjects had a record of having been admitted to a state hospital in New York before 1971. This is not surprising since there are relatively few young persons admitted to such institutions (New York State Department of Mental Hygiene, 1972). This is also a relatively gross index to presence of psychopathology since only severely disturbed individuals get admitted to such institutions; in addition, there are social class and regional biases affecting admission rates. However, in the 13th grade we administered to each subject a personality inventory, the MMPI (Dahlstrom *et al.*, 1972), probably a more sensitive instrument for detecting psychopathology than admission to a state hospital. As an indication of psychopathology we used the sum of scores on the psychotic tetrad (scales 6, 7, 8, and 9 — labeled paranoia, psychasthenia, schizophrenia, and hypomania, respectively). There is evidence that this is a valid index to potential and actual psychotic behavior (Dahlstrom *et al.*, 1972). In this chapter we will again treat results for boys and girls separately because the findings for the two sex groups are so dissimilar that the subjects in them do not seem to be drawn from the same population.

BOYS

It will be recalled from previous chapters that there were four types of antecedent variables measured when the subjects were eight years old that related to aggression in boys — instigators, contingent responses by parents to aggression, identification, and social class. Although all four types were related to aggression contemporaneously, the latter two were more powerful in predicting aggression over a ten-year time span. While the effects of lack of identification with parents and social class position at the early period persisted into late adolescence, the effects of instigation and punishment for the most part dissipated with time. For prediction of psychopathology at age 19, however, the opposite seems to be true. It is the instigation and contingent responses to aggression which relate most closely to psychopathology for boys. This is apparent from the relation between these variables and psychopathology as determined in a multiple correlation analysis (see Table 5.1). Certain of the variables in these analyses were the same as those used in Chapter 3, with the addition of another variable obtained by peer rating: aggression anxiety. Here, however, the criterion score is the MMPI psychotic tetrad and not peer-rated aggression.

Precursors to Psychopathology

The multiple regression analysis which, as pointed out in previous chapters, can give an estimate of the relative causal contribution of antecedent variables to a criterion, indicates that an important antecedent factor to psychopathology in males at age 19 is rejection by parents at age eight (this is a score that is summed for mothers and fathers). Rejection, which was one of the most important predictors to aggression at age eight, was not related significantly to aggression at age 19 but was related to psychopathology at age 19. From the direction of the relation, it would seem that the more the son was rejected at age eight by his father and/or mother, the more likely he is to obtain a high psychopathology score at age 19.

However, Table 5.2, which shows the mean psychopathology score for boys according to level of rejection by fathers and mothers reveals that the average psychopathology score for boys varies significantly only with father's rejection, not mother's. This pattern of means (shown in Fig. 5.1) reveals something that is masked by the correlation coefficient. The greatest difference in psychopathology scores is between those boys whose parents score moderately high on the rejection scale and those who score very high. The difference between the high and low rejection groups was actually not significant. An examination of the content of the rejection scale suggests a reasonable interpretation for this finding. The rejection items deal with behaviors in the child which the parent feels are changeworthy — e.g., Do you think Johnny is too forgetful? Are you satisfied with Johnny's manners? Are you pleased with the quality of Johnnys' schoolwork? Parents who obtain very low scores on this scale, indicating that they feel their child needs little improvement, are possibly communicating unrealistic evaluations to their child. Parents in the middle classification, indicating there are some areas in which the child can improve his behavior, are perhaps communicating a more realistic appraisal; while parents with high scores are saying that the child can never measure up to their standards, thus communicating a very negative evaluation. The same pattern holds for both mothers and fathers. Thus it would seem that parents in the moderate range of the rejection scale are setting up reasonable expectations for their children, training them not to expect universal approval from everyone with whom they interact, but also not encouraging a defeatist attitude about their competencies. It would seem that a little rejection has positive effects. Siegelman (1973) has reported that "male and female college students with personality traits frequently associated with creativity, tended to describe both parents as more rejecting than loving when growing up" (p. 43).

Another important finding to emerge from the regression analysis is that contingent response to aggression is related negatively to psychopathology so that low punishment goes with increased disturbance (see Table 5.3 for table of means). Thus it seems that low punishment functions much like high rejection; both of these reflect a minimal amount of interaction with the child. The parent who does not punish his son for transgressions is perhaps communicating that he does not really care about him or how he behaves and, just as the highly rejecting parent does, also tends to discourage interaction between parent and child. It is in these early interchanges with his parents that the child practices interpersonal skills and learns how to evaluate his own behavior and its effects on others. Persons who score high on the psychopathology scales do not do these things well. Thus, it is not surprising that IQ also contributes to the psychopathology score, since duller children have fewer resources for interpersonal skills than do brighter children. In this regard, furthermore, it is interesting that the remaining variable which has significant predictive power in the regression analysis is the peer-rating measure of aggression anxiety taken at age eight. Boys who appear to be anxious about expressing aggression at age eight tend *not* to have high MMPI psychopathology scores at age 19. The items in the aggression-anxiety scale reflect a tendency to try to facilitate interpersonal relations ("who says excuse me even when they have not done anything bad?" "Who will never fight even when picked on?"). Such boys undoubtedly care about their interactions with others and have probably learned techniques that help them get along with others. Consequently, they are more apt to gain gratifications from interpersonal relations and will not develop the maladaptive, defensive behaviors that are tapped by the MMPI items. A number of studies by other researchers have shown that severely maladjusted adults are deficient in social skills (Kelly *et al.*, 1971; Lerner, 1963; Senf *et al.*, 1956). Children who have not had sufficient practice in developing interpersonal skills in their primary groups or have not had competent tuition in such behaviors by their parents (Siegelman *et al.*, 1970) are more maladjusted as adults than children who have had more opportunity for social interaction with their primary caretakers. A study by Sherman and Farina (1974) demonstrates that nonacquisition of adequate skills for dealing with others is an important aspect of psychopathology and that inadequate skills are taught to the child by socially inadequate parents.

The final variable which had some predictability to the psychopathology score in the multiple regression analysis for boys was ethnicity, or the number of generations in which the child's family has been resident in the United States. Results with this variable indicate that the sons of more recent immigrants tended to obtain higher psychopathology scores. However, when considered in conjunction with the other third-grade predictors, ethnicity accounted for only a small portion of the variation in psychopathology. Thus, these data can hardly be cited as contradicting the evidence (Goldhammer and Marshall, 1953) that immigrant status has little effect on incidence rates of mental illness.

The procedure used to cross-validate the multiple regression analyses, as described in Chapters 2 and 3, indicated that ethnicity was actually of poor validity as a predictor to psychopathology in boys. Fair validity was ascribed to rejection and punishment, while aggression anxiety and IQ at age eight were of excellent validity as predictors of later psychopathology in boys.

Correlations Between Psychopathology and Individual Child-Rearing Variables

Not all of the measures obtained from parents and children during the first wave of the study were put into the multiple regression analysis, since each additional variable that is included increases the likelihood of chance relations emerging. Thus, only those variables that had theoretical relevance or were believed from previous experience to have strong predictive relations to aggression were included. However, there were significant correlations between psychopathology and variables that had not entered the multiple regression analysis (see Table 5.4). Among these were fathers' and mothers' rating of boys' home aggression (r = .15 and .18, respectively).

It is interesting that these positive correlations between home aggression at age eight and psychopathology at age 19 are about the same as those between home aggression at age eight and aggression at age 19 rated by peers (r = .12 for fathers and .20 for mothers). Also the correlation between home aggression at age eight and psychopathology at age 19 is larger than the correlation between home aggression and peer-rated aggression when both were measured at age eight (r = .00 for mothers and .13 for fathers). Perhaps the rating of aggression at home made by the parents when these boys were eight years old really served as an indirect measure of how disturbed the parent judged the child to be. Parents for whom aggressive behavior on the part of the child was salient possibly saw this as a manifestation of maladaptive (or at least, unusual) behavior and thus reported it to the interviewer who asked how aggressive the child was at home. In support of this hypothesis there is a highly significant relation between peer-rated aggression at age 19 and psychopathology for boys (r = .28, p < .001). The pattern of these relations gives us more confidence in the proposition that aggression, as defined in this study, is an aspect of psychopathology as stated in the beginning of this chapter. Furthermore, the variables that we termed instigators in the third grade, while not related to aggression ten years later, are related to the appearance of psychopathology in the later period.

However, the identification variables measured in third grade which predicted aggression at age 19 did not predict psycho-pathology — with the possible exception (r = .17) of the confessing measure. Whatever predictability to later psychopathology there is of a child not confessing transgressions to his parents may be a function of the quality of relationship it reflects between a parent and child. Confessing behavior on the part of the child is probably an indication of warmth and acceptance by the parent. The child who feels he can confess misdeeds freely to his parents is likely to have a warm relationship with them, interacting easily with them and thereby obtaining practice in communicating with others and developing social skills that lessen the probability of psychopathology.

RELATION OF PSYCHOPATHOLOGY TO AGGRESSION

Another way of looking at the relation between psychopathology and aggression is to separate the sample of subjects into high-aggressive and low-aggressive groups and do a discriminant function analysis between the two groups, predicting from each of the 13 MMPI scales (three validity and ten clinical scales) to the aggression categorization. This was done separately for boys and girls and for aggression as measured at age eight and at age 19. Subjects in the upper and lower quartiles of peer-rated aggression at each of these periods were called high and low aggressive. Additional analyses were done for those subjects who were classified in the same quartiles (high or low) at both periods. Because intelligence and social class have in the past been related to scores on the MMPI (Dahlstrom and Welsh, 1960), these two variables were included in the set of predictors. We found that the profile of scores discriminated signifi-cantly between high- and low-aggressive groups in all the cases.

Just as one can compute the best equation for predicting the score on one dependent variable from a whole set of independent variables, one can compute the best equation for discriminating between the high- and low-aggressive subjects from a set of independent variables. A coefficient is derived for each independent variable which repre-sents the variable's importance in discriminating between the high- and low-aggressive subjects. Thus, the discriminant coefficient of an MMPI scale would represent the contribution of that scale to predicting aggression independently of IQ and social class. Details of this analysis appear in Table 5.5.

The MMPI scales, in conjunction with IQ and social class, distin-guish significantly between males high and low in aggression at age eight. Which scales contribute significantly to this discrimination? Four scores discriminate between the two groups:

1) intelligence: low-aggressive boys have higher IQ scores;
2) hypochondriasis: high-aggressive boys have a higher number of physical complaints;
3) psychopathic deviate: high-aggressive boys have a greater tendency toward antisocial behavior;
4) psychasthenia: high-aggressive boys display more obsessive-compulsive behaviors.

All of the above MMPI scales separate the high- and low-aggressive groups about equally well as seen by the discriminant coefficients.

Using peer-rated aggression at age 19 to separate the boys into high- and low-aggression groups (Table 5.6), which scales contribute significantly?

1) k scale: low-aggressive males endorse more socially acceptable behaviors;
2) psychopathic deviate scale: high-aggressive males again tend more toward antisocial behavior;
3) psychasthenia: high-aggressive males again display more obsessive-compulsive behaviors.

The discriminant coefficients suggest that the k scale and the psychopathic deviate scale were slightly better discriminators than the psychasthenia scale; while the schizophrenia scale showed a tendency (p < .10) to discriminate between the two groups with high-aggressives displaying more bizarre behaviors.

When we compare males who are high on peer-rated aggression both at ages eight and 19 with males low in aggression at both times (Table 5.7), which scales discriminate?

1) intelligence: low-aggressive males have higher IQ scores;
2) psychasthenia: high-aggressive males display more obsessive-compulsive behaviors;
3) schizophrenia: high aggressive males admit to more bizarre behaviors.

In addition, the psychopathic deviate scale was almost a significant discriminator (p < .10) with a coefficient comparable to the above scales. It is quite apparent from these results that aggression can indeed be called a facet of psychopathology for boys.

Finally, it is instructive to look at the average MMPI profiles of boys who are high and low on peer-rated aggression. Figure 5.2 presents a profile of the mean scores on each of the MMPI scales for boys who were rated in the high quartile of aggression in both the third and 13th grades and for boys who were rated in the low quartile both times. The high-aggressive boys have significantly high scores, more than two standard deviations above the mean for normal subjects, on two scales — 9 (hypomania) and 8 (schizophrenia). The other high score, one and one-half stand deviations above the mean, was on scale 4 (sociopathic behavior). The 9-8-4 pattern is extremely rare in normal populations but not unexpected among delinquent boys, especially those who exhibit persistent and bizarre misbehavior (Hathaway and Monachesi, 1963). Lefkowitz (1966) found that, in a residential treatment school for delinquent males, such a pattern discriminated those boys who received irregular discharges from those who received regular discharges. The latter subjects exhibited an average profile showing highest scores on scales 4 and 9, but not 8. Lefkowitz (1966) ascribed the difference to a greater amount of psychopathology in the failure group. The irregular discharges had been awarded for such reasons as inability to make good use of the program; gross acting-out behavior (e.g., assault on staff or repeated running away), and severe emotional disturbance.

The low-aggressive boys as rated by their peers in both the third and 13th grades have an average profile that is well within normal limits (all scales less than two standard deviations above the mean for normal subjects). The mean scores on all scales are so similar that no real pattern is discernible. The high point obtained for scale 5 (feminity) is not unusual among normal male adults, especially college students and Peace Corp Volunteers, and indicates inhibition of manifest delinquent behavior (Dahlstrom et al., 1972).

When we compare the individual profiles of all male subjects who were in the high quartile of aggression in both the third and 13th grades with the individual profiles of all male subjects who were in the low quartile at both periods, the relation between aggression and psychopathology becomes even clearer (see Tables 5.8 and 5.9). Although the two groups are not significantly different in the number of individuals in each who have one or more clinical scales with scores equal to or greater than 70 (17/24 in the high group and 17/27 in the low group), the patterning and pile-up of scores is very different, indicating more pathology of the bizarre, acting-out variety in the high-aggressive group. In the high group of 24 subjects there are a total of 56 scale scores equal to or greater than 70; whereas in the low group of 27, only 43 such scores meet this criterion. In addition, seven subjects in the high (29 percent) as compared to two in the low group (seven percent) have F-scale scores greater than or equal to 70. High F-scale scores are associated with severity of pathology (Dahlstrom *et al.*, 1972). Further, the high-aggressive group contains 19 individuals (79 percent) who have the pattern 4-9-8, 4-9, 4-8, or 9-8 as their two or three highest scores; while the low-aggressive group contains only three individuals (11 percent) with such profiles.

Fourfold displays showing the incidence in both groups of individuals with T-scores over 70 on scales 4, 8, 9, and 5 appear in Table 5.10. It is apparent that high scores on scales which signify bizarre, acting-out behavior (scales 4, 8, 9) are more prominent in the high-aggressive group, while scores indicating inhibition of acting-out are more prominent in the low group (scale 5).

There can be little doubt from the above findings that aggression in boys is indeed an aspect of psychopathology. It should be pointed out again that the measures of aggression and psychopathology were obtained independently of each other. The former is a peer-rated measure and the latter a self-rated measure.

GIRLS

Precursors to Psychopathology

The results of the regression analysis for girls are quite different than those for boys and reveal a somewhat different pattern of contributions of parent variables and other measures taken in the third grade to psychopathology at age 19 (see Table 5.1). The most striking difference is that there is no relation between peer-rated aggression anxiety and psychopathology for girls, nor between punishment by parents and psychopathology. One possible reason for the difference is that the types of behavior reflected by the aggression-anxiety score are learned by most girls very early in life and approximate the norm of behavior for girls. Thus, these behaviors are probably not related to individual differences in the ability to get along with others, as they are in boys. Similarly, girls are usually punished so little for aggression that there would not be sufficient variability in scores on punishment by parents to relate to individual differences in psychopathology in the daughters.

The most important predictor to psychopathology in the regression analysis is preference for girls' games — i.e., girls who do not prefer to play girls' type games when they are eight years old tend to obtain higher psychopathology scores at age 19 than girls who at age eight prefer games deemed to be appropriate for their sex.

Also important in the multiple regression analysis, girls' third-grade peer-rated aggression and fathers' aggression are shown to have relevance for later psychopathology in girls. These results indicate that there is a tendency for girls who are rated by their peers as aggressive at age eight and who at that time have aggressive fathers as models to obtain higher psychopathology scores at age 19 than girls who were not seen as aggressive by their peers and did not have aggressive fathers as models. This is not at variance with the finding that preference for girls' games is a negative indicator of later psychopathology. Girls who are reputed to be aggressive and girls who model their behavior after aggressive fathers are also engaging in behaviors deemed inappropriate for females. And they have already thus been singled out by their peers at age eight. It should be pointed out that in the cross validations described previously, nonpreference for girls' games and activities demonstrated excellent validity as a predictor to psychopathology. Peer-rated aggression at third grade was of fair validity and fathers' aggression was of poor validity.

There are some correlations between psychopathology and other variables that were not included in the multivariate analysis for reasons explained above (see Table 5.4). Two of these — mother's education (r = .19) and father's acquiescence, a response tendency to agree with extreme statements, (r = .21) — are probably related to social class. The measure of acquiescence is taken from the Reversed F-scale (Christie *et al.*, 1958) on which lower class subjects are routinely reported to get high scores on acquiescence. Both of these measures (mother's education and father's acquiescence) are related to high psychopathology scores of the daughters. It is interesting that for boys there was no correlation between psychopathology and any of the indications of social class.

Relation of Psychopathology to Aggression

For females, the discriminant function analysis (see Table 5.11) relating third-grade aggression and MMPI scale scores at age eight yielded significant differences in the following:

1) intelligence: low-aggressive females have higher IQ scores;

2) masculinity: high-aggressive females are more masculine in interests, attitudes, and behaviors;
3) social isolation: low-aggressive girls tend to withdraw from social interaction more than high-aggressive girls.

The discriminant function analysis for females relating peer-rated aggression scores at age 19 to MMPI scales (Table 5.12) yielded significant differences on two scales. These were:

1) one of the validity scales, F: high-aggressive females said more unusual things about themselves;
2) psychopathic deviate: high-aggressive females tended more toward antisocial behavior.

When we compare females who are high on peer-rated aggression both at ages eight and 19 with females low in aggression at both times (Table 5.13), the discriminant function analysis again separates the two groups. However, only one scale contributed to this discrimination — social isolation: low-aggressive girls tend more to withdraw from interpersonal relations. In addition, the masculinity scale was almost a significant discriminator (p < .10) in the last two analyses, with a coefficient comparable to those scales that discriminated significantly.

It is interesting to compare the results of the discriminant function analysis for boys and girls. It is apparent that there is a strong relation between the aggression level of both female and male subjects and the manner in which these subjects endorse items on a set of scales measuring psychopathological deviance. However, there are more such relations between psychopathology and aggression for males than females. High-aggressive males are more prone to engage in antisocial, obsessive-compulsive, and other deviant behaviors. High-aggressive females are more masculine in their attitudes and interests, and low-aggressive females tend more to withdraw from social interaction than high-aggressive females. In both males and females higher aggression is associated with lower intelligence. It should be emphasized that the effect of IQ is independent of the other scales in this analysis, which accounts for the unique contribution of each variable to the criterion.

When we compare the composite MMPI profile, as in Fig. 5.3, of girls who were rated in the high quartile of aggression by their peers in both the third and 13th grades with girls who were rated in the low quartile at both periods, we do not find the extreme scores in either group or the differences that were obtained with the boys. Both sets of profiles are within normal limits. The high-aggressive girls do have a high 4-9 profile as would be expected (Dahlstrom *et al.*, 1972) but neither scale score is significantly high by itself. The low-aggressive girls have a composite profile not unlike that of the low-aggressive boys, except that instead of a high point 5, they have a low point 5 — both low-aggressive boys and low-aggressive girls say female things on female items. The latter is not uncommon in women (Dahlstrom *et al.*, 1972), especially those who admit to being somewhat dissatisfied with themselves but who are actually described in favorable terms by their peers.

The relative lack of differentiation between high- and low-aggressive groups of girls on the basis of psychopathology score is evident when we examine the individual MMPI profiles of girls in these groups. Four out of ten girls in the high-aggression group (Table 5.14) have profiles with one or more scale scores greater than or equal to 70; while seven out of 21 in the low-aggression group (Table 5.15) have such profiles; and there is no difference in the presence of 4-9, 4-8-9, or 8-9 profiles between the two groups, although there was such a difference for high- and low-aggressive boys. In addition, one girl in the high group had an F-scale score above 70, but there was no such occurrence in the low group.

It should be emphasized that the relation between psychopathology and aggression implied by the findings described in this chapter is not necessarily relevant to the incidence of violent acts among mentally ill persons. According to the reports of the Task Force on Individual Acts of Violence (Mulvihill and Tumin, 1969), "all studies to date indicate that the mentally ill are no more likely than the general population to be involved in such crimes as assault, rape or homicide" (p. 444). But the research on this topic is not entirely unequivocal. A recent study (Zitrin *et al.*, 1976) shows that arrest rates for mental patients were higher than those for the general population in that particular catchment area and higher than those for 4601 cities in the United States. Violent offenses are included in these arrest rates. As far as we know, none of our subjects was diagnosed as mentally ill. The indications of psychopathology that we used was the tendency to respond to a personality inventory in a manner similar to persons of known diagnosis.

However, the findings presented here on the relation between psychopathology and aggression are not unexpected when considered in the context of recent research in the diagnosis of child behavior disorders. Quay (1972) has stated: "almost without exception multivariate statistical studies of problem behaviors in children reveal the presence of a pattern involving aggressive behavior, both verbal and physical, associated with poor interpersonal relationships with both adults and peers" (p. 9). It would seem that the relations noted by Quay between aggression and interpersonal difficulties in childhood persist at least into late adolescence.

The multivariate studies of Peterson (1961) and Quay and his associates (1966) also corroborate the differential finding for boys and girls. These researchers have consistently found that conduct disorders are significantly more frequent among boys and personality disorders among girls. Also, in this regard, Eysenck (1963) in her factor analytic study on data collected from 6760 English schoolchildren ranging in age from seven to 16, found that girls obtain significantly higher neuroticism scores than boys. Boys, on the other hand, obtain significantly higher scores on extraversion than girls.

Boys and girls appear to be not unlike, however, when we consider the relation between intelligence and psychopathology. One of the better predictors of psychopathology at age 19 is a low IQ score at age eight for both males and females. The relation between mental illness and intelligence has been one of the most consistent findings in the area of psychopathology for at least half a century (Burdock and Hardesty, 1973). However, those studies have been concerned primarily with adult mental patients and have been interpreted as demonstrating the effect of mental illness on intellectual efficiency. The current findings would indicate that the lowered intellectual capacity is probably antecedent to the disturbance in interpersonal relations. These findings support Werry's (1972) conclusion that in childhood psychosis intellectual functioning at the time of diagnosis is "The best single predictor of final adaptive level . . ." (p. 222).

SOCIAL ATTAINMENT

So far, our efforts have been directed at illuminating the causes of the development of aggression in children and, to a lesser extent, the development of general psychopathology. However, it is also valuable to investigate the emergence of behaviors that appear to be the obverse of aggression. These behaviors — popularity and leadership — are important in that they may prevent the development of the negative aspects of personality such as aggression and psychopathology. By now, it is quite clear that a major factor in the control of aggressive behavior is the learning of nonaggressive behaviors

(Eron *et al.*, 1971; Patterson, 1972). If a youngster is to learn to be dependably low in aggression, he should learn nonaggressive behaviors to solve those problems that he might otherwise try to solve with aggressive behaviors.

As described in Chapter 2, *popularity* was measured in the third and 13th grades by asking a child's peers two questions: "Who would you like to sit next to in class?" and "Who are the children you would like to have for your best friend?" Also in the 13th grade a subject's *leadership* was measured by asking his peers "Who was a leader of a club or group?" It is no mean achievement for a developing youngster to be identified by his peers as their best friend or to be regarded by his peers as a leader of a group. During the period between ages eight and 19, the peer group increasingly becomes the main source of a child's social income. His age mates constitute one of the adolescent's major social resources. A young adult with high scores in popularity and leadership has resources useful to him in good times as well as in times of adversity. For example, there is some evidence that a highly prosocial individual who becomes "schizophrenic" is more likely to function as a reactive type of schizophrenic, being more able to rebound from his debility than a process type of schizophrenic (Phillips, 1968; Phillips and Zigler, 1961; Zigler and Phillips, 1961).

From the outset, it is clear that popularity and leadership are traits that are fairly stable over time. The correlation between popularity at age eight and at age 19 is .378 for boys and .458 for girls. This means that a young adult's social success, in terms of his popularity and leadership abilities, can be predicted, at least partially, on the basis of his popularity and leadership abilities as an eight-year-old. Of course, some of this stability may be due to a subject's peers remembering earlier social successes and rating the subject on them. However, as explained in Chapter 2, logic and data suggest that the scores were mostly measuring the behaviors occurring near the time the peer nominations were obtained.

The task, then, is to identify the determiners of social success in both males and females. Any events or characteristics of the child measured when the child was in the third grade that predict the child's positive social achievements ten years later would be of particular interest. Since the emphasis of our study was on the development of aggression, many obvious candidates for predictors were not measured (e.g., physical attractiveness). Nevertheless, an extensive enough portrait of each child's environment was obtained to permit us to draw some important conclusions about the development of prosocial behaviors.

What are some of the events that can predict achievements of these positive outcomes? As with the other dependent variables — aggression in Chapter 3 and psychopathology earlier in this chapter — we shall use four types of predictor scores: (1) the child's exposure to events that might be instigators to aggression, (2) the parents contingent responses to the eight-year-old child's aggression, (3) the opportunities the child has and takes to increase identification with parents or others, and (4) the sociocultural characteristics of the home. These four categories had been formulated to predict aggression, not positive social outcomes. Therefore, this classification scheme may need revision for the purpose of predicting non-aggressive interpersonal skills.

We might ask it any of these predictor variables involve positive nonaggressive behavior at age eight. The answer is *yes*. Several of these third-grade measures correlated significantly with third-grade *popularity*; they were *nurturance, aggression anxiety, preference for girls' games, profile identification, confessing, guilt,* and *IQ* (see Table 5.16). This look into our third-grade data for correlates of *popularity* demonstrates that, while we may not have the measures that would have been the most relevant, we may well have measures with sufficient relevance to permit the identification of some antecedents to these positive nonaggressive outcomes in young adults.

We computed the multiple correlation between the 25 third-grade predictor variables and popularity and leadership in the 13th grade. This also yielded multiple regression equations for predicting popularity and leadership from these 25 third-grade predictor variables (Table 5.17).

The independent variable that was found most useful in predicting from the third grade for both males and females ten years later is IQ. Thus, a person with a higher IQ in the third grade, other things being equal, is likely to achieve a higher positive social position in the 13th grade.

Is low IQ here functioning as a frustrator, as argued in Chapter 3? It is reasonable to believe that a youngster with a higher IQ is less deprived because he starts out in the third grade with more behavioral or skill resources and over the ten-year span acquires even more of these in comparison to the youngster with a lower IQ. He is likely to be more popular and regarded as a leader. The lower IQ child is not as likely to be popular, or lead, or gain the satisfactions that derive from these activities. He therefore will be more frustrated. These results are consistent with classifying low IQ as a frustrator and thus as an instigator to aggression.

The second most consistent predictor to both 13th-grade positive social outcomes is, not surprisingly, popularity in the third grade.[1] Popularity in the third grade, independently of other variables, predicts popularity in the 13th grade for both males and females. It also predicts leadership for males. For the females, an apparently corresponding predictor to leadership is third-grade aggression anxiety. However, for neither males nor females was aggression at age eight a predictor to popularity or leadership when considered in conjunction with the other variables. We might speculate why these third-grade predictors — IQ, popularity, and aggression anxiety — so consistently predict these positive outcomes.

It would be surprising if popularity and aggression anxiety were not predictors. The relations over a ten-year period may be stability of behavior. (See Tables 5.18 and 5.19 for the correlations for girls and boys.) This strong relationship may prevent the other 22 variables from showing their predictive power. We therefore re-computed the multiple correlations and regressions between the 13th-grade prosocial behaviors and the third-grade predictors without including popularity, aggression anxiety, and aggression (Table 5.20).

In these analyses, IQ and popularity in the third grade are joined by religiosity of the youngster's parents when the child was in the third grade as predictors to positive social outcome for both boys and girls. Religiosity of the parents reporting frequent church-synagogue attendance was found to be relevant to later popularity and leadership when the third-grade peer-nomination scores were excluded from the analysis; it appears more strongly for girls than for boys.

To gain more information about the causal relationship between religiosity and popularity, we can look at the pattern of correlations across time. Known as cross-lagged correlations, these analyses between religiosity and popularity are presented in Fig. 5.4 for boys and in Fig. 5.5 for girls.

It would appear that the amount of church-going professed by the parents ten years before is a source of influence on popularity, rather than the reverse. The more the parents go to church, presumably taking the child, the more likely the child is to be popular ten years later. Of course, this relation quite possibly might be due to the effect of a third variable, which is correlated with religiosity and popularity — e.g., a person who goes out to church or anywhere for that matter is more likely to meet more people. Also the more the parents went to church ten years before, the more the youngster went to church when he was 19 years old. Only for girls was there an influence from the parents' church going to the child's third-grade popularity. In sum, then, the amount of church-going by the parents when the child is eight years old is associated with a girl's popularity at both ages. A boy's church-going experience at age eight has only a longitudinal or delayed association to popularity. Church-going by the 19-year-old, male or female, while following to some extent the pattern that may have been set by the parents, does not have an influence on current popularity.

As in the previous chapters, we shall attend to the differences between boys and girls. In both sex groups, one can predict over a ten-year time span to positive outcomes from popularity, IQ, and parent's religiosity (the latter more for girls than for boys).

BOYS

For boys, the instigators are more important components than for girls. When the three third-grade peer-nomination scores are excluded from the list of 25 potential predictors to positive social outcome, parental disharmony and rejection by parents appear to join IQ, especially in predicting leadership. For girls, only IQ is a significant component from the instigator category.

Two sociocultural variables are significant predictors, whether or not the third-grade peer-nomination scores are included in the analyses. These third-grade variables are mobility aspiration and generation level. Thus, the more the parents of a third-grade boy say they are willing to sacrifice to get ahead socially, the more likely he is to be a leader ten years later. Similarly, the more recently a boy's family has come to his country, the less likely he is to be popular at age 19. This is not so for girls.

GIRLS

For girls, five third-grade variables are distinctive predictors of positive social outcomes: parents' education, preference for TV violence, hours of TV watched, guilt, and parents' use of punishment. The higher the education of a girl's parents when she was in the third grade, the more likely she was to be a leader ten years later. Not so for boys. The correlation between parents' education and daughter's popularity in both the third and 13th grades is about .20.

The reports of parents concerning the TV programs girls preferred to watch and the number of hours of TV they watched both related positively to 13th-grade popularity in the multiple regression analysis. To understand the roles of these two TV variables, we examined the correlations between the preference for violent TV programs and popularity at the third and 13th grades and between TV hours watched and popularity at both of the grade levels. There was no relation between preference for TV violence and popularity across time; however, there were significant correlations between the hours of TV watched and a girl's popularity. This effect can best be illustrated by examining the correlations in a cross-lagged arrangement as presented in Fig. 5.6.

The pattern of correlations strongly suggests that less popular girls in the third grade begin to turn more and more to watching TV, perhaps as a substitute for the gratifications received by more popular girls from interpersonal relations. Furthermore, this substitute behavior shows its effect ten years later in a contemporary relation between unpopularity and number of TV hours watched. This is an excellent example of how causal relationships can be detected from correlational data in a field study.

Another finding of note is that when parents of third-grade girls could detect guilt from their daughter's actions, these girls were more likely to be popular ten years later. Finally, the parents who reported that they punished their third-grade girls less harshly tended to have daughters who at age 19 were more likely to be popular.

PORTRAIT OF THE POPULAR AND LEADING CHILD

What kind of an eight-year-old child achieved popularity ten years later? What kind achieved leadership? It is clear from previous discussions in this book as well as from other sources (e.g., Money and Ehrhardt, 1972) that sex of the child is such a powerful moderator variable that we must rephrase the questions, emphasizing the child's sex.

Perhaps to simplify this discussion we may note that correlations between popularity and leadership at the 13th grade approach the size of correlations between identical measures ($r = .64$ for boys and $r = .72$ for girls). It is defensible to assert that popularity and leadership at age 19 are two related aspects of positive social position. Thus, we can ask of these data, "What kind of an eight-year-old boy went on to achieve positive social position ten years later?" and "What kind of an eight-year-old girl went on to achieve this type of position?"

The *boy* who achieved a positive social position at age 19 was popular and somewhat polite with his peers at age eight, and had a higher IQ. His parents stated that they would sacrifice pleasures and convenience to get ahead socially. They were church-going folks who may have taken their son to church or synagogue quite regularly. This family had not arrived in this country recently. The parents tended to be satisfied with the way their eight-year-old son was developing; however, there was some controversy between the parents, perhaps about how best to do their parenting. There is some suggestion that the eight-year-old boy and his father were closely identified.

The *girl* who achieved a positive social position at age 19 was, like her male counterpart, popular at age eight. As noted elsewhere (Eron *et al.*, 1971; Flor-Henry, 1974) girls in general tend to have more skills that do not involve aggressive behaviors than do boys. Therefore, politeness does not emerge as a predictor to positive social position for girls as it does for boys. In addition, this girl also had a higher IQ and had parents who had gone further in their own education. The parents were church-going folks who may have taken their daughter to church or synagogue quite regularly, which helped to increase her popularity then and later on through this ten-year period. Her popularity at age eight provided her with friends then and through late adolescence. Having friends apparently made it less necessary to watch TV, so that activities with people tended to replace TV programs that were rated as more violent. Her parents believed that they could tell from her facial expression whether she had broken a rule. And they tended to punish her less harshly when she did transgress.

SUMMARY

In this chapter we have discussed the relation between high aggression and psychopathology and low aggression and positive social outcomes. At the outset of this longitudinal study, we had hypothesized that aggression was one aspect of psychopathology. However, we were unable to collect data on extent of psychopathology among our subjects until the second wave of the study. These data included the sum of the scores on scales comprising the psychotic tetrad of the MMPI, which each subject took during the follow-up interview.

It was found that aggression was indeed an aspect of psycho-pathology at least for boys. Similar child-rearing practices were associated with the later appearance of both psychopathology and aggression in boys. But punishment and rejection at age eight were more closely related to psychopathology at age 19 than to aggression. In addition to the moderately high positive correlation between psychopathology and aggression in boys, it was demonstrated that a number of individual MMPI scales discriminated significantly between high- and low-aggressive males. High-aggressive males had more hypochondriacal complaints, obsessive-compulsive defenses, and admitted to more schizophrenic-like behaviors than low-aggressive males. In general, high-aggressive males responded more like persons who engage in bizarre, acting-out behaviors, while low-aggressive males responded more like persons who inhibit such behavior.

Findings for girls and boys differed. Important childhood precursors to psychopathology for girls were lack of preference for girls' games and high peer-rated aggression at age eight. Also related to high psychopathology scores for girls were indicators of lower social class position. It seems that girls who later had high psychopathology scores were singled out as deviant as early as age eight.

Correlates of low aggression were readily classifiable as social attainment or social success. Positive social position was most readily achieved by young adults who were intelligent, popular, and polite as young children. Their parents were not new to the country, attended church, and understood their children. Thus, this social achievement was reached by those who come from their childhood with intellectual and social behaviors that had been developing favorably in a family with parents who did their parenting positively, warmly, and with some enthusiasm.

NOTES

[1] Popularity in the third grade could have been viewed as an outcome or dependent variable then. We use it here as a predictor variable.

Table 5.1 Multiple Regression Analysis for Predicting Psychopathology in the 13th Grade from Third-Grade Variables

Third-Grade Predictor Variable	Females		Males	
	Standardized Coefficient	Significance	Standardized Coefficient	Significance
Aggression, Third grade	.15	.096		
Preference for girls' games	-.179	.05		
Father's aggressiveness	.132	.145		
Aggression anxiety			-.272	.002
Punishment			-.302	.001
I.Q.			-.200	.019
Rejection			.193	.025
Ethnicity			.136	.107

F = 3.09   df = 3/185   p < .01   F = 6.37   df = 5/122   p < .001

Table 5.2 Mean Scores on 13th-Grade Psychopathology as a Function of
Various Levels of Rejection

Father	Boy's Mother			
	LO	MED	HI	TOTAL
LO	245.10	233.86	245.29	241.42
MED	230.80	230.60	239.69	233.70
HI	276.16	252.43	256.01	261.53
TOTAL	250.68	238.96	247.09	245.55
	Girl's Mother			
LO	228.69	235.58	219.20	227.82
MED	228.24	236.45	213.71	226.13
HI	223.21	239.44	240.36	234.34
TOTAL	226.72	237.16	224.42	229.43

F (Father's Rejection) = 5.116   df = 2,131 $p < .008$

Table 5.3 Psychopathology Scores of Boys at Different Levels of Punishment

		Psychopathology Scores
	High	239.0
Punishment	Medium	239.8
	Low	247.3

Table 5.4   Correlations Between Third-Grade Antecedent Variables and
13th-Grade Psychopathology*

Variable	Female	Male
Aggression, third grade	.09	.14[a]
Aggression anxiety	-.08	-.27[b]
Preference for girls' games	-.14	-.08
Father's occupation	.10	.05
Father's Rejection	.15	.24[b]
Mother's rejection	.01	.17[a]
Father's rating of home aggression	-.06	.18[a]
Mother's rating of home aggression	-.03	.15[a]
Confessing	-.08	-.17[a]
Mother's punishment	.15a	-.06
Father's acquiescence	.21b	-.02
Mother's education	.19b	.05
TV hours watched	.16a	.07
IQ	-.10	-.23[b]
Punishment mother + father	.17a	-.08
Rejection mother + father	.09	.23[b]
**Aggression, Grade 13	.12	.28[b]

*   This table includes every antecedent (third-grade) variable for which
    there is a significant bivariate correlation with the psychotic tetrad
    score for either males or females.
**   This is not a third-grade antecedent variable but is included for
    illustrative purposes.

[a] $p < .05$ [b] $p < .01$

Table 5.5 Discriminant Analysis Between Boys High and Low in Aggression in Grade 3

| | Means | | Discriminant Coefficient | p |
	Low Agg.	High Agg.		
IQ3	111.31	99.17	.00110	< .001
Father's Occupational Status 13	3.96	4.12	.00149	
MMPI L	47.54	49.35	-.00036	
K	57.30	61.32	-.00004	
F	51.54	50.26	.00003	
1	53.38	53.61	.00096	< .05
2	55.97	55.91	.00009	
3	55.36	56.62	-.00052	
4	55.73	63.82	-.00085	< .05
5	60.80	58.94	.00003	
6	54.53	59.26	-.00029	
7	58.74	59.41	.00101	< .05
8	59.58	64.79	-.00057	
9	61.68	66.20	.00027	
MMPI 10	53.38	52.26	-.00030	

Overall Significance
$F = 3.17$ $df = 15, 92$ $p < .001$

Table 5.6 Discriminant Analysis Between Boys High and Low in Aggression in Grade 13

| | Means | | Discriminant Coefficient | p |
	Low Agg.	High Agg.		
IQ3	111.48	105.30	.00026	
Father's Occupational Status 13	3.83	4.34	.00110	
MMPI L	49.26	47.79	.00023	
F	56.02	66.58	.00001	
K	54.10	49.64	.00115	< .02
1	53.09	54.96	-.00003	
2	55.67	58.04	-.00007	
3	55.53	56.60	-.00001	
4	55.65	66.13	-.00123	< .01
5	60.00	58.52	.00029	
6	53.55	60.71	-.00005	
7	59.45	62.87	.00082	< .05
8	58.74	69.60	-.00066	< .10
9	59.33	69.39	.00014	
MMPI 10	54.64	51.67	.00049	

Overall Significance
$F = 4.36$ $df = 15, 95$ $p < .001$

Table 5.7 Discriminant Analysis Between Boys High and Low in Aggression in Both Grades 3 and 13

	Means		Discriminant Coefficient	p
	Low Agg.	High Agg.		
IQ3	113.7	98.5	.00385	< .01
Father's Occupational Status 13	3.9	4.8	-.00462	
MMPI L	47.3	48.1	.00188	
K	57.2	65.9	.00106	
F	54.5	51.3	-.00011	
1	53.9	52.6	.00487	< .02
2	57.2	58.0	-.00180	
3	56.0	57.0	-.00196	
4	56.5	68.1	-.00371	< .10
5	63.5	59.9	.00189	
6	54.3	60.8	-.00053	
7	60.1	61.7	.00547	< .02
8	59.8	70.4	-.00453	< .05
9	60.5	71.7	-.00006	
MMPI 10	54.5	50.6	-.00075	

Overall Significance
$F = 3.55$ df = 15, 32 $p < .001$

Table 5.8 Individual MMPI Scale Scores of Male Subjects Who Were in High Quartile of Aggression in Both Third and 13th Grades

L	F	K	HS 1	D 2	HY 3	PD 4	MF 5	PA 6	PT 7	SC 8	MA 9	SI 0
63	55	59				71						
44	46	59										
44	76	48				81		79	79	99	75	73
2	53	68										
40	68	53				76				74	73	74
46	60	51										
50	55	38		75			73					
46	100	44		96			95	91				
56	92	49		80	73	83	76	79	73	74	73	
56	104	51				74		73	87	94	82	
46	66	55							81	101		
44	86	36								94		
44	46	53								84	93	
50	66	42		70				82	71	92		
46	66	44								74	70	
63	55	57			80				77		75	
40	76	44				71		70		80	75	
66	76	49						76		73	81	
40	48	53								88		
40	62	51				74					73	
44	48	62										
46	53	57										
44	62	48								82	73	
46	53	51									81	

Table 5.9 Individual MMPI Scale Scores of Male Subjects Who Were in Low Quartile of Aggression in Both Third and 13th Grades

L	F	K	HS	D	HY	PD	MF	PA	PT	SC	MA	SI
			1	2	3	4	5	6	7	8	9	0
56	60	4			71	79	82	73	71	71	75	
46	48	61										
40	55	46										
46	70	49	98	94	82		71		89	99		74
46	58	40										
50	48	72			71							
0	44	50		75	77							
46	46	53										
60	68	55								73	78	75
2	36	66										
0	44	50								73		74
53	62	57										
53	64	57					74		71		75	
66	48	59										
36	70	48					71					
44	55	36										
50	60	51	70						73	80	70	
50	62	59					80				75	
46	60	51										
46	50	59										
46	60	61										

Table 5.9 Individual MMPI Scale Scores of Male Subjects Who Were in Low Quartile of Aggression in Both Third and 13th Grades (Cont'd.)

L	F	K	HS 1	D 2	HY 3	PD 4	MF 5	PA 6	PT 7	SC 8	MA 9	SI 0
53	58	74										
50	58	51					76	76				70
44	46	61		80			71		75	73		
56	58	57									70	
40	53	49					71					
46	50	59										

Table 5.10 Frequency of T-Scale Scores over 70 on Selected MMPI Scales for High- and Low-Aggressive Boys

Aggression	Scale 4*		Scale 8		Scale 9		Scale 5*	
	Presence	Absence	Presence	Absence	Presence	Absence	Presence	Absence
High	8	16	13	11	12	12	2	22
Low	1	26	6	21	6	21	8	19
			$X^2 = 5.52$		$X^2 = 4.29$			
			df $= 1$		df $= 1$			
			$p < .025$		$p < .05$			

*Test of statistical significance not possible because of low frequency in one cell.

Table 5.11 Discriminant Analysis Between Girls High and Low in Aggression in Grade 3

| | Means | | Discriminant Coefficient | P |
	Low Agg.	High Agg.		
IQ3	108.61	97.26	.00047	< .01
Father's Occupational Status 13	3.79	4.13	-.00037	
MMPI L	49.29	50.59	-.00062	
K	54.09	59.03	-.00027	< .10
F	53.16	52.23	.00079	
1	50.30	51.33	.00042	
2	52.45	53.85	.00005	
3	54.61	54.72	-.00010	
4	57.31	62.31	-.00017	
5	46.55	54.03	-.00077	< .01
6	56.72	57.51	.00046	
7	55.92	56.61	-.00029	
8	55.56	59.82	-.00044	
9	59.05	62.74	.00026	
MMPI 10	53.10	51.20	.00091	< .02

Overall Significance
$F = 3.06$ $df = 15, 103$ $p < .001$

Table 5.12 Discriminant Analysis Between Girls High and Low in Aggression in Grade 13

| | Means | | Discriminant | |
	Low Agg.	High Agg.	Coefficient	p
IQ3	108.22	102.80	-.00002	
Father's Occupational Status 13	3.91	4.02	-.00061	
MMPI L	49.41	50.29	-.00026	
F	50.86	59.17	-.00104	< .01
K	53.91	52.44	.00056	
1	48.65	50.98	.00028	
2	51.66	52.85	-.00032	
3	52.66	55.02	-.00003	
4	54.50	64.72	-.00062	< .05
5	46.38	52.80	-.00055	< .10
6	54.67	58.07	-.00006	
7	55.52	55.98	.00078	
8	54.60	58.78	.00019	
9	57.60	63.30	-.00002	
MMPI 10	54.14	50.76	.00077	

Overall Significance
$F = 3.78$ $df = 15, 96$ $p < .001$

Table 5.13 Discriminant Analysis Between Girls High and Low in Aggression in Both Grades 3 and 13

| | Means | | Discriminant Coefficient | p |
	Low Agg.	High Agg.		
IQ3	107.3	97.3	.00140	
Father's Occupational Status 13	4.1	4.0	-.00373	
MMPI L	50.84	53.12	-.00231	
K	50.73	60.46	-.00210	$< .10$
F	54.30	53.50	.00331	
1	48.91	52.00	-.00065	
2	51.39	54.17	-.00041	
3	52.85	54.50	.00105	
4	54.03	65.12	-.00133	
5	47.48	54.91	-.00201	$< .10$
6	54.58	58.91	.00110	
7	54.45	57.87	-.00218	
8	53.24	59.75	.00179	
9	56.54	63.75	.00094	
MMPI 10	54.48	50.75	.00475	$< .01$

Overall Significance
$F = 3.02$ $df = 15, 41$ $p < .005$

Table 5.14 Individual MMPI Scale Scores of Female Subjects Who Were in High Quartile of Aggression in Both Third and 13th Grades

L	F	K	HS 1	D 2	HY 3	PD 4	MF 5	PA 6	PT 7	SC 8	MA 9	SI 0
63	58	49										
56	53	62										
50	55	51										
56	48	60										
44	62	51				79					73	
63	80	59						85		89	75	
50	58	49										
56	46	57										
40	66	46				76					70	
56	55	40				71						

Table 5.15 Individual MMPI Scale Scores of Female Subjects Who Were in Low Quartile of Aggression in Both Third and 13th Grades

L	F	K	HS 1	D 2	HY 3	PD 4	MF 5	PA 6	PT 7	SC 8	MA 9	SI 0
46	55	48										
56	55	57										
44	53	55										
50	50	60									81	
56	46	59										
53	48	49										
73	46	64										
50	46	64										
50	50	59					71		70		70	
50	55	54									70	
40	62	46										
66	53	51										
44	64	49								78	70	
63	46	53										
40	64	35										
50	60	59					71				70	
53	48	48										
50	58	51										70
63	46	59										
50	48	62										
44	50	53										

Table 5.16 Correlations Among Generally Positive Third Grade Nonaggressive Interactions for 120 Girls (above Diagonal) and 128 Boys (below Diagonal)

	1	2	3	4	5	6	7	8
1. Third grade aggression anxiety		.11	-.17	.10	.15	.13	.68	.01
2. Child's preference for girls' games	.15		-.04	.08	.13	.22	.18	.05
3. Child's identification with father	.16	-.01		.11	.09	.19	.20	-.02
4. Confessing to mother	.19	-.07	.02		.50	.23	.08	-.09
5. Child's guilt	.21	-.02	.03	.51		.20	.21	-.12
6. Child's IQ	.13	-.04	.25	.12	.07		.21	.10
7. Third grade popularity	.73	.06	.27	.19	.14	.27		.03
8. Parental nurturance of child	.20	-.10	.04	.26	.20	.01	.17	

For N = 128: $r_{.05} = .17$; $r_{.01} = 23$

For N = 120: $r_{.05} = 20$; $r_{.01} = .25$

Table 5.17 Multiple Regression Analyses+ for Predicting 13th-Grade Prosocial Behavior from Third-Grade Variables including Peer Ratings

Third-Grade Predictor Variable	Type	Females		Males	
		13th-Grade Popularity	13th-Grade Leadership	13th-Grade Popularity	13th-Grade Leadership
Parental rejection of child	Instigator				
Parental disharmony	Instigator				
Child's IQ	Instigator	.185*	.147	.293***	.182*
Parental nurturance of child	Instigator				
Parental punishment of child	Contingent	-.178*			
Child's identification with father	Identification				
Father's aggressiveness	Identification				
Child's identification with mother	Identification				
Mother's aggressiveness	Identification			.127	
Television violence	Identification	.223**			
Hours TV watched by child	Identification	.142			
Child's guilt	Identification				
Child's confessing to parents	Identification				
Child's preference for boys' games	Identification				
Child's preference for girls' games	Identification				

+The regressions were computed in a stepwise manner. Stepping was stopped when no predictor variable could be entered which would explain at least 2% of the variance in the outcome variable.

Table 5.17 Multiple Regression Analyses[+] for Predicting 13th-Grade Prosocial Behavior from Third-Grade Variables including Peer Ratings

Third-Grade Predictor Variable	Type	Outcome Variables			
		Females		Males	
		13th-Grade Popularity	13th-Grade Leadership	13th-Grade Popularity	13th-Grade Leadership
Father's occupational status	Sociocultural				
Parents' mobility orientation	Sociocultural				-.128
Parents' religiosity (frequency of church attendance)	Sociocultural	.170*			
Parents' educational level	Sociocultural		.235**		
Ethnicity of family	Sociocultural			.210**	
Third grade aggression	Peer Ratings				
Third grade aggression anxiety	Peer Ratings		.293***		
Third grade popularity	Peer Ratings	.336***		.288***	
R		.579***	.471***	.508***	.433***
df		6/113	3/116	4/123	3/124

*p ≤ .05; **p < .01; ***p < .001

[+]The regressions were computed in a stepwise manner. Stepping was stopped when no predictor variable could be entered which would explain at least 2% of the variance in the outcome variable.

Table 5.18 Basic Statistics of and Intercorrelations Among Six Positive Social Achievement
Variables for Girls

	1	2	3	4	5	6
1. Third-grade aggression anxiety						
2. Third-grade popularity	.70					
3. 13th-grade aggression anxiety	.28	.25				
4. 13th-grade popularity	.36	.46	.41			
5. 13th-grade leadership	.38	.39	.28	.72		
6. 13th grade MMPI						
psychotic tetrad	-.08	-.13	-.09	-.02	-.03	
Mean	20.36	25.04	23.98	61.13	3.88	230.81
Standard Deviation	13.69	14.81	29.03	50.18	6.63	32.10
N	216	216	216	216	216	216

Table 5.19 Basic Statistics of and Intercorrelations Among Six Positive Social Achievement Variables for Boys

	1	2	3	4	5	6
1. Third-grade aggression anxiety						
2. Third-grade popularity	.70					
3. 13th-grade aggression anxiety	.31	.18				
4. 13th-grade popularity	.22	.38	.18			
5. 13th-grade leadership	.29	.40	.18	.64		
6. 13th-grade MMPI psychotic tetrad	-.27	-.13	-.20	-.10	-.13	
Mean	16.70	25.29	19.69	58.77	3.69	244.01
Standard Deviation	12.33	16.63	24.49	49.10	6.48	39.34
N	211	211	211	211	211	211
Skewness	0.77	0.79	1.95	0.87	2.68	0.73

Table 5.20 Multiple Regression Analyses[+] for Predicting 13th-Grade Prosocial Behavior from Third-Grade Variables

Third Grade Predictor Variable	Type	Outcome Variable			
		Females		Males	
		13th-Grade Popularity	13th-Grade Leadership	13th-Grade Popularity	13th-Grade Leadership
Parental rejection of child	Instigator				-.197*
Parental disharmony	Instigator				.198*
Child's IQ	Instigator	.181*	.143	.329***	.242**
Parental nurturance of child	Instigator	.128			
Parental punishment of child	Contingent	-.191**			
Child's identification with father	Identification			.190**	
Father's aggressiveness	Identification				.092
Child's identification with mother	Identification				
Mother's aggressiveness	Identification				
Television violence	Identification	.155*			
Hours TV watched by child	Identification	.185*			
Child's guilt	Identification	.222*			
Child's confessing to parents	Identification				
Child's preference for boys' games	Identification			-.128	
Child's preference for girls' games	Identification	.106			

[+]The regressions were computed in a stepwise manner. Stepping was stopped when no predictor variable could be entered which would explain at least 2% of the variance in the outcome variable.

Table 5.20 Multiple Regression Analyses+ for Predicting 13th-Grade Prosocial Behavior from Third Grade Variables (Cont'd.)

Third Grade Predictor Variable	Type	Outcome Variable			
		Females		Males	
		13th-Grade Popularity	13th-Grade Leadership	13th-Grade Popularity	13th Grade Leadership
Father's occupational status	Sociocultural	-.140			
Parents' mobility orientation	Sociocultural				-.141
Parents' religiosity (frequency of church attendance)	Sociocultural	.224**			.143
Parents' educational level	Sociocultural		.303**	.252**	
Ethnicity of family	Sociocultural				
R		.548***	.388***	.467***	.415***
df		8/111	3/116	4/123	6/121

*p ⩽ .05; **p < .01; ***p < .001

+The regressions were computed in a stepwise manner. Stepping was stopped when no predictor variable could be entered which would explain at least 2% of the variance in the outcome variable.

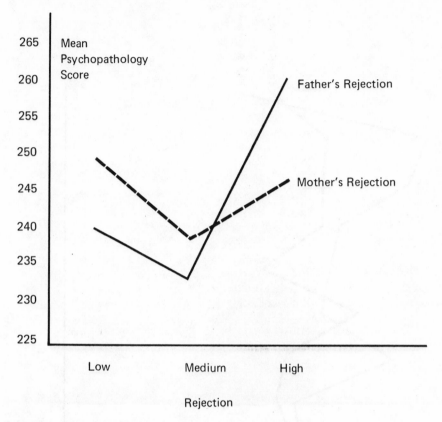

Fig. 5.1. Boys' mean score on psychopathology at age 19 for different amounts of parental rejection.

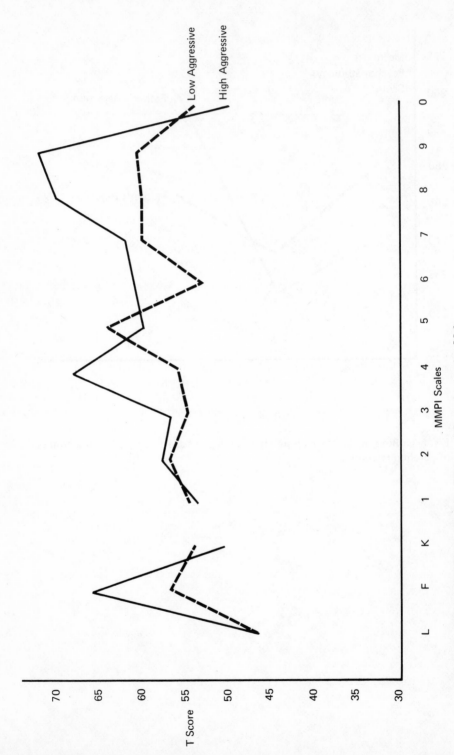

Fig. 5.2. Average MMPI Profiles for High- and Low-Aggressive Males.

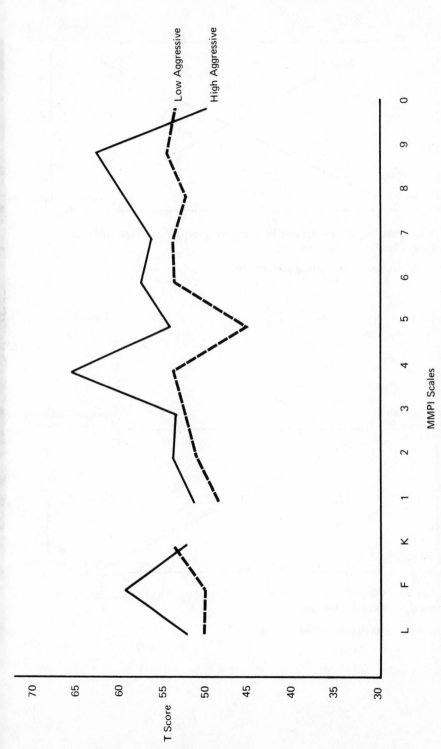

Fig. 5.3. Average MMPI Profiles for High- and Low-Aggressive Females.

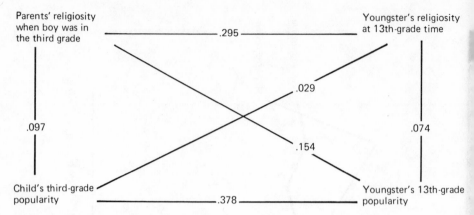

Fig. 5.4. Cross-lagged Correlations Between Religiosity* and Popularity at Third and 13th Grades for Boys.

*Reported frequency of church attendance.

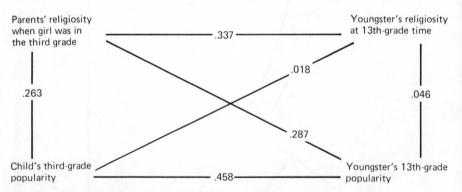

Fig. 5.5. Cross-lagged Correlations Between Religiosity+ and Popularity at Third and 13th Grades for Girls.

+Reported frequency of church attendance

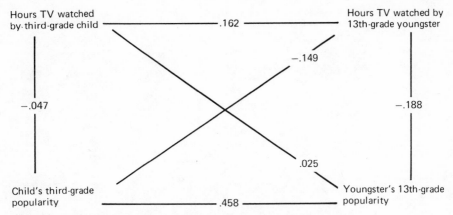

Fig. 5.6. Cross-lagged Correlations Between Hours TV Watched and Popularity at Third and 13th Grades for Girls.

6
Implications of the Results for
Theory and Practice

In Chapter 1 we reviewed the major theoretical positions on the provenance and ontogenesis of aggressive behavior. The first wave of the field study in 1959 took its cue largely from learning theory and, to a lesser extent, from dynamic psychology. In the second wave, begun in 1970, our model was largely derived from social learning theory. However, we were aware of the potential contribution of other factors, including neurophysiological antecedents.

INNATE AGGRESSIVENESS

In our view, the theory of innate aggression as applied to man, in which spontaneously generated aggression serves as a primary drive, is untestable chiefly because of its metaphysical character. We also reject the theoretical foundation of the frustration-aggression model, although we used the suggestions offered by the Yale theorists (Dollard *et al.*, 1939) as to what might be likely instigators to aggression. Aggressive drive providing the impetus to aggression from within the organism as a consequence of frustration strikes us as a concept that is lacking in parsimony and is essentially tautologous. Because the existence of this drive is always inferred from one or more aggressive acts, which are then attributed to the drive, nothing is explained. Unlike sex and hunger drives, the physiological and motivational components of the "aggression drive" have not yet been found. With fair accuracy, for example, we can predict the behavior of animals deprived of food and sex. What forecasts can be made about animals, particularly humans, who are deprived of the expression of aggression? None! However, if we know something about an animal's past experiences and the present situation, we can make fair predictions about its aggressive behavior. The work of Scott and his students suggests that pacific behavior perpetuates such behavior. In Scott's terms ". . . by being peaceable an individual learns to be peaceable" (1973, p. 8). Young mice not permitted to observe other mice fighting fought very little as adults compared to other mice who witnessed such early fighting scenes.

Supporters of innate aggression theory would argue that aggression, unless released, builds up and then explodes (Lorenz, 1966). However Stewart (1972), working in Scott's laboratory, found that dogs deprived of the opportunity to "express" aggression by being muzzled fought significantly less after removal of the muzzles than an unmuzzled control group.

THE SOCIAL LEARNING OF AGGRESSION

In conjunction with our dissatisfaction with drive theories of aggression, the results of the first wave of our study carried out in 1959-60 (Eron *et al.*, 1971) impressed us with the importance of situational or environmental variables as determinants of aggressive behavior. For example, prior to our examination of the third-grade results, our interest in modeling was limited. But, when we encountered the finding that a child's preference for violent television was significantly associated with the manifestation of aggressive behavior in school, we viewed the potential strength of modeling with more respect. Cumulatively, the effect of such findings was to reinforce our belief in a pull rather than push theory to better explain the development of aggressive behavior. In short, we felt that it would prove more fruitful to study conditions in the environment that might induce an individual to act aggressively than to assume that individuals were predisposed to do so. Thus, our study emphasized the contribution of experiential rather than innate variables to the manifestation of aggressive behavior.

CEREBRAL MECHANISMS AND AGGRESSION

In Chapter 1 we discussed how certain sequelae of insult to the central nervous system may be internal impellers to aggression. These are clinical conditions that probably occur statistically with relative infrequence. However, we attempted to explore certain relations between pregnancy and birth complications and aggressive behavior. Our finding of some evidence of a relation between male aggressive behavior in late adolescence and mother's age at time of delivery — albeit qualified — is in accord with other research (Mark and Ervin, 1970) which illustrated an association between central nervous system aberrations and aggressive behavior.[1] Indeed, the plethora of evidence from other studies suggesting a causal relationship between neurophysiological impairment and aggression cannot be overlooked.

In the broad sense, however, central nervous system damage is also an environmental event inasmuch as injury to the brain of the fetus or neonate can be attributed to factors in the environment (such as socioeconomic, child rearing, nutrition, or toxic substances). Consequently, when central nervous system insult — from whatever cause — is identified as an antecedent of aggression, an essential distinction must be made between this type of antecedent and the notion of an aggressive drive. Although both may be categorized as internal impellers, since the stimuli to behave aggressively inhere within the organism, the frequency of central nervous system damage in the population can be mitigated if not eliminated by modifying conditions in the environment — for example, by means of improved public health and social services. On the other hand, the notion of aggressive drive connotes immutability because of its putative phylogenetic origin. In this sense it is viewed as unequivocally innate by theorists of this persuasion, such as Lorenz (1966).

HORMONES AND AGGRESSION

Our findings that males are more aggressive than females at the ages of both eight and 19 years may be interpreted to support both the hormonal and social learning theories of aggression. Endocrinologically, males have higher levels of testosterone than females but the behavioral expression of this physiological condition, as we have seen, is shaped by social expectations and contingencies. The difference in aggression between boys and girls is even more pronounced at age 19 than at age eight. As boys and girls mature physically and socially, the levels of androgens and estrogens increase, respectively: males become increasingly stronger than females and the effects of differential reinforcement sustain male aggression and discourage female aggression. In young adulthood this pattern of aggressive males and passive females may be mutually reinforcing in the short run. Each person's behavior is reinforced by the responses of the person of the opposite sex.

PREDICTORS OF AGGRESSION

A major finding emerging from our field study was that aggression at age eight is the best predictor we have of aggression at age 19 irrespective of IQ, social class, or parents' aggressiveness. This suggests that aggressiveness may be largely maintained by such learning factors as external reinforcement, vicarious reinforcement, and self-reinforcement. The stability of this behavior over time (as noted in Chapter 3) and the importance of its apparent trait-like qualities for both the individual and the society will be discussed more extensively below.

In general our four major categories of independent variables — instigators, contingent responses, identification, and sociocultural factors — predicted aggression. The best predictors to immediate aggression were the instigators, identification, and sociocultural variables. However, the best predictors to later aggression were identification and sociocultural variables. From our earlier work (Eron *et al.*, 1971), we can surmise that the effects of contingent response (punishment) on aggression are complicated and mediated by other variables. For example, in that study we found that punishment reduced aggressive behavior only for certain boys who were strongly identified with their fathers. When high identification was not present, punishment (especially physical punishment) was positively and strongly associated with aggression. Finally, the longitudinal data indicate that moderate punishment by parents in the long run produced less aggressive children than either no punishment or harsh punishment. One implication of this finding for child rearing is that punishment, when used in moderation, seems to be effective in diminishing aggressive behavior. However, when harsh punishment is used, particularly with children who weakly identify with their parents, aggression is heightened — probably as a result of modeling. At the same time, permissiveness, as indicated by no punishment, is equally deleterious according to our data.

An important exception to the idea that instigators do not have a long-term effect was the nurturance variable. Lack of nurturance, which is a strong contemporaneous predictor of aggression, does seem to have a modest long-term relation to aggression. On the other hand, rejection of the child by the parents, which had the strongest immediate effect on aggression, had no long-term effect, although rejection and psychopathology were positively related over time (as discussed in Chapter 5). It seems clear that close communication with one's child has both immediate and long-term effects in reducing aggression.

Whereas parents or parent surrogates may have control of punishment, rejection, or amount of nurturance rendered, their control over a predictor to aggression, such as IQ, is much less obvious due both to the unknown and subtle determinants of this factor. In our discussion of this variable in Chapter 3, we suggested that not low IQ per se but a general incompetency factor, of which low IQ is a part, could be one cause of aggression. Because low IQ impedes learning, a child with this condition, in addition to incompetency, will have been handicapped in learning the variety of prosocial behaviors achieved by his brighter peers. The high correlation both in our study and in the general population between IQ and academic achievement is exceedingly pertinent inasmuch as a major characteristic of the violent youthful offender is alienation and disaffection with school in conjunction with academic retardation often associated with low IQ. Also correlated with low IQ is a style of life characterized by low socioeconomic status and its concomitant ills. Interestingly, we found strong evidence that a child's recognition of his own academic incompetence causes him to view more and more TV where he can experience success vicariously. The same holds true for children who are unpopular. Furthermore, low-IQ children think TV is more realistic and are therefore more susceptible to its modeling effects.

The motto that "things get done with fist and gun" is reinforced on the television screen many times each day and evening by gun-toting, two-fisted hero policemen and soldiers, by criminals with similar equipment, and by Kung Fu and karate experts. This diet of violent television in conjunction with the ready availability of handguns and knives, could provide the low-IQ child, the one with few positive social behaviors in his repertoire, with a "proven" solution to the problem of attaining those premiums upon which society places greatest value: material and sexual objects. In the first eight months of 1974, compared with the same period a year ago, arrests in the 7-19 year age group increased by 33 percent for rape, 13 percent for assault and five percent for robbery (*New York Times*, 1974a). Whether or not raising IQ and thus mitigating general incompetency and faulty social learning would indeed reduce aggressive and violent responding is a question requring empirical verification through research.

Low IQ and consequent poor school achievement and general incompetency is a problem requiring early intervention and is of the magnitude to necessitate a sweeping effort at all levels of society. Part of this effort should include the elimination of malnutrition in children and women of child-bearing age. The fact that IQ and mental deficiency are in part the result of malnutrition has been amply demonstrated (Birch and Gussow, 1970; Kaplan, 1972; *Maternal, Fetal and Infant Nutrition*, 1973; Scrimshaw and Gordon, 1968).

Equal emphasis needs to be placed on effective learning environments in all of the child's natural habitats. Specifically, educational institutions should try to teach, even those children difficult to teach, effective prosocial techniques for dealing with the environment. These recommendations regarding IQ may well require fundamental changes in our social philosophy and priorities. However, the benefits could be twofold: an increase in the intellectual competence of many children and a decrease in aggressive and violent behavior of many children.

The next set of independent variables to be discussed with respect to their relevance for aggression is classified under identification. Our concept of identification is most closely related to imitation by modeling as understood in its broad sense. Thus, it is possible for a child to identify with his parents, with a television actor, or with a particular sex role by copying or imitating the manifest behavior of the models. Similarly, children are able to copy the value systems of parents and internalize these as their own. This process, as discussed in Chapter 3, is facilitated when expression of these values by the child is positively reinforced by the parents. We found, as we had hypothesized, that children who copied their parents' expressive behaviors and adopted their parents' values concerning unacceptable behaviors were lower in aggression than children who did not identify with their parents. Moreover, we found that exposure to violent television models results in increased aggression. Indeed, the longitudinal design and the statistical analyses we imposed on the data permit us to speak of a causal relation between viewing violent models on television and aggressive behavior of male viewers. The heightened aggression occurs in childhood and extends at least to young adulthood. When placed in conjunction with similar findings generated by laboratory and other field studies (see e.g., Bandura, 1973a; Berkowitz, 1962; Liebert *et al.*, 1973), the evidence substantiating the pernicious effect of this kind of identification is rather overwhelming. Given the proclivity of so many members of our society for violent behavior and the easy availability of weapons, the offerings of violent television may serve as the catalyst in part responsible for the ever-increasing rate of violent behavior witnessed across the nation. Notwithstanding the equivocation and denial of network television (*Hearings*, 1972), the United States Surgeon General, Dr. Jesse Steinfeld, based on the findings of his Scientific Advisory Committee on Television and Social Behavior, stated that:

> After review of the committee's report and the five volumes of original research undertaken at your request, as well as a review of the previous literature on the subject, my professional response today is that the broadcasters should be put on notice. The overwhelming consensus and the unanimous Scientific Advisory Committee's report indicates that televised violence, indeed, does have an adverse effect on certain members of our society.
>
> While the committee report is carefully phrased and qualified in language acceptable to social scientists, it is clear to me that the causal relationship between televised violence and antisocial behavior is sufficient to warrant appropriate and immediate remedial action. The data on social phenomena such as television and violence and/or aggressive behavior will never be clear enough for all social scientists to agree on the formulation of a succinct statement of causality. But there comes a time when the data are sufficient to justify action. That time has come.
>
> I would also emphasize that no action in this social area is a form of action: it is an acquiescence in the continuation of the present level of televised violence entering American homes. (Hearings, 1972, p. 26)

Unfortunately, the acquiescence continues and the networks have been derelict in policing themselves, contrary to the assurances all three major networks (ABC, CBS, and NBC) gave to Senator Pastore, Chairman of the Communications Subcommittee of the U.S. Senate Committee on Commerce (*Hearings*, 1972). Three years later the problem of exposure of children to television violence, if anything, has become more pronounced. A sense of desperation is conveyed in a report (*New York Times*, 1974b) in which Senator Pastore and Representative MacDonald, Chairmen of the Communication Sub-committees of the Senate and House, tell the Federal Communications Commission ". . . that it must somehow act on the violence . . . problem." Since the television networks are not licensed, they cannot technically be regulated by the FCC. Moreover, the FCC moves in a treacherous strait between the Scylla of TV violence and the Charybdis of censorship. Governments which interpret television violence to be a "clear and present danger" just as they might smallpox or bubonic plague resort to more extreme action. Mexico serves as a current example, where 37 mostly American television series have been banned (*New York Times*, 1974c) because ". . . their violent content is harmful to the country's youth." One counter-vailing force in the United States which has managed to marshal some resistance against the exploitation of children by the television industry is the Massachusetts-based group, Action for Children's Television. The thrust of ACT's program is to exert pressure on Congress to upgrade children's television and to eliminate com-mercialism on children's programs. To date, the group has had conspicuous success in reducing commercialism but little in mitigat-ing the amount of violence on television to which a child could be exposed. Acquiescence on the part of the public may be one reason and the vast power of commercial television another. Liebert *et al.* (1973) note that the aim of commercial television is to make money for the networks; in 1970 net revenues of about three billion dollars were earned through advertising. One producer states:

"Filmmaking for television is a business of merchandising and profit making. We are manufacturing a product and we want it to attract the largest possible audience, short of prostitution" (Baldwin and Lewis, 1972, p. 313).

More than a decade ago, Newton Minnow, the Chairman of the Federal Communications Commission, termed television "a vast wasteland." An editorial in *The Nation* (1974) cites a distinguished jurist, Chief Judge David L. Bazelon of the U.S. Court of Appeals for the District of Columbia, who terms television ". . . mass appeal pablum, designed to titillate a sufficiently large majority to enable the broadcasters to sell the most advertising." He cited leaders of the television industry for ". . . their abuse of the immense power of television for the private profit of a few" (p. 581). This *Nation* editorial goes on to state that:

... the predominance of material warranted to bore any civilized person is the least of the evils that commercial television perpetrates, year in, year out. The worst aspect of today's programming is the emphasis on violence and the aseptic form in which murder, rape and cruelty are invariably presented. The Television Code, to which most stations subscribe, proscribes 'detailed presentation of brutality or physical agony by sight or by sound.' The physical and psychological horrors of murder, torture and other forms of violence are thus concealed, leaving the way open for conversion of violence into pure entertainment. The effect on children and susceptible adults is hardly edifying. Today, in quite respectable neighborhoods, elderly people are attacked by groups of children, beaten and robbed and sometimes senselessly killed — murder having become a form of sport. In view of the amount of time that children, especially slum children, spend in front of the tube, common sense would seem to point to a connection between TV and real-life violence, but the industry's bosses have always denied that possibility. (p. 581)

However, more than common sense dictates the recognition of a relation between TV violence and real-life violence. The empirical findings reported in this book when added to the evidence acquired by others points to excessive exposure to televised violence as a major cause of aggression.

Why is violence so ubiquitous on television? Television violence is profitable. Because it attracts a mass audience, a sales technique so reinforcing to an already powerful industry is unlikely to be relinquished voluntarily. Consequently, we feel that violence in television programing will not be controlled until public officials are convinced that it is as much a hazard to safety as cigarette smoking is to health. Actually, substantial evidence exists (Lesser, 1974) that it is not violence per se but action (movement) and suspense that attract mass audiences. The vast success of such children's programs as *Sesame Street*, The *Electric Company*, and *Zoom* demonstrate that nonviolent action programs can be even more popular than violent programs.

The remaining identification variable which predicted inversely to aggressive behavior (for males) at both eight and 19 years of age was preference for girls' games and activities, our measure of identification with a particular sex role. Why should a boy's choice of feminine activities as early as eight be associated with ratings of lower aggressive behavior at that age and, more remarkably, ten years later? And why, in our sample, should the choice of masculine activities be associated with increased aggression at both ages? In Chapter 3 we suggested that the two behaviors might be incompatible. Identification by males, to this extent, with a feminine sex role resulted in a lower rating of aggression probably because of the cultural expectations that define the constellation of feminine behaviors comprising a feminine sex role. At least for the first wave of our subjects, this constellation of feminine behaviors tended to preclude aggression from the cultural expectation. Although this explanation might be consonant with the findings of cultural anthropologists (see, e.g., Alland, 1972), it does not answer the question of why a boy would opt for a feminine sex role.

At least two plausible explanations exist. One is physiological and the other social learning. In the former, evidence from several areas of research suggests that hormonal differences (Harris and Levine, 1965; Joffe, 1969, Chapter 5; Young *et al.*, 1964; Flor-Henry, 1974; Levine, 1966) may determine sex-role behaviors. In the case of social and brain differences learning, differential reinforcement and the availability of models (Bandura, 1973b) are avenues by which sex-role behaviors may be determined.

SOCIOCULTURAL VARIABLES

The final group of variables to be discussed for their implications are those we classified as sociocultural. Perhaps the most interesting finding and that having greatest import for theory was that high occupational status of fathers and upward social mobility of parents varied concomitantly with high aggression of their sons and daughters. There has been a fair amount of research suggesting an inverse relationship between socioeconomic status and aggression (see e.g., Miller and Swanson, 1960; Zigler and Child, 1969). However, a few studies, like the present one, have found either no consistent relation between socioeconomic status and aggression (Maas, 1954) or a positive relation (Body, 1955; Eron *et al.*, 1971). In fact, our longitudinal data permit us to state that the conventional view of aggression as a behavior that enhances achievement, particularly of material goods, has some validity. To some extent, the difference between our findings and earlier studies may be a function of the population and particular surround. Recall that these subjects were reared in a semirural area where the largest city contained approximately 12,000 inhabitants. Neither in 1960, during the first wave of data collection, nor in 1970, during the second wave, did the extremely stressful conditions associated with low socioeconomic status in heavily populated urban areas exist in Columbia County. Ghetto dwelling was virtually nonexistent and, although poverty was certainly present, the hardships of the low socioeconomic family may have been tempered by country living and low-density populations in the towns and cities. Germane to this argument is the evidence showing higher rates of psychopathology in urban as compared to rural areas (Dohrenwend and Dohrenwend, 1974). Consequently, in the absence of some of the usual instigators to aggression, a passive or perhaps stoical acceptance of life might become the style. But passivity is not the best avenue to upward mobility and attainment of material worth, particularly in the ambiguous situation where occupational status is high and formal educational achievement is low. We conclude that this combination of high occupational and low educational achievement for the father produces the most aggressive children. The father with these attributes, we reason, is under considerable stress to maintain high — and atypical — occupational status in view of his relatively low formal education. Finally, as already noted in Chapter 3, a father's upward mobility orientation is the best single predictor of his son's aggressiveness ten years later. Upwardly mobile fathers apparently serve as salient models of striving and aggressive behavior for their sons. Identification of child with parent, mediated by modeling, probably accounts for the positive correlation between upward mobility and aggression. It appears then that a father with low education, high occupational status, and a strong upward mobility orientation, is most likely to raise highly aggressive children.

Complicating this analysis, but important for its implication, was the discovery that by the time our subjects became age 19 an inverse relation between the father's current occupational status and the son's aggression existed. This relation was based on subjects' report of their fathers' occupational status. To explain the seeming paradox of the reversed direction of this relationship, we theorized (see Chapter 3) that the instigating conditions inherent in lower socioeconomic status homes which produce aggressive behavior are cumulative. Consequently, these conditions do not reach threshold effect until some time after childhood, at which time the relation between social class and aggression becomes negative. In a child's early years, however, the model of parental behavior dominates and the child's aggressiveness correlates directly with his parent's social status.

If this theorizing is valid, it would suggest that aggressive behavior can be mitigated, insofar as it is contingent upon social class conditions, by changing these conditions early on. In one instance, modification of the behavior of upwardly mobile, aggressive models is necessary and, in the other, some modification of the oppressive circumstances that prevail in lower social class homes.

THE STABILITY OF AGGRESSION

One of the most salient findings to emerge from our study is the consistent manifestation of aggression both across time and across situations. Boys and girls rated as aggressive by their peers in the third grade tended to be rated in a similar fashion in the 13th grade. Our third-grade measure of aggression, which appeared to tap different kinds of aggressive behavior (e.g., physical, verbal, indirect), was actually shown to be a response class comprised of behaviors whose common feature was its irritating or injurious effect on another person. Moreover, third-grade peer-rated aggression was significantly correlated with various self-ratings of aggression ten years later. Also subjects who were rated as aggressive by their peers in a classroom context, significantly more often witnessed aggressive acts and were victims of such acts. Is aggression in our subjects a trait that is reflected in consistent behavior over a wide range of situations? G.W. Allport (1961), the examplar of trait psychology, defines a trait as a neuropsychic structure that is able to make many stimuli functionally equivalent and that guides behavior in meaningfully consistent forms. A great deal of effort has gone into research attempting, by means of factor analysis, to sort our fundamental trait dimensions (see e.g., Hall and Lindzey, 1970, for a discussion of the major protagonists of trait factors). Other writers (Bandura, 1973a; Skinner, 1974) argue that the search to uncover trait dimensions or inner causes of behavior is a teleological exercise (also see Chapter 1) and, according to Berkowitz (1969c) a ". . . backwater in the mainstream of psychological research" (p. 70). Situational determinants and environmental contingencies according to these researchers are the major forces that shape and maintain behavior. Skinner (1974) says, "Many supposed inner causes of behavior, such as attitudes, opinions, traits of character, and philosophies, remain almost entirely inferential . . . Nevertheless, terms referring to traits of character are freely used in explaining behavior" (p. 159). For example, ambition, greed, and moral callousness are termed traits of character "... where no evidence of the inner causes is available except the behavior attributed to them" (p. 159).

Yet Berkowitz (1969c) argues that although the definition of what a trait is may have to be reformulated by giving a greater role to situational determinants, the trait idea still has a place in psychology. A highly aggressive person would be expected to show a good deal of consistency in this behavior because of stimulus generalization and response generalization (Berkowitz, 1962). Even across situations, it has been shown that hyperaggressive boys as compared to normals respond with a narrower band of behaviors, which are mostly aggressive (Dittman and Goodrich, 1961). Perhaps a more parsimonious explanation than stimulus generalization and response generalization to account for such trait-like consistency in aggressive responding is one we advanced earlier (see Chapter 3) concerning the constricting effect of lower IQ on the behavior repertoire of aggressive children. Specifically, lower intelligence limits the range of subtle or oblique behaviors a child can learn. Thus he is left with aggression as the most convenient response to instigators. In addition, for reasons other than low IQ (e.g., differential reinforcement), some children learn a limited number of ways of interacting with other persons.

By this discussion of traits we seem to have come full circle to Chapter 1 and the questions raised about aggression and the nature of man by the social philosophers of the 17th and 18th centuries and currently by the ethologists. Is aggression the result of some neuropsychic structure (Allport, 1961), some essential innate substance (Lorenz, 1966), or, following Skinner (1974), need we look for inner causes at all? The consistency with which our study population expresses aggression in various situations and over a time span of ten years leads us to conclude that this behavior is a trait, but only phenotypically — i.e., a visible characteristic. Consequently, our definition would preclude the notion of essence, or genotype. Acceptable would be the meaning of a trait suggested by Marlowe and Gergen (1969): "... some relatively enduring or chronic attribute of the individual usually assessed by a personality test" (p. 640). Actually, Skinner's admonition against seeking inner causes for aggression has not gone unheeded. We would postulate, therefore, that the genotype is *not* the constitutional predisposition to aggress, but rather the predisposition to learn certain response modes to deal with stress. What we observe in our subjects is the phenotypic expression of one such mode: aggression. This position is consonant with Bandura's (1973b) formulation of arousal-prepotent response. Emotional arousal can elicit a variety of behaviors: help seeking, increased achievement, withdrawal, aggression, somatic reactions, drug use, or an intensification of constructive efforts to mitigate or eliminate the source of stress. Most likely to occur is the behavior the individual has found in the past to be relatively effective in coping with stress. It is, therefore, superfluous to posit inner causes when a learning model such as Bandura proposes accounts for what we think is a trait of aggression and involves fewer assumptions. Furthermore, our data suggest that the array of positive behaviors which it is possible to learn may narrow as intelligence decreases.

There is no inherent contradiction between adopting a social learning hypothesis to explain what we observe to be a trait and our position earlier embracing endocrine and neurophysiological hypotheses. Viewing behavior in a multivariate and probabilistic context, we would reject the notion of inner causes when this notion means that aggression is innate and invariant as implied in the theories of Hobbes (1969), James (1890), and Lorenz (1966). While contributing factors to aggression (such as levels of testosterone, differential hemispheric efficiency, chromosomal anomalies, or central nervous system insult) may be "inner" with respect to their loci, they are far from innate or invariant causes. Shaped by individual experience and the "cultural envelope" (Eisenberg, 1972), these inner conditions contribute to aggression only in complex interaction with the environment in which they are expressed. For example, although sex differences in aggression are probably significantly associated with levels of testosterone, the behavior itself can be modified — in either direction — by early socialization practices. Phenotypic behavior (aggression) is thus the result of an interaction in some complex manner of a genotype with its environment. Prediction of aggression is complicated not only because of this interaction but also because phenotype itself interacts with environment in a manner capable of altering that environment. Consequently, only when these state variables are controlled — such as in a multivariate model — can the best predictions of aggression be made.

CONTROL OF AGGRESSION

For the purposes of this discussion, control can be divided into treatment and prevention. The distinction is somewhat academic because prevention and treatment are frequently attempted simultaneously.

Perhaps the most common treatment of persistently violent behavior is by some form of mental-penal institutionalization. The term "treatment" is used very loosely in this sense inasmuch as the goal of institutionalization is not primarily to treat but to incarcerate persistently antisocial individuals. At the very best, for juveniles and young offenders, the period of institutionalization may serve as a psychosocial moratorium during which time controls over behavior develop more as a function of the passage of time than because of any treatment effect of the program. Actually, from our data we are able to conclude that aggressive behavior probably does not decrease and may even increase due to the exposure to violent models, brutality, and other situational determinants likely to elicit violent response. In the more benign training schools and penal institutions the treatment program is usually unfocused and consists of work, education, religious activities, recreation, and individual or group psychotherapy. No rigorous attempt has been made to evaluate the effect of such programs in mitigating violent behavior. Rigorous evaluation requires random assignment of individuals to institutional or community programs. For ethical and political reasons, judges are reluctant to countenance such experimentation. There is no evidence that unfocused treatment programs generalize to behavior in the community after an individual's discharge. More likely, institutional experience that is not designed to modify a specific target behavior, such as aggression, will have no effect on this behavior in the community. In a study comparing the effect of long-term (9.6 months) versus short-term (4.4 months) institutionalization of female juvenile delinquents (Lefkowitz, 1975), no difference in social restoration measured after return to the community was found. (Antisocial behavior was one component of this measure.) Even more remarkable was the finding that degree of social restoration — for either group, or groups combined — was unrelated to length of institutionalization or institutional experiences, which included perceptibly different but unfocused programs. This finding is similar to those for mental patients (Anthony et al., 1972) that traditional therapies — individual, group, work, and drugs — have no differential effect on the discharged patients' community functioning.

Incarcerating habitually violent men in maximum security prisons, rather than isolating them from society in a protective way, is thus seen to be a useless experience (Bach-y-Rita, 1974): "These patients spend their lives in holding institutions that are only barely able to contain their behavior; certainly their life pattern is not changed" (p. 1020).

An overview of 34 studies (Davidson and Seidman, 1974) concerned with behavior modification techniques in dealing with specific target behaviors of juvenile delinquents provides some promising but ambiguous findings. Behavior modification seems to be effective in reducing aggressive behavior in the institutional setting. But, again, the question of scientific rigor is raised because, in addition to other methodological problems in these studies, 82 percent had no control group and only 18 percent had follow-up data. Nevertheless, on the basis of the success of behavior modification in other areas, and on the basis of our data concerning modeling, we feel that behavior modification might be one of the most promising approaches to mitigate aggressive behavior. Unfortunately, the term "behavior modification" has been abused and misused to cover a multitude of unethical and nonbehavioral procedures which do not use the principles of behavior modification. Some examples are punishment-oriented programs, psychosurgery, and drug therapy programs. Such misuse has created a climate in which even promising behavior modification programs are widely banned. Given no evidence to the contrary, it seems reasonable to conclude that penal institutions and training schools probably have no lasting effect in lessening aggressive or violent behavior.

Treatment of violent behavior has also been attempted by pharmacotherapy and psychosurgery. The control of aggressive-assaultive behavior in state institutions has been significantly reduced by the use of major tranquilizers classified under the phenothiazines. "Combativeness disappears and relaxation and cooperativeness become prominent" (Jarvik, 1965, p. 177). A survey of 403 Boston psychiatrists (Tardiff, 1974) reported 18 percent used major tranquilizers to treat violent behavior. The minor tranquilizers classified under the benzodiazepines, have been shown to be fairly effective in reducing aggressive excitability, hostility, and irritability (Moyer, 1971). Two preparations, chlordiazopoxide and diazepam, are used for sedatives and skeletal muscle relaxation.

For children suffering brain dysfunction (frequently expressed in hyperkinetic aggressive behavior, temper tantrums, and rage), certain psychomotor stimulants such as the amphetamines and methylphenidate have been used successfully to mitigate such behavior (Conners, 1972a; 1972b). On the other hand, the major anticonvulsant drug, diphenylhydantoin, has proven unsuccessful in controlled studies (Conners, 1972a; Lefkowitz, 1969), in mitigating disruptive behavior or severe temper tantrums of juvenile delinquents.

Actually, the physiochemical mechanism by which psychotropic drugs mediate aggressive behavior is far from clear. Neuropharmacological experimentation on these mechanisms, for ethical reasons, is restricted largely to animals. Generally, these drugs seem to alter synaptic activity, which in turn affects the level of neurotransmitters (Avis, 1974). Another point of view (Crane, 1973) is that the reduction of belligerent behavior by psychoactive drugs is probably a secondary effect due to the general lessening of psychopathology. But Crane cautions that long-term exposure to such "powerful chemical agents" is potentially dangerous and may produce permanent neurological disorders.

Psychosurgery

In the 1950s psychosurgery was considered to be an acceptable mode of treatment for intractable aggressive behavior. Prefrontal lobotomy and temporal lobectomy were widely used techniques.

The lobotomy has become much less popular and has been replaced by stereotaxic surgery. This procedure allows tiny electrodes to be implanted in the brain through a small opening in the skull. Guided to deep target structures by a stereotactic machine, the electrodes are used to destroy a very small number of cells in an exactly demarcated area. (See Mark and Ervin, 1970, pp. 72-83, for photos of the seven stages in this technique.) One-tenth as much tissue is destroyed as in a lobectomy and, once implanted, the electrodes — not harmful to the patient — can be used to ascertain which cells are firing abnormally, thereby producing symptoms of seizures and violence. Mark and Ervin claim that they can initiate or terminate violent behavior in patients suffering temporal lobe disease by stimulating different loci in the amygdala and hippocampus.

What is known of the efficacy of stereotactic surgery in treating patients with violent behavior is based entirely on clinical observation. Summarizing this knowledge, Mark and Ervin (1970) state ". . . there is a significant and growing body of clinical and especially surgical evidence to indicate that the production of small focal areas of destruction in parts of the limbic brain will often eliminate dangerous behavior in assaultive or violent patients" (p. 87).

A major argument made against this procedure is that conclusive evidence is lacking correlating specific brain structures with specific behaviors. Perhaps the impetus for the current interest in psychosurgery has been the increasing crime rate and the violence that has characterized the late 1960s and early 1970s. Proponents of psychosurgery argue that while environmental and social variables are undoubtedly important in the violence and urban riots that have occurred throughout the country, it is entirely one-sided to ignore the possible role played by focal lesions in the brain which initiate assaultive and destructive behavior. Opponents argue that "psychosurgery is an abortion of the brain and is being used to repress and vegetablize the helpless: the poor, the women, the black, the imprisoned, and the institutionalized" (Holden, 1973, p. 1110). Not nearly enough, they feel, is known about the brain to justify such operations. Those opposed conclude that psychosurgery is a failure of medicine.

Perhaps we have dwelt on stereotactic surgery at some length because it appears to be a dramatic treatment procedure for literally extirpating violent behavior. However, even if controlled research were to support these clinical observations, the treatment would be applicable only to those cases where focal brain abnormalities exist. Furthermore, even when applicable, the likelihood of its general use as a treatment mode is remote because of its awesome nature.

Unfortunately, no technique has been developed to treat chronically aggressive or violent individuals that can claim long-term success and is also feasible to use. The soaring rate of violent crime supports this conclusion. Law enforcement officials are beginning to view as a myth the notion that criminals can be rehabilitated. In this regard, the former United States Attorney General, William B. Saxbe, believes — based on studies funded by the Law Enforcement Assistance Administration — that habitual violent offenders cannot be rehabilitated (APA Monitor, 1975). Thus, he argues, probation may not only be meaningless but dangerous to society.

PREVENTION

In 1959, when we began this longitudinal investigation, our premise was that aggressive behavior was one aspect of mental illness. One of our goals at that time was to determine the incidence and distribution of this disordered behavior in a countywide population of third grade schoolchildren. That this premise is still current is evidenced in the decision taken by Hugh C. Carey, the Governor of New York, to place youthful violent offenders in the facilities of the Department of Mental Hygiene rather than the State Training Schools of the Division for Youth. The implication of this decision is that psychiatric treatment of these youth can be effected.

Indeed, our premise — that aggression was an aspect of psychopathology — has been supported by our longitudinal findings (see Chapter 5). Furthermore, we found that aggressive children were viewed by their peers as unpopular and lacking in leadership qualities. These results have certain implications for preventive programs. Those who would arrange situations designed to reduce aggressive behavior are also likely to reduce psychopathology, especially in boys. Concomitantly, they would promote prosocial behavior such as leadership and popularity.

Aggressive behavior transcends the classification of solely a mental health problem and should be viewed as a problem of public health and safety. The concern of the United States Surgeon General with the effects of television violence on social behavior supports this contention as does the nationwide concern with crimes of violence. Since programs for the treatment and/or rehabilitation of violent offenders for the large part have been unsuccessful in terms of lasting results, the focus must be on prevention. Since the causes of violent behavior as we now understand them are so vastly complicated, the launching of a preventive approach must have the full support of appropriate government agencies.

Prevention of aggressive behavior in any one individual begins even before that individual's conception, inasmuch as the mother's physical and nutritional status are major determinants of complications of pregnancy and birth. Such complications may produce brain damage in the fetus, which is sometimes an antecedent of aggressive behavior. Furthermore, it follows that other conditions leading to postnatal brain damage may be implicated in aggressive behavior.

Subsequent to birth, the development of aggressive behavior, psychopathology, and prosocial behavior seems to be affected most by child rearing and sociocultural variables. These variables comprise the cultural envelope (Eisenberg, 1972) in which the individual develops. This envelope may provide all the stimuli for the development of aggressive behavior or it may serve to potentiate aggressive behavior by providing a milieu which interacts with certain conditions in the individual such as brain dysfunction, low IQ, or testosterone level. For the large part, we feel that the thrust of any preventive effort must be on this cultural envelope.

To produce a diminution in the level of violence, a broad change in values must be effected, hopefully through socioeducational means. In contemporary American society aggression and violence are glorified and celebrated in major areas of endeavor: industry and commerce, labor, military, politics, and most forms of entertainment. When violence is successful in winning a cause, the perpetrators are reinforced and a model for emulation is created. This apotheosis of violence and the implements of violence are the child's earliest fare provided by television, movies, books, parents, and peers. In real life he sees the daily successful application of aggression as he matures. These conditions in conjunction with the saturation of the environment with all kinds of weapons, but especially guns, literally makes for a tinder box. Guns are particularly noxious because they allow a transient impulse to aggress to be realized easily, cleanly, and lethally. Certainly it would require a monumental preventive effort to institute a change in values to deglorify violence. Even when a violent act is manifestly "bad" (for example, murder or arson), the news media make the event salient, which on the one hand serves, for many, to reinforce the act by making it a publicly recognized "achievement" and on the other to increase the probability of contagion so aptly described by Bandura (1973b).[2]

In 1973 there were 13,070 gun murders in the United States as compared to 35 in England and Wales where gun controls are strict. Germane and worthy of repetition, is Etzioni's (1973) rhetorical question of how many people Charles Whitman would have killed from atop the University of Texas Tower had he only a coke bottle instead of a rifle. Scheibe (1974) cites the grim statistic of approximately 20,000 gun deaths each year in the United States and notes the estimate that in Detroit one of every three residents possesses a handgun. He asks, "If these weapons did not exist, would the assailants go to the trouble of stabbing, or, more work still, of killing with the bare hands" (p. 582)? Ratiocinating, Scheibe hypothesizes that if higher primates were provided with deadly weapons their conspecific homicide rate would be greatly increased. He makes a fairly convincing argument against the thesis popularized by Lorenz (1966) that man is unique among species in the animal kingdom for conspecific killing.

In terms of prevention, stringent gun control laws — or, in Etzioni's terms (1973), domestic disarmament — are relatively easy to achieve when compared with the task of modifying a value system in which violence is glorified. It is beyond the scope of this book to present a program for such value modification. However, certain general guidelines are ineluctably suggested by the data presented so far. There appears to be a "clear and present danger" to the public from aggression. Celebrating violence by publicizing and glorifying it, particularly for profit, must be regulated. In a democracy, such regulation ideally is expected to be self- rather than government-imposed. When profit interest groups — such as the television industry — refuse to regulate themselves, then government regulation may be obligatory. Since, as we have demonstrated, aggression is a facet of psychopathology and is of epidemic proportions, then the problem is one for the National Institute of Mental Health and other appropriate government agencies. Regulation need not take the form of absolute censorship. There is little evidence that media violence has lasting deleterious effects on adults. Yet some way must be found to control the exposure of children to television violence. We offer as an example a film such as "The Godfather." This film shattered many box-office records and, according to *The New York Times* (1974d), also established some sort of record in "the pornography of violence." The sum of ten million dollars was paid by NBC Television for the rights to this film, which shows two garrotings, eight murders, one attempted murder, a man beaten insensible, a woman machine-gunned in bed, another one blown up by a bomb, and a final machine gun scene is which scores of bullets are pumped into the victim. Televised on a Saturday night from 9 to 11 PM in the East and 8 to 10 PM in the Central Time Zone, this film was viewed by millions of children and adolescents. Questions *The New York Times* (1974d): "This is family entertainment?" The Godfather, Part II, equally saturated with violence and gore is also smashing box-office records and eventually will be telecast.

A preventive approach to violence would mandate that films and programs in this genre be shown on television only after 11 PM local time and be restricted to adult viewers. Since the media have not lived up their responsibilities in this regard, government must intervene. In addition, if the news media cannot desensationalize their reporting of crime news, Congress and the courts must enforce procedures that protect the rights of the accused, the rights of the victim, and the rights of the public not to be taught that violence pays. Education in violence prevention, like sex education, should be part of the elementary school curriculum. Finally, citizen education in violence prevention should receive as intensive a thrust as that given to educational efforts in heart disease, cancer, and against driving while intoxicated.

In our discussion of prevention up to this point, the focus has been largely on events in the individual's environment. But how can prevention be applied to those conditions associated with aggression which seem to have their locus more in the individual than the social context? Examples are: central nervous system insult, chromosomal anomalies, testosterone level, morphology, and the behavior which results from those child-rearing practices that we have shown in our research to be associated with aggression (see Chapter 3). We would agree with Bandura (1973a) that predictions of aggressive behavior are generally more accurate when based on knowledge of the social context than on knowledge of the individual. For example, irrespective of the performer's personality, we could safely predict that aggressive behavior would more frequently occur on a ghetto sidewalk than in a church. Thus, the thrust of preventive measures would likely be more successful when directed at the social context. Consonant with the major premise of our research effort, this approach to prevention assumes that, in the main, aggression is a socially learned phenomenon. Nevertheless, no opportunity to prevent aggression can be overlooked; as we have already indicated, complications of pregnancy and birth often associated with brain damage and lowered IQ are preventable. On the other hand, there are certain conditions which, while organismically normal — such as sex differences in testosterone levels — seem to be implicated in aggressive behavior. We would argue that although this difference may be one of genotype, the phenotypic behavior (greater male aggression) is not necessarily immutable. Just as some females can learn to be aggressive, males can learn *not* to be aggressive. The significant variables are the values and expectations a society holds for the expression of aggressive behavior in one sex rather than another and the rewards it provides when that behavior is expressed.

In discussing the implications of our findings, rather broad ramifications have emerged. But, throughout, it has been our assumption that aggression, for the large part, is a socially learned behavior and that manipulation in certain ways of a set of social conditions will produce an aggressive individual, whereas manipulation of these conditions in another way will produce a non-aggressive individual. For obvious reasons, we had no hand in the experimental manipulation of any of these variables. Nevertheless, variation in these conditions which we have termed our set of four predictor or independent variables did occur, very probably, willy nilly. Our aim as behavioral scientists was to discover this set of conditions governing aggressive behavior and the principles or laws by which they operate. Since this behavior appears inimical to the species, a second aim was to explore and recommend techniques for the control of these conditions. Insofar as our data would permit, we believe that these aims have been accomplished.

NOTES

[1] As mentioned in Chapter 3, an equally tenable interpretation of these findings is that older mothers use different child-rearing methods than younger mothers.

[2] *Item*: Just as this section is being written, a 17-year-old high school honor student in Olean, New York, barricaded himself in a school building and with a rifle fusillade indiscriminately killed three people and wounded nine others (*The New York Times*, 1975a). According to a classmate, guns were this youth's whole life and were on prominent display in his bedroom. When captured, the youth was dressed in combat fatigues, camoflaged for jungle warfare, and had also provided himself with a gas mask. The very next day, in another part of the state, a man used a shotgun to kill a mail carrier, following which he walked into a nearby police station and seriously wounded two policemen (*The New York Times*, 1975b). Prominent local and statewide coverage was given to these two acts by the news media. Subsequently an editorial (*The New York Times*, 1975c) advocating strong gun control laws suggested that the second event might be attributable to the contagion of violence.

REFERENCES

Alland, A., Jr. *The human imperative.* New York: Columbia University Press, 1972.

Allport, G.W. *Pattern and growth in personality.* New York: Holt, Rinehart and Winston, 1961.

Anthony, W.A., Buell, G.J., Sharrott, S., and Althoff, M.E. Efficacy of psychiatric rehabilitation. *Psychological Bulletin,* 1972, **78**, 447-456.

APA Monitor. Saxbe: The myth of rehabilitation. January 1975, p. 10.

Ardrey, R. *The territorial imperative.* New York: Dell, 1966.

Armour, D.J. Measuring the effects of television on aggressive behavior, RAND Corp. R-1759-MF, Santa Monica, April 1975.

Avis, H.H. The neuropharmacology of aggression: A critical review. *Psychological Bulletin,* 1974, **81**, 47-63.

Azrin, N.H. "Some effects of noise on human behavior." *Journal of Experimental Analysis of Behavior,* 1958, **1**, 183-200.

Azrin, N.H. and Holz, W.C. Punishment. In W.K. Honig (Ed.), *Operant behavior.* New York: Appleton-Century, 1966.

Bach-y-Rita, G. Habitual violence and self-mutilation. *The American Journal of Psychiatry,* 1974, **131**, 1018-1020.

Bailyn, L. Mass media and children: A study of exposure habits and cognitive effects. *Psychological Monographs,* 1959, **73**(1), 1-48.

Baldwin, T.F. and Lewis, C. Violence in television: The industry looks at itself. In G.A. Comstock and E.A. Rubinstein (Eds.) *Television and social behavior.* Vol. 1: *Media content and control.* Washington: U.S. Government Printing Office, 1972, 290-373.

Bandler, R.J., Jr., and Flynn, J.P. Neural pathways from thalamus associated with regulation of aggressive behavior. *Science,* 1974, **183**, 96-99.

Bandura, A. "Vicarious process: A case of no-trial learning." In L. Berkowitz (Ed.) *Advances in experimental social psychology.* Vol. 2. New York: Academic Press, 1965.

Bandura, A. *Principles of behavior modification.* New York: Holt, Rinehart and Winston, 1969.

Bandura, A. *Aggression — a social learning analysis.* Englewood Cliffs: Prentice Hall, 1973a.

Bandura, A. Social learning analysis of aggression. Paper presented at the meeting of the American Psychological Association, Montreal, September 1973b.

Bandura, A., Ross, D., and Ross, S.A. Transmission of aggression through imitation of aggressive models. *Journal of Abnormal and Social Psychology,* 1961, **63**, 575-582.

Bandura, A., Ross, D., and Ross, S. Vicarious reinforcement and imitative learning. *Journal of Abnormal and Social Psychology*, 1963a, **67**, 601-607.

Bandura, A., Ross, D., and Ross, S.A. Imitation of film-mediated aggressive models. *Journal of Abnormal Psychology*, 1963b, **66**, 3-11.

Bandura, A. and Walters, R.H. *Social learning and personality development*. Holt, Rinehart, Winston, 1963.

Bergson, Henri. *Creative evolution*. New York: Henry Holt, 1911.

Berkowitz, L. *Aggression: A social psychological analysis*. New York: McGraw-Hill, 1962.

Berkowitz, L. *Roots of aggression: A re-examination of the frustration aggression hypothesis*. New York: Atherton Press, 1969a.

Berkowitz, L. Simple views of aggression, an essay review. *American Scientist*, 1969b, **57**, 372-383.

Berkowitz, L. Social motivation. In G. Lindzey and E. Aronson (Eds.) *The handbook of social psychology*, 2nd ed., vol. 3. Reading, Massachusetts: Addison Wesley, 1969c, 50-135.

Berkowitz, L., Corwin, R., and Heironimus, M. Film violence and subsequent aggressive tendencies. *Public Opinion Quarterly*, 1963, **27**, 217-229.

Birch, H.G. and Gussow, J.D. *Disadvantaged children*. New York: Harcourt, Brace & World, 1970.

Body, M.K. Patterns of aggression in the nursery school. *Child Development*, 1955, **26**, 3-12.

Boelkins, R.C. and Heiser, J.F. Biological bases of aggression. In D.N. Daniels, M.F. Gilula, and F.M. Ochberg (Eds.) *Violence and the struggle for existence*. Boston: Little, Brown, 1970.

Bronson, F.H. and Desjardins, C. "Aggression in adult mice: Modification by neonatal injections of gonadal hormones." *Science*, 1968, **161**, 705-706.

Brown, R.M. Historical patterns of violence in America. In H.D. Graham and T.R. Gurr (Eds.) *Violence in America: Historical and comparative perspectives*. Vol. 1. Washington, D.C.: U.S. Government Printing Office, 1969.

Brown, J.L. and Hunsperger, R.W. Neuroethology and the motivation of agonistic behavior. *Animal Behavior*, 1963, **11**, 439-448.

Brownmiller, S. "Street fighting woman." *The New York Times*, April 18, 1973, Op. Ed. Page.

Burdock, E.I. and Hardesty, A.S. A multivariate analysis of the relations between intelligence and psychopathology. In M.

Hammer, K. Salzinger, S. Sutton (Eds.) *Psychopathology: Contributions from the social, behavioral and biological sciences.* New York: Wiley, 1973, 427-430.

Buss, A. Aggression pays. In J.L. Singer (Ed.) *The control of aggression and violence.* New York: Academic Press, 1971.

Chaffee, S.H. Television and adolescent aggressiveness. In G.A. Comstock and E.A. Rubinstein (Eds.) *Television and social behavior.* Vol. III: Television and adolescent aggressiveness. Washington, D.C.: U.S. Government Printing Office, 1972.

Chasdi, E.H. and Lawrence, M.S. Some antecedents of aggression and effects of frustration in doll play. In D. McClelland (Ed.), *Studies in motivation.* New York: Appleton-Century-Crofts, 1955.

Chiswick, N. "An experimental study of the effects of punishment and permission on aggression and anxiety." Unpublished doctoral dissertation, University of Illinois at Chicago Circle, 1973.

Christie, R., Havel, J., and Seidenberg, B. Is the F scale irreversible? *Journal of Abnormal and Social Psychology,* 1958, 56, 143-159.

Cline, V.B., Croft, R.G., and Courrier, S. Desensitization of children to television violence. *Journal of Personality and Social Psychology.* 1973, 27, 360-365.

Comstock, G.A. Television violence: Where the Surgeon General's Study leads. Rand Corporation Paper P-4831, Santa Monica, California, May 1972.

Conners, C.K. Pharmacotherapy of psychopathology in children. In H.C. Quay and J.S. Werry (Eds.), *Psychopathological disorders of children.* New York: Wiley, 1972a.

Conners, C.K. Symposium: Behavior modification by drugs, II. Psychological effects of stimulant drugs in children with minimal brain dysfunction. *Pediatrics,* 1972b, 49, 702-708.

Cowie, J. and Kahn J. XYY constitution in prepubertal child. *British Medical Journal,* 1968, 1, 748-749.

Crane, G.E. Clinical psychopharmacology in its 20th year. *Science,* 1973, 181, 124-128.

Dahlstrom, W.G. and Welsh, G.S. *An MMPI handbook.* Minneapolis: University of Minnesota Press, 1960.

Dahlstrom, W.G., Welsh, G.S., and Dahlstrom, L.E. *An MMPI handbook.* Vol. 1. *Clinical interpretation,* Minneapolis: University of Minnesota Press, 1972.

Dalton, K. *The premenstrual syndrome.* Springfield, Illinois: Thomas, 1964.

Darlington, R.D. "Multiple regression in psychological research and practice." *Psychological Bulletin,* 1969, 69, 161-182.

Davidson, W.S. II and Seidman, E. Studies of behavior modification and juvenile delinquency: A review, methodological critique, and social perspective. *Psychological Bulletin*, 1974, 81, 998-1011.

Delgado, J.M.R. Social rank and radio-stimulated aggressiveness in monkeys. *Journal of Nervous and Mental Disease*, 1967, 144, 383-390.

Dittman, A.T. and Goodrich, D.W. A comparison of social behavior in normal and hyperaggressive preadolescent boys. *Child Development*, 1961, 32, 315-327.

Dohrenwend, B.P. and Dohrenwend, B.S. Social and cultural influences on psychopathology. In M. Rosenweig and L. Porter (Eds.), *Annual review of psychology*, vol. 25, Palo Alto, California: Annual Reviews, 1974, 417-452.

Dollard, J., Doob, L.W., Miller, N.E., Mowrer, O. H., and Sears, R.R. *Frustration and aggression.* New Haven: Yale University Press, 1939.

Ehrhardt, A.A., Epstein, R., and Money, J. Fetal androgens and female gender identity in the early-treated androgenital syndrome. *Johns Hopkins Medical Journal*, 1968, 122, 160-167.

Ehrhardt, A.A. and Money, J. Progestin induced hermaphroditism: IQ and psychosexual identity in a study of ten girls. *Journal of Sex Research*, 1967, 3, 83-100.

Eisenberg, L. The *human* nature of human nature. *Science*, 1972, 176, 123-128.

Eron, L.D. Relationship of TV viewing habits and aggressive behavior in children. *Journal of Abnormal and Social Psychology*, 1963, 67(2), 193-196.

Eron, L.D., Huesmann, L.R., Lefkowitz, M.M., and Walder, L.O. "Does television violence cause aggression?" *American Psychologist*, 1972, 27, 253-263.

Eron, L.D., Walder, L.O., and Lefkowitz, M.M. *Learning of aggression in children.* Boston: Little, Brown, 1971.

Eron, L.D., Walder, L.O., Toigo, R., and Lefkowitz, M.M. "Social class, parental punishment for aggression and child aggression." *Child Development*, 1963, 34, 849-867.

Etzioni, A. Public policy and curbing violence. *International Journal of Group Tensions*, 1973, 3, 76-95.

Eysenck, S.B.G. *Manual for the junior Eysenck personality inventory.* San Diego: Educational and Industrial Testing Service, 1963.

Feshbach, S. Aggression. In P.H. Mussen (Ed.), *Carmichaels' manual of child psychology*, 3rd ed., Vol. 2. New York: Wiley, 1970.

Feshbach, S. and Singer, R.D. *Television and aggression.* San Francisco: Jossey-Bass, 1971.

Flor-Henry, P. Psychosis, neurosis and epilepsy. *The British Journal of Psychiatry*, 1974, **124**, 144-150.

Freud, S. *The ego and the id.* London: Hogarth, 1923.

Freud, S. Beyond the pleasure principle. In J. Strachey (Ed.), *The standard edition of the complete psychological works of Sigmund Freud*, Vol. 18. Toronto: The Hogarth Press, 1955.

Freud, S. Why war. In J. Strachey (Ed.), *Collected papers*, Vol. 5. New York: Basic Books, 1959.

Fried, M.H. Letters. *The New York Times*, November 30, 1969, **4**, 13.

Goldhammer, H. and Marshall, A.W. *Psychosis and civilization:* Glencoe, Illinois: Free Press, 1953.

Goranson, R.E. Media violence and aggressive behavior: A review of experimental research. In L. Berkowitz (Ed.), *Advances in experimental social psychology*, Vol. 5. Academic Press, 1970.

Greenberg, B.S. and Gordon, T.F. *Critics and public perceptions of violence in TV programs.* Michigan State University: Dept. of Communication, 1970.

Hall, C.S. and Lindzey, G. *Theories of personality*, 2nd ed. New York: Wiley, 1970.

Hamburg, D.A. Effects of progesterone on behavior. In R. Levine (Ed.), *Endocrines and the central nervous system.* Baltimore: Williams & Wilkins, 1966.

Hamburg, D.A., Moos, R.H., and Yalom, I.D. Studies of distress in the menstrual cycle and postpartum period. In R.P. Michael (Ed.), *Endocrinology and human behavior.* London: Oxford University Press, 1968.

Harper, P.A. and Wiener, G. Sequelae of low birth weight. *Annual Review of Medicine*, 1965, **16**, 405-420.

Harris, G.W. and Levine, S. Sexual differentiation of the brain and its experimental control. *Journal of Physiology*, 1965, **181**, 379-400.

Hathaway, S.R. and McKinley, J.C. *The Minnesota Multiphasic Personality Inventory.* New York: The Psychological Corporation, 1969.

Hathaway, S.R. and Monachesi, E.D. *Adolescent personality and behavior: MMPI patterns of normal, delinquent, dropout and other outcomes.* Minneapolis: University of Minnesota Press, 1963.

Hearings before the Subcommittee on Communications of the Committee on Commerce, United States Senate, Serial No. 92-52. Washington: U.S. Government Printing Office, 1972.

Heise, D.R. Causal inference from panel data. In E.F. Borgatta and G.W. Bohrnstedt (Eds.), *Sociological methodology*. San Francisco: Jossey-Bass, 1970.

Hinde, R.A. The nature of aggression. *New Society*, March 2, 1967, 302.

Hobbes, T. *Leviathan.* New York: Penguin, 1969.

Holden, C. Psychosurgery: Legitimate therapy or laundered lobotomy? *Science*, 1973, **179**, 1109-1112.

Hook, E.B. Behavioral implications of the human XYY genotype. *Science*, 1973, **179**, 139-150.

Huesmann, L.R., Eron, L.D., Lefkowitz, M.M., and Walder, L.O. Television violence and aggression: The causal effect remains. *American Psychologist*, 1973, **28**, 617-620.

Huesmann, L.R., Eron, L.D., Lefkowitz, M.M. and Walder, L.O. Change analysis as applied to the analysis of television violence and aggression: a reply to Armour, Technical Report, Department of Psychology, University of Illinois at Chicago Circle, July, 1975.

James, W. *Principles of psychology.* 2 Vols. New York: Holt, 1890.

Jarvik, M.E. Drugs used in the treatment of psychiatric disorders. In L. Goodman and A. Gilman (Eds.), *The pharmacological basis of therapeutics*, 3rd ed. New York: Macmillan, 1965.

Jarvik, L.F., Klodin, V., and Matsuyama, S.S. Human aggression and the extra Y chromosome: Fact or fantasy? *American Psychologist*, 1973, **28**, 674-682.

Joffe, J.M. *Prenatal determinants of behavior.* Braunschweig, Germany: Pergamon Press, 1969.

Kaada, B. Brain mechanisms related to aggressive behavior. In C.D. Clemente and D.B. Lindsley (Eds.), *Aggression and defense.* Berkeley, California: University of California Press, 1967.

Kaplan, B.J. Malnutrition and mental deficiency. *Psychological Bulletin*, 1972, **78**, 321-334.

Kaufmann, H. *Aggression and altruism.* New York: Holt, Rinehart & Winston, 1970.

Kelly, F., Farina, A., and Mosher, D. Ability of schizophrenic women to create a favorable or unfavorable impression on an interviewer. *Journal of Consulting and Clinical Psychology*, 1971, **36**, 404-409.

Kenny, D. Threats to the internal validity of cross-lagged panel inference as related to "Television Violence and Child Aggression: A Follow-up Study." In G.A. Comstock and E.A. Rubinstein (Eds.), *Television and social behavior.* Vol. III. *Television and adolescent aggressiveness.* Washington, D.C.: U.S. Government Printing Office, 1972.

Kessler, S. and Moos, R.H. XYY chromosome: Premature conclusions. *Science*, 1969, **165**, 442.

Kirchner, E.P. The fight question: A mirror of differential socialization and instance of discrimination against little boys? *Developmental Psychology*, 1974, **10**, 300.

Knobloch, H. and Pasamanick, B. Prospective studies on the epidemiology of reproductive casualty: Methods, findings, and some implications. *Merrill-Palmer Quarterly of Behavior and Development*, 1966, **12**, 27-43.

Lefkowitz, M.M. Some relationships between sex role preference of children and other parent-child variables. *Psychological Reports*, 1962, **10**, 43-53.

Lefkowitz, M.M. MMPI Scores of juvenile delinquents adjusting to institutionalization. *Psychological Reports*, 1966, **19**, 911-914.

Lefkowitz, M.M. Effects of diphenylhydantoin on disruptive behavior: Study of male delinquents. *Archives of General Psychiatry*, 1969, **20**, 643-651.

Lefkowitz, M.M. Short-term institutionalization for delinquent girls. *Evaluation*, 1975, **2**, No. 2, 22-23.

Lefkowitz, M.M., Eron, L., Walder, L., and Huesmann, L.R. Television violence and child aggression: A follow-up study. In G.A. Comstock and E.A. Rubinstein (Eds.), *Television and social behavior*, Vol. III. Washington: U.S. Government Printing Office, 1972.

Lefkowitz, M.M., Eron, L.D., Walder, L.O., and Huesmann, L.R. Preference for televised contact sports as related to sex differences in aggression. *Developmental Psychology*, 1973, **9**, 417-420.

Lefkowitz, M.M., Eron, L.D., Huesmann, L.R., and Walder, L.O. The effects of perinatal complications on the development of aggressive behavior. Paper presented at the meeting of the International Society for Research on Aggression, Toronto, Canada, August 1974.

Lefkowitz, M.M., Walder, L.O., and Eron, L.D. Punishment, identification and aggression. *Merrill Palmer Quarterly of Behavior and Development*, 1963, **9**, 159-174.

LeMaire, L. Danish experiences regarding the castration of sexual offenders. *Journal of Criminal Law and Criminology*, 1956, **47**, 294-310.

Lerner, L.J. Hormone antagonists: Inhibitors of specific activities of estrogen and androgen. *Recent Progress in Hormone Research*, 1964, **20**, 435-490.

Lerner, M. Responsiveness of chronic schizophrenics to the social behavior of others in a meaningful task situation. *Journal of Abnormal and Social Psychology*, 1963, **67**, 295-299.

Lesser, G.S. *Children and television: Lessons from Sesame Street.* New York: Random House, 1974.

Levine, S. Sex differences in the brain. *Scientific American,* April 1966, **214,** 84-90.

Liebert, R.M., Neale, J.M., and Davidson, E.S., *The early window: Effects of television on children and youth.* New York: Pergamon Press, 1973.

Locke, J. *Treatise on civil government.* London: Cadell, 1781.

Lorenz, K. *On aggression.* New York: Harcourt, Brace and World, 1966.

Maas, H.S. The role of member in clubs of lower-class and middle-class adolescents. *Child Development,* 1954, **25,** 241-252.

Maccoby, E.E. Sex differences in intellectual functioning. In E.E. Maccoby (Ed.), *The development of sex differences.* Stanford: Stanford University Press, 1966.

Maccoby, E.E. and Jacklin, C.N. Sex differences and their implications for sex roles. Paper presented at the meeting of the American Psychological Association, Washington, D.C. September 1971.

MacFarlane, J.W., Allen L., and Honzik, M.P. A developmental study of the behavior problems of normal children between twenty-one months and fourteen years. *University of California publications in child development, Vol. II.* Berkeley: University of California Press, 1954

Mark, V. and Ervin, F. *Violence and the brain.* New York: Harper & Row, 1970.

Marlowe, D. and Gergen, K.J. Personality and social interaction. In G. Lindzey and E. Aronson (Eds.), *The handbook of social psychology,* 2nd ed., Vol. 3, Reading, Massachusetts: Addison-Wesley, 1969.

Maternal, fetal and infant nutrition. Part I — Consequences of malnutrition, Series 73/MFI 1. Washington: U.S. Government Printing Office, 1973.

McCord, W., McCord, J., and Zola, I.K. *Origins of crime: A new evaluation of the Cambridge-Somerville Youth Study.* New York: Columbia University Press, 1959.

McDougall, W. *An introduction to social psychology.* London: Methuen, 1908.

McNeill, W.H. *The rise of the West.* New York: The New American Library, 1963.

Mednick, S.A. Breakdown in individuals at high risk for schizophrenia: Possible predispositional prenatal factors. *Mental Hygiene,* 1970, **54,** 50-63.

Milavsky, J.R. and Pekowsky, B. Exposure to TV "violence" and aggressive behavior in boys, examined as process: A status report of a longitudinal study. Unpublished manuscript, Department of Social Research, National Broadcasting Company, 1973.

Milgram, S. Behavioral study of obedience. *Journal of Abnormal and Social Psychology*, 1963, **67**, 371-378.

Milgram, S. *Television and antisocial behavior.* New York: Academic Press, 1973.

Miller, D.R. and Swanson, G.E. Inner conflict and defense. New York: Holt, Rinehart and Winston, 1960.

Miller, N.E., Sears, R.R., Mowrer, O.H., Doob, L.W., and Dollard, J. The frustration-aggression hypothesis. *Psychological Reveiw*, 1941, **48**, 337-342.

Mischel, W. "Sex-typing and socialization." In P.H. Mussen (Ed.), *Carmichael's manual of child psychology*, 3rd ed., Vol. 2. New York: Wiley, 1970.

Money, J. and Ehrhardt, A.A. *Man & woman, boy & girl.* Baltimore: Johns Hopkins University Press, 1972.

Montagu, M.F.A. The new litany of "Innate depravity", or original sin revisited. In M.F. Ashley Montagu (Ed.), *Man and aggression.* New York: Oxford University Press, 1968.

Morgan, C.T. *Physiological psychology.* New York: McGraw-Hill, 1965, pp. 306-338.

Morris, D. *The naked ape.* New York: McGraw-Hill, 1967.

Moyer, K.E. Kinds of aggression and their physiological basis. *Communication in Behavioral Biology*, 1968, **2**, 65-87.

Moyer, K.E. The physiology of aggression and the implications for aggression control. In J.L. Singer (Ed.), *The control of aggression and violence.* New York: Academic Press, 1971.

Mulvihill, D.J. and Tumin, M.M. *Crimes of violence*, Vol. 12. Staff Report to the National Commission on the Causes and Prevention of Violence. Washington, D.C.: U.S. Government Printing Office, 1969.

Munro, R.L. *Schools of psychoanalytic thought.* New York: Dryden, 1955.

The Nation. Abuse of power. December 7, 1974, p. 581.

Neale, J.M. Comment on "Television violence and child aggression: a follow-up study." In G.A. Comstock and E.A. Rubinstein (Eds.), *Television and social behavior*, Vol. III, *Television and adolescent aggressiveness.* Washington, D.C.: U.S. Government Printing Office, 1972.

New York State Department of Mental Hygiene, Office of Statistical and Clinical Information Systems, 1972.

The New York Times. Youthful violence grows and accused are younger. November 4, 1974, p. 1.(a)

The New York Times. TV sex and violence: New move highlights problems. November 28, 1974, p. 66.(b)

The New York Times. Mexico banning violent TV series. September 30, 1974, p. 71.(c)

The New York Times. 'Godfather for Xmas.' December 23, 1974, p. 26.(d)

The New York Times. Sniper's classmate says guns were 'whole life.' January 1, 1975, p. 1.(a)

The New York Times. Rifleman slays a mailman; shoots 2 in police station. January 1, 1975, p. 34.(b)

The New York Times. Guns against society. January 3, 1975, p. 26.(c)

Osgood, C.E., Suci, G.J., and Tannenbaum, P.H. *The measurement of meaning.* Urbana: University of Illinois Press, 1957.

Parlee, M.B. The premenstrual syndrome. *Psychological Bulletin,* 1973, **80,** 454-465.

Parton, D.A. The study of aggression in boys with an operant device. *Journal of Experimental Child Psychology,* 1964, **1,** 79-88.

Pasamanick, B. and Knobloch, H. Retrospective studies on the epidemiology of reproductive casualty: Old and new. *Merrill Palmer Quarterly of Behavior and Development,* 1966, **12,** 7-26.

Patterson, G.R. Reprogramming the families of aggressive boys. In C.E. Thoreson (Ed.), *Behavior modification in education.* Chicago: The National Society for the Study of Education, 1972.

Patterson, G.R., Littman, R.A., and Bricker, W. Assertive behavior in children: A step toward a theory of aggression. *Monographs of the Society for Research in Child Development,* 1967, **32,** No. 5, Serial No. 113.

Peterson, D.R. Behavior problems of middle childhood. *Journal of Consulting Psychology,* 1961, **25,** 205-209.

Peterson, R. Aggression as a function of retaliation and aggression level of target and aggressor. *Developmental Psychology,* 1971, **5,** 161-166.

Phillips, L. A social view of psychopathology. In P. London and D. Rosenham (Eds.), *Foundations of abnormal psychology.* New York: Holt, Rinehart & Winston, 1968.

Phillips, L. and Zigler, E. Social competence, the action-thought parameter and vicariousness in normal and pathological behaviors. *Journal of Abnormal and Social Psychology,* 1961, **63,** 137-146.

Quay, H.C. Patterns of aggression, withdrawal and immaturity. In

H.C. Quay and J.S. Werry (Eds.), *Psychopathological disorders of childhood.* New York: Wiley, 1972, 1-29.

Quay, H.C., Sprague, R.L., Shulman, H.S., and Miller, A.L. Some correlates of personality disorder and conduct disorder. *Psychology in the Schools,* 1966, **3**, 44-47.

Rader, D. The sexual nature of violence. *The New York Times,* October 22, 1973, 31.

Robinson, B.W. The physiology of fighting and defeat. Paper presented at the meetiof the American Association for the Advancement of Science, Dallas, December 1968.

Rosenthal, R. *Experimenter effects in behavioral research.* New York: Appleton-Century-Crofts, 1966.

Rosvold, H.E., Mirsky, A.F., and Pribram, K.H. Influences of amygdalectomy on social behavior in monkeys. *Journal of Comparative and Physiological Psychology,* 1954, **47**, 173-178.

Rousseau, J.J. *Emile.* New York: Dutton, 1911.

Rousseau, J.J. The social contract. In R.M. Hutchins (Ed.), *Great books of the Western World, Montesquieu, Rousseau.* Chicago: Encyclopedia Britannica, 1952.

Rozelle, R.M., and Campbell, D.T. More plausible rival hypotheses in the cross-lagged panel correlation technique. *Psychological Bulletin,* 1969, **71**, 74-79.

Scheibe, K.E. Legitimized aggression and the assignment of evil. *American Scholar,* 1974, **43**, 576-592.

Schram, W., Lyle, J., and Parker, E. *Television in the lives of our Children.* Stanford: Stanford University Press, 1961.

Scott, J.P. That old time aggression. *The Nation,* January 9, 1967, 53-54.

Scott, J.P. Biology and the control of violence. *International Journal of Group Tensions,* 1973, **3**, 4-19.

Scrimshaw, N.S. and Gordon, J.E. (Eds.), *Malnutrition learning and behavior.* Cambridge: MIT Press, 1968.

Semler, I.J. and Eron, L.D. "Replication report: Relationship of aggression in third-grade children to certain pupil characteristics." *Psychology in the Schools,* 1967, 4, 356-358.

Senf, R., Huston, P., and Cohen B. The use of comic cartoons for the study of social comprehension in schizophrenia. *American Journal of Psychiatry,* 1956, **113**, 45-51.

Sherman, H. and Farina, A. Social adequacy of parents and children. *Journal of Abnormal Psychology,* 1974, **83**, 327-330.

Siegelman, M. Parent behavior correlates of personality traits related to creativity in sons and daughters. *Journal of Consulting and Clinical Psychology,* 1973, **40**, 43-47.

Siegelman, M., Block, J., Block, J., and Van Der Lippe, H. Antecedents of optimal psychological development. *Journal of Consulting and Clinical Psychology*, 1970, **35**, 283-289.

Sigg, E.B. Relationship of aggressive behavior to adrenal and gonadal function in male mice. Proceedings of the symposium on the Biology of Aggressive Behavior, Milan, May 1968.

Singer, J.L. *The child's world of make believe: Experimental studies of imaginative play.* New York: Academic Press, 1972.

Skinner, B.F. Operant behavior. In W.K. Honig (Ed.), *Operant behavior.* New York: Appleton-Century, 1966a.

Skinner, B.F. The phylogeny and ontogeny of behavior. *Science*, 1966 b, 1205-1213.

Skinner, B.F. *About behaviorism.* New York: Knopf, 1974.

Stewart, J.M. Social disorganization and the control of fighting in dogs. Unpublished doctoral dissertation, Bowling Green State University, 1972.

Sullivan, E.T., Clark, W.W., and Tiegs, E.W. *California short-form test of mental maturity.* Los Angeles: California Test Bureau, 1957.

Tardiff, K.J. A survey of psychiatrists in Boston and their work with violent patients. *The American Journal of Psychiatry*, 1974, **131**, 1008-1011.

Telfer, M.A., Baker, D., Clark, G.R., and Richardson, C.E. Incidence of gross chromosomal errors among tall criminal American males. *Science*, 1968, **159**, 1249-1250.

Tinbergen, N. On war and peace in animals and man. *Science*, 1968, **160**, 1411-1418.

Tinklenberg, J.R. and Stillman, R.C. Drug use and violence. In D.N. Daniels, M.F. Gilula, and F.M. Ochberg (Eds.), *Violence and the struggle for existence.* Boston: Little, Brown, 1970.

United States Bureau of Census. *Classified index of occupations and industries.* Washington, D.C.: U.S. Government Printing Office, 1960.

Walder, L.O., Abelson, R., Eron, L.D., Banta, T.J., and Laulicht, J.H. Development of a peer-rating measure of aggression. *Psychological Reports*, 1961, **9**, 497-556.

Warner, W.L., Meeker, M., and Eells, K. *Social class in America.* New York: Harcourt, 1960.

Wechsler, D. *Manual for the Wechsler Preschool and Primary Scale of Intelligence.* New York: Psychological Corporation, 1967.

Werry, J.S. Childhood psychosis. In H.C. Quay and J.S. Werry (Eds.), *Psychopathological disorders of childhood.* New York: Wiley, 1972.

White, L. Organic factors and psychophysiology in childhood schizophrenia. *Psychological Bulletin*, 1974, **81**, 238-255.

Wicker, T. In the nation: Only one kind of war. *The New York Times*, December 2, 1969, 54.

Winick, M. In *Select Committe on Nutrition and Human Needs.* United States Senate. To save the children, 26-462. Washington: U.S. Printing Office, 1974.

Young, W.C., Goy, R.W., and Phoenix, C.H. Hormones and sexual behavior. *Science*, 1964, **143**, 212-218.

Zigler, E. and Child, I.L. Socialization. In G. Lindzey and E. Aronson (Eds.), *The handbook of social psychology*, 2nd ed. Vol. 3. Reading, Massachusetts: Addison-Wesley, 1969.

Zigler, E. and Phillips, L. Social competence and outcome in psychiatric disorder. *Journal of Abnormal and Social Psychology*, 1961, **63**, 264-271.

Zitrin, A., Hardesty, A.S., Burdock, E.I., and Drossman, A.K. Crime and violence among mental patients. *The American Journal of Psychiatry*, 1976, **133**, 142-149.

Author Index

Subject Index

LEARNING OF AGGRESSION IN CHILDREN

Leonard D. Eron, Leopold O. Walder, Monroe M. Lefkowitz

"In American society today we are probably witnessing the deleterious effects of *unplanned* yet systematic education for aggressiveness."

This is both the subject and the conclusion of careful empirical study of aggression, whose causes are often obscured in social, philosophical, and genetic confusions and complexities. Based on an extensive survey of children in New York state, this book makes explicit those features of the school and home environment of children that *instigate, support,* and *maintain* aggressive behavior.

In an America seeing more and more social violence and its increasing acceptability by our population, there is a vital need to understand aggressive behavior. Considerable care was taken in the study to distinguish environmental conditions that determine the *learning* of aggressive behavior from other possible sources, including the concepts of "frustration" (the frustration-aggression hypothesis) and of "instinct" and other biological and evolutionary determinants (Lorenz, Tinbergen, and others).

Having reviewed the behavior-theoretical and psychoanalytical literature on the causes of aggressive behavior, the authors assert that the important "antecedents" to aggressive behavior are *instigation, reinforcement,* and *identification,* and that various socio-cultural factors influence the expression and formulation of these antecedents. Each antecedent is then systematically examined with reference to relevant data from the four-year research study.

The authors conclude that a major stimulant of aggressive behavior in children is a general lack of favorable support from their parents, which in turn tends to reduce the effectiveness of the punishment that may later be necessary to prevent destructive forms of aggressiveness. Moreover, parents who are more punitive actually tend to increase their children's aggressiveness.

Finally, the authors discuss the social and ethical questions raised by the possibility of using proven behavior modification techniques to reduce aggressiveness, in particular, by providing parents with the means to change their own habits that serve to constantly strengthen children's aggressiveness.

Contents: Chapter 1: Introduction. Chapter 2: Theoretical Orientation to Learning of Aggression in Children. Chapter 3: Methodological Considerations. Chapter 4: The Reinforcement and Punishment of Aggression. Chapter 5: Instigation to Aggression. Chapter 6: Identification and Aggression. Chapter 7: Sociocultural Variables and Aggressive Behavior. Chapter 8: The Learning Conditions of Aggression. Chapter 9: Implications for Child-Rearing. Appendix I: Classroom Measures. Appendix II: Parent Interview Measures. Appendix III: Reinforcement Measures. Appendix IV: Attempted Measures of Identification. Appendix V: Summary Statistics. Appendix VI: The Environmental Management of Aggression.

242pp   1971   0 08 020929-7 microfilm
0 08 021119-4 microfiche
0 08 020930-0 flexi copyflo
0 08 021120-8 hard cover copyflo

CLASSROOM MANAGEMENT:
THE SUCCESSFUL USE OF BEHAVIOR MODIFICATION —
Second Edition
Edited by K. Daniel O'Leary and Susan G. O'Leary,
State University of New York at Stony Brook

"The best compendium of materials on this subject we have found yet."
The WES Education Bulletin

". . . a useful handbook presenting principles, data, and procedures which will provide the teacher with clear solutions to many of the problems they face in their classrooms daily . . ." Journal of Reading

Based on the thesis that behavior modification procedures can lead to successful classroom management, this volume presents both principles and data which provide clear solutions to a variety of common classroom problems. In providing the reader with a set of principles for changing problem behavior, this work also places those principles within the historical context of the development of childhood treatments. Research evidence documenting the efficacy of procedures described is offered, while the final chapter deals specifically with the ways in which teachers can utilize these approaches in their classrooms.

An advanced undergraduate text for students in education and psychology, this book will also prove useful to experienced teachers and to clinical, educational and school psychologists who consult with teachers on educational problems.

Special features of this new edition:

- Introductory and concluding chapters have been updated to reflect new trends and recent research findings.

- New sections on Organizational Assessment and Change and on Behavioral Ecology have been included.

- Stronger emphasis has been placed on self-management with descriptions of how to teach self-control in the classroom.

1977   0 08 021395-2 (ppk.)
                  0 08 021396-0 (h)

THE EARLY WINDOW:
EFFECTS OF TELEVISION ON CHILDREN AND YOUTH
by Robert M. Liebert, John M. Neale,
State University of New York at Stony Brook,
and Emily S. Davidson, Vanderbilt University

*". . . an eminently readable as well as informative text which is likely to appeal
to professional psychologist and lay parent alike. . ."*   Behavior Therapy

*"THE EARLY WINDOW is an important book on a topic of great interest to my
students. It's thorough and well-written. . . . Too many 'relevant' books are
superficial; THE EARLY WINDOW is based on the later empirical studies and
deals with the issues in depth."*   Dianne Horgan, Northern Illinois University

"The case against television's present offerings is clear," say the authors of this
important contribution to the discussion of television and youth. They base
their conclusions on evaluations and original research which they contributed to
the Surgeon General's Report on the impact of televised violence. In addition to
a review of the major theoretical and methodological issues, the book covers the
gamut of television production from ideas to commercials. A special chapter
discusses the politics of investigation and regulation of the television industry.

Contents: Chapter 1: From Birth to Maturity in Twenty Years. Chapter 2:
Television Today; Production and Content. Chapter 3: Television and Aggres-
sion: The Problem and the Issues. Chapter 4: Television and Aggression:
Laboratory Studies. Chapter 5: Television and Aggression: Field Studies.
Chapter 6: Television's Potential: Prosocial Effects. Chapter 7: The Commercial
Interests. Chapter 8: Control of Content: The Government and the Industry.
Chapter 9: The Past—And the Future.

200 pp   1973   0-08-017780-8 (ppk)
0-08-017091-9 (h)

CHILD BEHAVIOR AND THERAPY
By Donna M. Gelfand and Donald P. Hartmann,
University of Utah

A comprehensive guide to the practice of child behavior modification, this book is directed toward child treatment workers and students studying to enter the field. The book also covers the often neglected issues of ethical questions involved in implementing a behavior change program. Emphasis is on the measurement of behavior and behavior change and the techniques necessary to carry out a behavior modification program step by step, from the identification of a changeworthy behavior, through the planning, application and evaluation of an intervention method.

200 pp   1975   0 08 018228-3 (ppk.)
                      0 08 018229-1 (h)

CHILD BEHAVIOR MODIFICATION:
A MANUAL FOR TEACHERS, NURSES, AND PARENTS
By Luke S. Watson, Jr.,
Columbus State Institute, Ohio

Written in laymen's language, this book is designed to teach the principles of behavior modification to teachers, occupational therapists, nurses, psychiatric aides, and other paraprofesionals who work with mentally retarded, psychotic and emotionally disturbed children. It provides sufficient information to deal with all problems that such persons encounter with children of this type in educational, institutional and home settings. All phases of the behavior modification method are covered, with special emphasis placed on the problems of securing and maintaining the child's attention and cooperation. Testing materials are used to ensure that the reader understands the essential points of the book.

162 pp   1973   0 08 017061-7 (ppk.)
0 08 016823-X (h)

ECOLOGICAL ASSESSMENT OF CHILD PROBLEM BEHAVIOR: A CLINICAL PACKAGE FOR HOME, SCHOOL, AND INSTITUTIONAL SETTINGS
By Robert G. Wahler, University of Tennessee,
Alvin E. House, Illinois State University, and
Edward E. Stambaugh, III, Eastern Michigan University

A manual providing to mental health workers a set of objective guidelines for assessing a child's interactions with his social environment. This unique assessment device differs from traditional approaches in that it permits measurement of the child's behavior in his natural environment. The authors develop in detail the utility of this device in conducting and evaluating treatment for the troubled child.

98 pp   1976   0 08 019586-5 (ppk.)

ADAPTIVE LEARNING:
BEHAVIOR MODIFICATION WITH CHILDREN
Edited by Beatrice A. Ashem and Ernest G. Poser,
McGill University

One of the few publications bringing together major contributions to the rapidly growing literature on behavior modification with children, this work skillfully integrates the collected readings with excellent introductory and summary chapters. The book deals not only with techniques used in modifying deviant behaviors that occur in emotionally disturbed and psychotic children, but also includes a chapter on the modification of behavior within the normal range. The final chapter demonstrates the wide variety of professional and nonprofessional persons who can be helpful in bringing about therapeutic behavior change in children.

459 pp   1973   0 08 017683-6 (ppk.)
0 08 016822-1 (h)